MEDICO-PHILOSOPHICAL TREATISE ON MENTAL ALIENATION

Produced and printed by Servier as a service to medicine

MEDICO-PHILOSOPHICAL TREATISE ON MENTAL ALIENATION

Second Edition, Entirely Reworked and Extensively Expanded (1809)

Philippe Pinel

Translated by

Gordon Hickish
David Healy
Louis C. Charland

A John Wiley & Sons, Ltd., Publication

This edition first published 2008, © 2008 John Wiley & Sons Ltd

Wiley-Blackwell is an imprint of John Wiley & Sons, formed by the merger of Wiley's global Scientific, Technical and Medical business with Blackwell Publishing.

Registered office: John Wiley & Sons Ltd, The Atrium, Southern Gate, Chichester, West Sussex, PO19 8SQ, UK.

Other Editorial Offices:
9600 Garsington Road, Oxford, OX4 2DQ, UK
111 River Street, Hoboken, NJ 07030-5774, USA

For details of our global editorial offices, for customer services and for information about how to apply for permission to reuse the copyright material in this book please see our website at www.wiley.com/wiley-blackwell

ISBN: 978-0-470-99746-8(H/B)

A catalogue record for this book is available from the British Library.

Typeset in 10/12pt Times by Aptara Inc., New Delhi, India.
Printed in England by CPI Antony Rowe, Chippenham, Wiltshire

CONTENTS

FOREWORD

Why translate, for the first time, the second edition of a Treatise published in French two hundred years ago? Because it provides historians of medicine and psychiatrists in the English-speaking world with an authoritative overview of mental illnesses as they were understood at the birth of modern psychiatry. This work, by Philippe Pinel (1745–1826), the founder of psychiatry in France at the time of the French Revolution, made the author world-famous. But he became known mainly as the doctor who freed the insane from their chains – which is true mainly in a symbolic way: his assistant Jean Baptiste Pussin did so three years before Pinel followed suit.

In 1806, an English translation of the first edition of his Treatise of 1800 appeared. This was one year after Napoleon had defeated the British at Austerlitz. No wonder the translator, a patriotic obstetrician from Sheffield, called France 'a vast Bicêtre,' the asylum for insane men where Pinel served as physician in 1793–1795.

Further bad luck befell Pinel in the English-speaking world after the publication, in 1813, of Samuel Tuke's *Description of the Retreat a York*. 'Now we understand Pinel,' the English public seemed to say; 'Pinel is the French Tuke.' And so Pinel entered the English-language literature of psychiatry as the French counterpart of a rich Quaker tea merchant, and the twins 'Tuke–Pinel' have appeared together in the Anglo-American medical literature for two centuries, while the obstetrician DD Davis's wretched translation is still quoted as the only available English version of the *Traité médico-philosophique de l'aliénation mentale ou la manie* of 1800.

By 1800, Pinel had been professor of internal medicine at the reformed Paris medical school for five years and had published his *Philosophic Nosography,* the textbook in which all French medical students learned diagnosis and the clinical approach, and that went through six editions in twenty years. Pinel was also about to be elected to the Academy of Sciences, an honor he took very seriously since he believed that medicine could only progress by adopting the scientific method. What is most important for the present book, however, is that Pinel was appointed physician-in-chief of Salpêtrière Hospice, the huge Parisian establishment for mentally ill women, in 1795, and he served in that position for thirty-one years, until his death.

By 1809, the date of the second edition of the *Traité*, Pinel had important new information to present to the medical, scientific and, indeed, to the socio-political world. He had conducted what he called an 'experiment' with the help of his assistant AJ Landré-Beauvais. They had, over almost five years, 1802–1805, closely examined some one thousand mentally ill women hospitalized at the Salpêtrière, or about to be admitted. The doctors elaborated and published a table of data that classified these women into the four traditional categories of mania, melancholia, dementia and idiocy, but also used personal information and a differential diagnosis. But the real purpose of the experiment was to calculate the probability of cure.

The focus on cure tells us that this professor, medical scientist and administrator was first of all a doctor. The omnipresence of case histories in the present text serves to prove this point, as well as to enliven the argument. But his finding, that only about 9 % of the women surveyed in 1802 were curable, revealed troubling problems. Pinel was a pioneer who had broadened the purview of medicine, proclaiming that the mentally ill are not culprits or madmen but patients and that it behooves the medical profession to care for them. The revolutionary message of the citizen-patient's equal right to medical treatment emphasized that point. But where were the buildings, the doctors, the nurses and the funding to care for this throng of indigent melancholic, demented and idiot patients, even assuming that the curable ones, mainly maniacal patients, could be taken care of? His student Esquirol would address this problem and prod the government into passing the Law of 1838 that still regulates the internment of mental patients in France.

Pinel realized that he was working on a new, burdensome, troubling and hugely expensive issue. That is why, it would seem, he decided to present his 'experiment' to the Academy of Sciences rather than to the medical faculty. Statesmen, scientists and mathematicians such as Chaptal, Fourcroy, Tenon, Cuvier, Lamarck, Laplace, Lagrange and Monge were in his audience on June 25, 1805 and February 9, 1807, and he made much of his mathematical approach: the calculus of probability of the patients' recovery.

The academicians were so impressed that they decided to get this report published in the *Moniteur universel*, the official government newspaper, the following Sunday. But the response to his findings was disappointing.

Pinel knew that his evidence was incomplete and his complaints on that subject, in the 1809 *Traité*, reveal dramatic details, hitherto unknown, about the practice of hospital psychiatry in early 19th century France. The process of admission was chaotic: women were often brought in by the police having been picked up on the streets. No information was available, unless the woman herself was willing and able to volunteer it. Similarly, many women were escorted from the Admitting Office near Notre Dame cathedral and, though they were interviewed here, information was not forwarded. The same was true of patients transferred from the Hôtel-Dieu, where mental patients traditionally underwent three months of 'treatment': venesection and purging, as they lay strapped to their beds. If not cured, they were shipped to the Salpêtrière or Bicêtre as incurable. Here again, Pinel received no medical information for about one-third of the patients admitted, and he complains bitterly. A related specific problem was that, having no information about any treatments or medications previously administered to one-third of his patients, he could not accurately foresee the effect of any therapy he might prescribe. This situation invites comparison with British practice where the voluntary hospitals selected the patients they admitted, rejecting the mentally ill: indigent 'madmen' were sent to Bethlem, paying patients to private 'madhouses.' The 'apothecary' at

Bethlem, John Haslam, faced a situation similar to that of Pinel who knew, and appreciated, his writings.

Pinel repeatedly mentions the careful daily notes he took on each patient, and also that he had to fill out certificates for discharge and, quite often, provide a medical opinion for legal proceedings. Worried about possible indiscretions should these notes and papers become known, he destroyed them all. To make matters worse for the biographer, neither his correspondence nor his manuscripts can be found.

So he proceeded with the administration of a service for the mentally ill that usually held about three hundred patients, while also caring for an equal number of patients in the general infirmary. In the present book he describes at length how his reforms improved the premises and lodgings, food and medications, and especially the psychological treatment – oddly known as 'moral' treatment – of the patients with varied problems and diseases. His reliance on the superintendent Jean Baptiste Pussin and his wife Marguerite Jubline are documented here, as are his troubles with supplies and with the servant girls. He does not mention the lay Sisters who had administered patient care for well over a century: he just tells us that they gradually resigned. (It would seem, however, that they set important precedents regarding the distribution of the patients and their daily routines.)

This book presents the far-sighted concerns of a medical scientist and civil servant, the physician-in-chief of Europe's largest public hospice. It documents his innovative attempt to apply the statistical approach to the study of illness and curability. At the same time, it gives us an intimate look at a deeply humane physician who spent countless hours in conversation with patients, trying to ascertain whether their 'alienation' might be reversible, aiming to classify their illness correctly, according to his nosology, and lodging them appropriately.

We find Pinel repeatedly denouncing the police and the civil service for bringing women to the hospice without information about their medical history; advocating psychological therapy instead of strong medications; experimenting with temporary home leave. Pinel never wavered from attention to the patient and the patient's history as the necessary focus of the physician's attention and care. That is why he shared every day of his life, for thirty years, with the mental patients of the Salpêtrière.

Dora B. Weiner PhD
Professor of the Medical Humanities & History, UCLA

TRANSLATORS' PREFACE

The impetus for this book came in the first instance from Dee Mangin, an academic primary care physician in Christchurch, New Zealand, who drew the attention of one of us to a famous quote from Pinel: 'It is an art of no little importance to administer medicines properly: but it is an art of much greater and more difficult acquisition to know when to suspend or altogether to omit them' (1).

Chasing the context of this quote further made it clear that this came from Pinel's 1800 Treatise on mental Alienation, and that his 1809 Treatise, his definitive work, had never been translated into English. Not only that but, as we were told by Dora Weiner, the translation of the 1800 Treatise was likely the worst translation of all time of any major work (2).

The 1809 Treatise is a landmark work in the study of the mind. In these pages Pinel can be seen grappling with the enduring issues of insanity and their intersection with his time. He had to accommodate, on the one hand, contributions on the issue of insanity stretching back to the Greeks, while at the same time disengaging from the claims of other authorities such as the Church when it came to dealing with pathological piety or religious delusions, for instance; and he had to negotiate these issues at a time of unparalleled social upheaval.

The tensions come through dramatically at points where he outlines clinical interventions to destroy religious materials he suspects have aggravated the condition of his patient, and where he blames misguided spiritual advice for leading to relapses. They also come through at points where he insists that remarkably different mental abilities may be differentially affected by illness. The reader may wonder why Pinel insists on what is for us so unremarkable, but in fact these observations that seem so mundane posed a profound threat to the doctrine of the unity of the soul.

This was a point in history where long-standing domains of influence were being reconfigured (3). Where once authorities such as the Church and traditions that stemmed from the ancients were unchallengeable, Pinel's generation hoped that the science of ideas (as we have translated ideology) might triumph and lead to progress of the kind produced within the physical and biological sciences (4). As a prerequisite of such a science, it was necessary to cast aside tradition and observe patients.

The emerging asylums gave him an opportunity to chart the course of his patients' disorders, and he described their situations and their problems with a vividness not seen since Hippocrates, and charted the course of their disorders in a way that had never been done before. He was the first to introduce the dimension of time into the consideration of mental illness, most evidently in his new notion of *folie périodique,* which helped lay the basis for the clinical approach to mental illness that flowered with Kahlbaum and Kraepelin, giving rise to our concepts of dementia praecox and manic-depressive illness.

Pinel hung his argument on these clinical descriptions, in a manner that is truly modern. While his classification of disorders may take some getting used to for modern readers, he outlines a range of clinical phenomena that readers will readily recognise – such as the role of expressed emotion in aggravating conditions, the concepts of relapse and relapse prevention, notions of an iatrogenic overlay on a primary condition, and problems that stem from polypharmacy – actually employing the term *polypharmacie* (paragraph 279).

For those interested in historical antecedents to modern notions, this is the text to cite not only for the origins of these psychiatric notions, but also as the first text to advocate clinical trials, as well as a recourse to probabilities and statistics to assess the efficacy of a treatment, and the first to call for an evidence based medicine.

When one gets used to the words being used, the classification Pinel suggests is in fact less alien than many might suspect, in that he distinguishes between shifting or multipolar states and conditions which show invariance or unipolarity in a manner that anticipates later 20th century thinking on unipolar and bipolar dichotomies (5). In outlining these ideas he gives new meanings to the terms mania (*'manie'*) and melancholia (*'mélancolie'*), which had previously referred essentially to overactive and underactive insanity.

Of all the terms in the book we have struggled with none more than with *manie.* Mania was the equivalent English term of the time, but mania then and mania now are two completely different things. Over half of the patients admitted to a facility for the mentally ill from Pinel's day through to 1900 had mania. Patients who would now be diagnosed as having schizophrenia or agitated depression, were diagnosed as having *manie.* Emil Kraepelin's creation of dementia praecox and manic-depressive in 1896 led to the demise of this form of mania, and the diagnosis shrank rapidly in frequency thereafter (5).

Manic-depressive illness remained a rare disorder for a century but in recent years we have succumbed to a 'mania' for bipolar disorder that is leading to all sorts of patients being diagnosed as having manic episodes who until 10 years ago would never have been diagnosed in this way, including overactive infants. A mania diagnosis now leads on to treatment with mood-stabilizing drugs. Even the briefest reading of Pinel's Treatise will make it clear he would never have condoned this.

There is in brief almost no commonality of meaning between Pinel's *manie* and this 21st century mania and so we have struggled to find the right term for *manie.* Initially we translated it as insanity. There was one big disadvantage to this approach, which is that it conceals Pinel's realisation that *'manie'* was one of the species of madness rather than the primary genus of mental alienation. This realisation led him to a change in title between the first edition of the Treatise entitled, *'Traité médico-philosophique sur l'aliénation mentale ou la manie,'* and the second edition entitled *'Traité médico-philosophique sur l'aliénation mentale'.*

Following input from Dora Weiner we finally settled on maniacal insanity, having rejected manic insanity en route as manic is to closely linked to the modern usage of mania. Maniacal in contrast paints a picture of overactivity, disorganisation and agitation that appeared to fit the bill quite well.

This brought us to *mélancolie*. Pine's new definition of melancholia focussed attention on the single delusional system that these patients typically had. This brought his melancholia quite close to the form of disorder that attracted this diagnosis for the greater part of the twentieth century. On this basis we opted to hold on to melancholia.

One of the problems both Pinel had as a clinician, and we as translators have had, is that the term delusion was not available to him. Mad patients with what would now be called delusions were then termed delirious (*délirants*). This led him to coin terms like exclusive or selective delirium ('*délire exclusif*'). In translating the text we have grappled with issues like this and used delusion rather than delirium where indicated. The problem is that the French word 'délire' does not clearly distinguish between the states referred to by the English terms 'delusion' and 'delirium' (6).

Combining these difficulties, Pinel also famously introduced the concept of '*manie sans délire*' to designate 'moral', 'emotional' or affective insanity, a notion easily confused with and invariably mistakenly associated with psychopathy (7). Reading the Treatise however makes it clear that Pinel was distinguishing these states from 'cognitive' insanity characterised by delusions and that he had in mind a range of conditions without frank delusions or confusion that would for the most part today be categorised as mood disorders, or obsessive compulsive or other disorders. We have opted to translate this as insanity without delusions.

He illustrated the new disorder in a number of vivid vignettes, none better than his description of what happened when the Bicêtre was stormed by revolutionaries expecting to find, and hoping to liberate, many who had been inappropriately incarcerated (paragraph 161). Thinking they had found one such individual, on the basis that he did not appear to have frank delusional ideas, they swept him off triumphantly, only to return him a short while later conceding that he was indeed mad. In the case of this and other concepts such as '*folie raisonnante*', the quintessential French antecedent of the modern delusional disorder, we have translated the concept but retained the original French term also.

Pinel also uses dementia and idiocy as classificatory terms, but many readers will suspect from the descriptions he gives that included among the dementias, and even among those with acquired idiocy, are some patients with dementia praecox.

We have also had to grapple with words like '*chagrin*'. Key to Pinel's thinking was the possibility that the passions, of which chagrin is the most commonly mentioned, might give rise to insanity. This word was also common in English in 1809 and referred to a powerful affective state. But the word is rarely used in Britain now, while in America it is commonly used but refers to an inconvenient embarrassment rather than the kind of re-sentiment that might lead to madness. We have opted to translate it for the most part as chagrin, and sometimes as deep sorrow. The use of lost concepts like chagrin and misanthropy, which once featured prominently in our efforts to understand ourselves, might hopefully act as a reminder that there have been other ways to see some of the issues at stake. Looking back can sometimes make visible the way forward – *reculer pour mieux sauter*.

While advocating an awareness of the passions as triggers to insanity, Pinel holds in conjunction all possible triggers to the conditions his patients evince, noting the physical changes in bodily functioning which he argues may lead on to secondary mental changes, and then outlining case histories in which events and circumstances that lead to powerful passions such as chagrin or anger trigger identical mental disorders to those that seem to have physical antecedents. This is an aetiological account that to this day still elicits support from all sides of psychiatry's divides.

But he pierces to the heart of psychiatry's divides in the treatment domain. Firstly and famously he advocates moral treatment. As translators we have had to struggle with this term (8). While it is often translated as psychological treatment, and the word psychology had been in existence from 1682, the idea of a psychotherapy did not come into existence before Freud and Janet almost a century later, and using a term like psychological treatment risks importing ideas into the mix that were just not available to Pinel. The term behaviour therapy maps well onto what he actually did, and behaviour therapists now cite him as the originator of their discipline (9), but equally this is a twentieth century term that risks misleading. There are also ethical senses of the term moral that need to be carefully noted and held at arms' length (10).

We have opted in most instances for mental treatment as a way forward. This is a concept that can accommodate psychodynamic, behavioural and other possibilities. It opens a space for clinical wisdom of the type Pinel approves when he refers to Galen's diagnosis and treatment of a women in love – outlined in Note 3 of his Introduction. There are at least three versions of this story in ancient medicine, of which the best known may be the Stratonica story. In this version, Seleucus, the King of Syria, then in his sixties is given the young Stratonica in marriage. His son Antiochus falls in love with her and wastes away, until the King's physician makes the diagnosis on the basis of changes in the youths pulse whenever she is near (11). Pinel makes clear his approval of clinical skill of this kind and his book is an attempt to build on this approach.

Finally, he also advocates the use of a new institution purpose built to treat the mentally ill – one that he refers to as a hospice, which his pupil Esquirol later called an asylum. This would differ from the facilities in which the mad were previously confined in that patients would be separated according to the state of their disorder, would have their treatment plans tailored to their state and where they might not only have their wits restored but where they might have had the opportunity to consolidate their recovery.

At a time when the height of fashion is to advocate treatment at home and to avoid admission to any kind of facility, Pinel offers a persuasive case against home treatment (paragraphs 229–231, 275–276, 309, 352, 364, 395). He is confident in the capacities of an enlightened institution, with responsible people at its head, to improve the lot of the afflicted. He contrasts such an institution with the kinds of facilities previously available, such as the Hotel-Dieu, where patients were likely to be brutalised by unsupervised care staff and debilitated by the treatment and procedures advocated by medical staff.

Pinel's hospice is a far cry from the total institutions that Erving Goffman in his book *Asylums*, 150 years later, claimed created the clinical pictures that mental health staff categorised as illnesses (12). It was a facility where recoveries were consolidated through work, and this example led on to the tradition of asylum farms and sewing rooms. Today we are apparently rediscovering the values of rebranded ecotherapy and ergotherapy, but it seems following Goffman's total stigmatization of the asylum recovering the notion of an asylum is just not possible.

In part, we have stuck with Pinel's designation of the mental health facility within the Salpêtrière as a hospice as the word asylum was not available to him. But in part we have also opted for hospice rather than asylum as the latter has been so stigmatised in our day that another word is needed to convey the benefits that enlightened institutional care might offer. To deny any possible benefits is fashionable but in a wider frame of reference risks looking more like a romantic denial of illness itself.

This book can be read on many different levels. On one level there are a series of human dramas that Pinel so deftly sketches. He is first and foremost a clinician – one of the first modern clinicians, as Dora Weiner brings out in her preface to this volume and in her biography of Pinel (13). On another level there is his articulation of the merits of the public domain, and its institutions, guided by the latest science. This is not just a matter of public versus private monies but rather, as he makes clear, is a matter of the progress that can be expected when competing interests are brought to the light of day – a public morality that will be built on the progress of science.

In our own day confidence in public science is low. There is it seems a greater confidence in business and market solutions. But on this point Pinel throws down a challenge to the marketplace. Physical and mental treatments can all be marketed, as can a humane and decent delivery of these treatments, but the market cannot readily handle 'No'. The market comes with a bias toward action and doing, ever giving another treatment if the first fails, or combining treatments in ever more elaborate cocktails. But there is here a fundamental retreat from wisdom, as the 1800 quote cited above illustrates. This quote is not repeated verbatim in the 1809 Treatise, but its thrust comes through repeatedly in the text. While Pinel advocates evaluating treatment, his treatment approach is ultimately underpinned by wisdom, a wisdom that may sometimes simply mean interfering as little as possible with the healing powers of nature – a central premise of his 'médecine expectante' (paragraph 157). This was a wisdom that seemed to him more secure in the public domain.

David Healy, Louis C. Charland, Gordon Hickish

NOTES TO TRANSLATORS' PREFACE

1. Mangin D, Sweeney K and Heath I (2007), Preventive health care in elderly people needs rethinking. *BMJ*, **335**, 285–287.
2. Weiner, DB (2000), Betrayal! The 1806 Translation of Pinel's Traité médico-philosophique sur l'aliénation mentale, ou la manie. *Generus*, **57**: 42–50.

3. Weiner, DB (2002), *The Citizen-Patient in Revolutionary and Imperial Paris*. Johns Hopkins University Press, Baltimore.
4. 'Ideologie' stemmed from the ideas of Cabanis, Destutt de Tracy and others who, following Locke, believed that ideas in the environment could change people's thoughts and behaviour, and as such needed controlling ideally by a scientific approach.
5. Healy D (2008), *Mania*. Johns Hopkins University Press, Baltimore.
6. Berrios, GE (1996), *A History of Mental Symptoms*. Cambridge University Press, Cambridge.
7. Berrios, GE (1999), Introduction to 'J.C. Prichard and the Concept of Moral Insanity', Classic Text No. 37, **10**: 111–116. See also, Shorter, E (2005), *A Historical Dictionary of Psychiatry*. Oxford University Press, Oxford, pp 213, 239–240.
8. King, LS(1964), A note on so-called 'moral treatment,' *Journal of the History of Medicine*, July, 297–298.
9. Marks, I (1998), Marketing the Evidence, in Healy, D (Ed.), *The Psychopharmacologists II*, Arnold, London, pp 543–560.
10. Charland, LC (2007), Benevolent Therapy: Moral Treatment at the York Retreat. *History of Psychiatry*, **18**(1): 61–80.
11. http://collection.aucklandartgallery.govt.nz/collection/ Search under Stratonica.
12. Goffman, E (1961), *Asylums: Essays on the Social Situation of Mental Patients and Other Inmates*, Anchor Books, Garden City, New York.
13. Weiner DB (1999), *Comprendre et Soigner: Philippe Pinel (1745–1826)*, Fayard, Paris.

ACKNOWLEDGEMENTS

We have worked from the recent French reissue of the 1809 Traité: Pinel P, *Traité médico-philosophique sur l'aliénation mentale*, Les Empêcheurs de penser en rond, Paris, 2005.

We gratefully acknowledge a huge input with key French words and passages from Dora Weiner, who co-edited the recent edition of the 1809 Traité with Jean Garrabé.

We had further input on concepts and practices from Monique Debauche and Philippe Pignarre, the publisher of the 2005 edition. Marilyn Gower helped us to translate sentences from Latin.

PREFACE

The first edition of this book unavoidably left several gaps to be filled, for at the time I only had the psychiatric patients at Bicêtre to look after, with very restricted facilities. It was only when I had moved to the Salpêtrière that I was able to resume the same projects, greatly aided by the hospice administration which had relocated the care of psychiatric patients there. The premises were huge, convenient and readily divided up; and abuses in the service could not possibly have escaped the zeal and sharp eyes of the new supervisor, Mr Pussin, then responsible for maintaining order in this part of the hospice. The gothic use of iron chains (1) was abolished, as had happened three years earlier at Bicêtre, and care from then on progressed steadily following a new method. It is this method that I will elaborate upon in detail in this second edition, devoted to clarifying the special and harmonious combination of factors conducive to the restoration of lost reason, especially in cases regarded, as much in England as in France, as incurable.

I also describe the successful results obtained at a similar establishment (that of Doctor Esquirol) modelled on the same principles: that is, based on observation and on experience.

One would ignore the real notions of insanity if one did not seek its most common cause – human passions rendered vehement or embittered by intense vexations. So it was first necessary to indicate their distinctive characteristics and their gradual progress to a complete loss of reason, something which could only become understood through numerous examples. There are in fact so many points of contact between Medicine and the story of the human race!

The words derangement, maniacal insanity, melancholia and dementia might be understood as equivalent to common words like madness, delirium, eccentricity, loss of reason etc used in everyday life. To avoid any ambiguity I felt I had to identify the physical and mental characteristics that distinguish the first group, looked upon as illnesses, before going on to subsequent considerations. Besides, how can there be common agreement unless, like natural scientists, we designate each object by its manifest signs (2), thereby enabling us to distinguish it from all others?

Mental illness can show countless varieties but many of these have particular similarities that seem to bring them together. This gives rise to special abstract terms embraced in the broader concept of mental illness of which they constitute distinct species. Thus the term maniacal insanity implies more particularly a general delirium with variable agitation or a state of rage. Likewise a delusion limited to one object, or a particular series of objects, takes the name of melancholia, whatever its other varieties may be. Similarly, I identify the terms dementia and idiocy by other specific characteristics.

Maniacal patients are particularly distinguished by recurring ramblings, the most intense irascibility, and a state of perplexity and agitation which seems to go on indefinitely or at least only gradually to subside. A single centre of authority must always be present in their imagination for them to learn to control themselves and to master their impetuous hotheadedness. Once this objective is accomplished, one only has to gain their confidence and earn their respect to restore their reason completely once their illness subsides and they reach convalescence. Therefore these patients need public or private establishments that are subject to strict rules of in-house regulation, and everyday experience shows how the smallest infraction of these rules can be harmful or even dangerous.

One can accept that in simple cases mental and physical management can bring about a full recovery in a given time; but in how many other cases does one have to resort to certain internal or external remedies depending on age, gender, the underlying cause, or indeed varieties in the individual constitution! How complicated are the ailments which can come from the suppression of menses or from their natural cessation, whereupon mental illness sets in! Do not spasms, generalised convulsions, intestinal colic, fever and all the consequences of voluntary abstinence often combine, leading to a lapse in reason: and do they not all require the most varied help? And I must add that, in every well run establishment, one often has also to put right the more serious effects of earlier badly conceived or rash treatment, and that medicine often has to undo the ill effects which other inept hands have brought about in her name.

The educated man has better things to do than sing the praises of his cures. He has always to be his own harshest critic, and the way to avoid mistakes is simple especially if he is in charge of a big establishment. This is to make inventories of the patients, month by month and year by year, and to see, after a fixed time, what the results are of treatment which, even though wise, should still give him some doubts. He finds out what the ratio is between the total number of patients treated and the number of cures obtained. He is happier if this ratio is favourable, but to avoid any relaxation of zeal, so natural with the human species, he carries out similar checks each following year. That is what I did with regard to the psychiatric patients at the Salpêtrière, working out the probabilities. Doctors who do not approve of my treatment method are free to apply the same analysis to that which they have adopted, and a simple comparison will show which is the better.

Obstacles to the curing of mental illness can be varied and stem from the structure of the brain or the skull, from hereditary predisposition, from a deep-rooted form of the disease, or from the breaking of certain fundamental rules of treatment. Understanding of these completely or relatively incurable cases is linked as much to scientific progress as are treatment methods, and alas there are always human limitations.

The most difficult part in the study of natural history is undoubtedly the art of correctly observing internal illnesses and distinguishing them in terms of their special characteristics. But mental illness presents yet fresh problems, and obstacles of many kinds to overcome, be it because of unusual behaviour and tumultuous agitation, or of a disorderly and inconsequential babble, or of a repulsive appearance of rustic and savage harshness. If one hopes to make sense of the observed phenomena, there is another stumbling block to look out for. This is mixing metaphysical discussions and ideological theorisings with the science of facts. Besides, psychiatric patients are of extreme subtlety unless they have completely lost their reason, and it would be a blunder to show the obvious intention to observe them and penetrate the secrets of their thoughts. Furthermore, how often is one left in ignorance, at the time of their admission, of the underlying cause and the increasing development of their delusion? These are the obstacles I have had to confront in order to endow the facts I relate with as much precision as they are capable of and organise them into a consistent methodological whole.

The internal lay-out and amenities of the premises are of such great importance in a psychiatric hospice that we must hope to see one day the inauguration of a new kind of establishment especially designed for this purpose and worthy of a powerful and enlightened nation. But will the architect yet again model his buildings on the places where ferocious animals are confined? Does the mentally ill patient not also need clean and healthy air to breathe?

NOTES TO PREFACE[1]

1. I have very carefully examined the effects which the use of iron chains had on psychiatric patients, compared with the results of their abolition, and I can no longer entertain any doubts about wiser and gentler restraint. The very patients, confined to chains for long stretches of years, who had remained in a constant state of rage, thereupon walked about calmly in a simple straight jacket, conversing with everybody, whereas previously nobody could go near them without being in great danger. There was no more menacing yelling or shouted threats, and their agitated state progressively passed away. They themselves asked for the straight jackets to be put on, and everything came under control.
2. I have always very greatly valued the Semeiology, whether general or individual, and have seen with pleasure that M. Landré-Beauvais made it a particular object of his research. I have no doubt that his Traité des Signes des Maladies (1 vol. in-8°, Paris, 1809. Chez Brosson, lib.) will have all the success it rightfully deserves.

---

[1] *Pinel used a series of footnotes in his Treatise. For clarity, generally the longer footnotes have been extracted as notes, which are given at the end of each section; Pinel's shorter footnotes have been retained as footnotes. Footnotes added by the translators by way of explanation are indicated thus – Ed.*

INTRODUCTION TO THE FIRST EDITION

It is a bad choice to take mental alienation as the specific subject for research, as this opens one up to vague discussions about the seat of the understanding and the nature of its various faults, and nothing is more obscure or more impenetrable than this. But if one confines oneself within sensible limits, keeping to a study of the distinctive varieties of derangement as shown by outward signs, and only adopts the results of enlightened experience as principles of treatment, one then follows the path widely followed in all branches of natural history. Then, by proceeding with reserve in doubtful cases, there is much less fear of going astray.

Mental alienation seems to call urgently for the keen attention of genuine observers, because of the incoherent and confused hotchpotch it presents. On the one hand, there are empirical methods, contradictory opinions or blind routine mistaken for orderly rule in a great number of private or public establishments dedicated to the insane. In other establishments, founded in England and France, we admire the felicitous results of the application of regular methods already confirmed by the most varied experience, and what has been learned from facts recorded in the collections of the most celebrated academies. And lastly, we acknowledge a general agreement on certain fundamental principles among the most enlightened ancient physicians and their modern counterparts (1). In a few hospices for psychiatric patients one can especially satisfy oneself that the supervision, the orderliness in the department, a certain harmony in all health matters, and the successful application of mental treatments, represent true knowledge much more appropriately than the popular pastime of coming up with elegant formulas about madness.

But do not the difficulties seem to be redoubled, from the outset, by the extent and the variety of additional knowledge required? Can the doctor remain a stranger to the history of the most intense human passions, for that is where the most common causes of alienation of the mind lie?

And should he not therefore study the lives of famous men ambitious for glory, scientific discoveries or enthusiasm for the fine arts, or for the austerity of a solitary life, or the transgressions of unhappy love? Will he be able to follow all the variations and distortions in the working of human understanding if he has not meditated deeply over the writings of Locke and Condillac and has not familiarised himself with their teaching? Can he precisely evaluate the innumerable events which pass before his eyes if he drags himself slavishly along beaten tracks, deprived equally of sound judgement and an ardent desire to learn? Is the history of insanity not bound up with all the mistakes and illusions of ignorant credulity, miracles, alleged possessions by the devil, divination, oracles and spells? Rousseau, in an outburst of caustic humour, invokes Medicine and bids her to come without the doctor, but he would have served humanity even better if he had raised his eloquent voice against presumptuous incompetence, summoning true talent to the study of this science, where deep and thorough understanding is so important.

From the earliest times narrow empiricism has led to the adoption of so-called specific remedies, whose virtues have been exaggerated and whose uses have multiplied in efforts to obtain success and avoid their dangers. Prescribing hellebore internally to cure insanity or other chronic illnesses, knowing how to select it, prepare it and specify how it should be used, was a sort of mysterious secret in Ancient Greece which seemed to be known only to a small number of devotees. Some of these precepts seemed wise, others meticulous and frivolous, stemming from popular prejudices or superstitious ideas. Is the hellebore from Mount Etna, from Galatea or that from Sicily to be preferred? Other subjects for grave discussion were the food to eat the night prior to taking it, the preliminary state of fullness or emptiness of the stomach and the drinks suitable to help its emetic action. Difficulties were often considerable on account of the spirited unruliness of the patients – how numerous were the ruses and tricks necessary to disguise the medication or combine it with foodstuffs! The art (2) of correcting or modifying the excessive or somewhat harmful action of this plant, and the precautions to be taken depending on individual dispositions and the duration of the illness, was a sophisticated practical matter for the cleverest men. But what a triumph the discovery of processes sure to achieve the success of treatment was for the ingenious sagacity of the doctors of the time! Repeated mouthwashes, lotions, strong smells, varieties of body positions, massage of the limbs. . . . Should danger of suffocation occur, or a spasmodic constriction of the throat, violent hiccough, syncope, or delirium, then all the subtleties of helleborism were deployed, together with swinging in suspended beds, fomentations, sneeze-provokers and countless expedients to relieve the stomach and bring an end to the symptoms.

The immense field of activity that Hippocrates created did not permit him to express partic- ular views on insanity, but he provided the first general example of the strictest descriptive method, and men who appreciate it take it as a model for their first drafts of the history and treatment of mental alienation. Nothing is more judicious than what Aretaeus has passed on to us about the distinctive traits of nervous disorders, their tendency to relapse, and the degree of physical and mental excitation they can produce, although he depends rather too much on assumed knowledge of the sciences and fine arts. The precepts which Celsus gives are of even more immediate usefulness in curing psychiatric patients, and bear on his habit of being a spectator of their breakdowns. He gives rules to manage them or in some cases to correct their false ideas, indications of methods of discipline sometimes to be used, or approaches of kindness and gentleness so often effective in disarming them. He also gives clear rules for sustained bodily exercise and hard labour. These are the opin- ions he expressed, and experience has for a long time confirmed their salutary effect. How can harsh treatments and aggressive actions, which he believed were only rarely needed to contribute to the curing of insanity, be authorised in his name? Cælius Aurelianus, so inferior to Celsus in elegance and purity of language, seems to have strived for another dis- tinction in his article on insanity. The precipitating causes of this illness, its warning signs and its distinctive symptoms are detailed with care in this part of his work. For psychiatric patients he recommends avoiding stimulating the sensory organs too actively. He outlines supervisory measures suitable to correct their disturbances, and he points out two stumbling blocks to be avoided by those managing them, namely unlimited indulgence and repressive harshness. The same author sets out a reasonable middle way between these two extremes: the great talent of approaching the patients, at the appropriate moment, with an attitude of solemn gravity, and at others with a simple air of true sensitivity. Each approach was aimed at winning their respect and esteem by a frank and open manner, so as to be continually cherished and feared. These are skills certain modern physicians have been credited with: I am here pointing to their source.

It is surprising that such brilliant and useful principles had not undergone any further development over a long succession of centuries, especially in the climates of Greece and Italy where alienation is so frequent and shows itself in such varied forms. But Galen, keen to achieve fame with new systems and by the application of Aristotle's doctrine to Medicine, imparted a new direction to contemporary thought. And there, undoubtedly, lies one of the greatest obstacles which mental medicine has had to face (3). He had to mount a continuous struggle against the different sects of dogmatists, methodists, empiricists and eclectics, and had the ambition to become the rival of Hippocrates himself and to be the dominant figure in the medical schools. While he had a quite wonderful prognostic skill, and did much to advance anatomy, this left him with neither the time nor the inclination to devote himself exclusively to one particular doctrine. The dominance he afterwards exercised over the science of the mind from then on drove away all except his superstitious worshipers, that is to say, almost all men working in medicine in Europe, Asia and Africa over more than sixteen centuries.

Disputes arising between Galenism and a flawed chemistry applied to medicine led to much bitter dispute without generating wisdom or certitude, so that the science of mental alienation produced nothing but meaningless compilations, lost in general systems of medicine filled with empty words and the sterile scholastic language. Sennert, Rivière, Plater, Heurnius, Horstius etc thought they had said and researched everything by constantly repeating words hallowed by use, *brain failure, diagnosis, prognosis, indications to fulfil* etc. They took advantage, as professors, to spread their doctrine on this and other matters, and to cultivate the admiration of their many students who were always keen to praise them and share in their glory. Nothing seemed easier, according to their elegant and learned explanations, than to cure alienation. Its cause was undoubtedly a *fiery and malignant indisposition of the spirits* or a humour one had to prepare to expel with preliminary medicaments. According to others it was offensive matter one had to divert from the brain and heart, cleverly alter it, and thereupon eliminate it as superfluous and harmful. The whole of nature seemed to contribute towards these learned operations by providing countless medicaments within easy reach, some endowed with *cold and dampening properties to thin black bile, followed by more or less active evacuants* etc; and it is easy to imagine that hellebore was not forgotten. The internal use of certain substances, such as narcotic powders, was thought helpful to strengthen the heart and brain, together with the external use of topical preparations applied to the head, heart and liver *to restore this organ,* as Heurnius put it. I shall not mention the mysterious specifics hallowed by blind credulity, and so worthy of being featured alongside the complicated formulae of Arab doctors.

The three famous schools which arose in Germany during the first half of the eighteenth century each concentrated separately on developing general systems of medical knowledge designed for teaching. But mental alienation, along with every other disease, was only treated as subordinate and as merely forming part of an enormous field, and so little progress was made. In a general account of insanity, Hoffmann merely introduced some vague theories in the prolix and redundant language of academia. Stahl shed the somber light of his profound and enigmatic doctrine. Boerhaave, gifted with a more cultivated mind, seemed to follow the opposite route, and characterized insanity in a precise and laconic style which he appears to have taken from Tacitus: '*Ut plurimum*', he said, '*immensum robur musculorum, pervigilium incredibile, tolerantia inediae et algoris, imaginationes horrendae*' (4). But how could he describe as fundamental, *princeps remedium*, a sudden immersion in water, which is just a dream of van Helmont's made into a precept? In the same period a limited number of case histories relating to insanity were recorded in academic collections or journals, where the results of research into organic lesions of the brain were occasionally reported. This was as much to pique the interest of scientists with some striking singularity as to contribute anything new to the advancement of medicine.

The monographs or personal treatises devoted to mental alienation in England (5) during the latter half of the eighteenth century, seemed to promise more tangible merits on account of the pains their authors had taken to focus their attention on a particular subject. But a rigorous critique reveals only a vague style of discourse, repeated compilations, scholastic conventions and just a few sparse facts. These serve from time to time as rallying points without offering an orderly body of doctrine based on repeated observations. This remark applies even more directly to the writings that have appeared on the same subject in Germany (6), where the art of skillful compilation is so perfected. One must however except Dr Greding, who has carried out long-term research on the most common illnesses of psychiatric patients and on the structural lesions or conformational defects which appear typical of them. Thus he has published his observations on the variations in the volume of the head in alienation, on the degree of strength or weakness of the skull, on the meninges, the brain in general, its ventricles, the pineal gland, the cerebellum, the pituitary gland and the irregularities of the base of the skull. But whilst one must praise his efforts to spread new light on the organic afflictions of psychiatric patients, can one establish any connection between the physical appearances after death and impaired intellectual function observed during life? How many similar variations might one not find in the skull and brain of people who have never shown any sign of loss of their reason! And then how shall one come to define the line separating what is natural from what may be associated with a state of illness.

The number of species of alienation is limited, but its varieties can be multiplied indefinitely. So it has been natural to seek to give a clear idea of many of these varieties by publishing a long series of detailed observations collected in a psychiatric establishment, directed according to fixed rules and agreed principles, and this is what Dr Perfect (7) has done in England. He has presented the causes and the typical progress of several cases of melancholia, sometimes associated with an irresistible urge to suicide. He has likewise characterised, with specific examples, plethoric hypochondria, maniacal insanity which pride has made incurable, as well as that which is complicated by the onset of apoplexy. He has similarly characterised that which follows childbirth or the menopause, or arises from excess fanaticism, or as a consequence of an exanthema, or follows alcoholism, or is hereditary. This interesting work contains one hundred and eight observations and deserves to be distinguished from many others, as much because of the prevailing tone of moderation and candour as on account of the variety and simplicity of the methods the author has used, which the success he achieved in a large number of cases seems to have justified. This is no doubt material to be included in a work that would combine this study with similar material from others. But what a far cry it is from this book to a consistent body of doctrine, and a general and profound treatise on mental alienation!

I leave it open whether analysis of the functions of human understanding has added much to our knowledge of loss of reason. But another analysis that is even more directly relevant is that of the passions, their nuances, their differing degrees of intensity, their violent explosion and their various combinations, when they are considered without reference to morality, as basic phenomena and facts of human life. Crichton became interested in expanding on the characteristics and basic effects of these psychological causes of alienation, and as examples he gives sorrow, terror, anger and above all love carried to delusion by the hardships it may undergo (8). He does the same for the feeling of joy, also prone to many varieties. Pleasure, which is one of its first stages, can spring directly from the possession of a desired object or simply from remembering it. We recall with interest the scenes of our first years, the follies of youth, emotions of long-ago experienced kindness, friendship, love, admiration and respect. In the same way we experience the delights of the productions of the fine arts, or reading tasteful books, or the discovery of scientific facts. These emotions result from a mixture of admiration for the superiority of the author, or from an inward satisfaction regarding one of the needs which our education or life style has created. Should one add to the list of feelings of joy those sudden bursts of jovial humour, and those thrills that provoke laughter, singing, or dancing, brought on by puns, quick and unexpected quips, grotesque imitations and satirical facial expressions, as though there is some form of effect of the brain on the diaphragm and respiratory organs? What a huge difference there is between playful sallies of convulsive gaiety and the calm and deep feelings which result from practicing domestic virtues, cultivating talents, their application to some great object of public good, or the imposing and majestic spectacle of the beauties of nature!

There are few subjects in medicine with so many contact points and inescapable associations with moral philosophy and the history of understanding as the science of insanity. There are even fewer areas of medicine where there are so many prejudices to be rectified and mistakes to be corrected. Derangement of the understanding, for instance, is commonly regarded as the product of an organic lesion of the brain and consequently as incurable, but this in a great number of cases is contrary to anatomical observations. The public asylums devoted to deranged patients have been regarded as places of seclusion and isolation for dangerous patients deserving to be confined away from society. Once admitted their keepers, who have often been among the most inhuman and unenlightened, have allowed themselves the most arbitrary acts of severity and violence. Experience, however, unceasingly shows the successful results of a conciliatory manner and of gentle and compassionate firmness. Empiricism has often profited from this consideration in setting up establishments favourable for psychiatric patients, and while many cures have resulted from this there has been little contribution to scientific progress with solid publications. The blind routine of many doctors has frequently revolved endlessly around the narrow circle of numerous blood-lettings, cold baths and harsh and repeated water jets, scarcely giving any attention to mental treatment.

So one way or the other we have neglected the purely philosophical aspect of alienation and the understanding and recognition of the physical and mental causes liable to produce it. We have ignored the distinction between its different species, the exact clinical history of its prodromal signs, the course and termination of episodes when it is intermittent, the in-house rules in different hospices, and the precise determination of the circumstances which make certain remedies necessary and those which make them superfluous. For with this illness, just as in many other branches of medicine, the skill of the doctor rests less in the repeated use of remedies than in the complex art of being able to use them at the right time and also being able to abstain from them when indicated.

Ferriar, the English author of whom I have already spoken, took on another subject in his special work on insanity. He tried out, one by one, different internal medicines which he used with a kind of empiricism, without distinguishing between the different kinds of insanity and the circumstances which might have dictated their choice and application. He has followed a course similar to that of Locher, the German doctor, and the whole difference between cases lay solely in the choice, the nature and the order of use of the medicaments. In contrast Chiarugi (9) always follows the beaten tracks, speaks of insanity in general in a dogmatic manner, then considers it specifically, returning again to that old scholastic order of *causes, diagnosis, prognosis and indications to fulfil*. The spirit of research hardly shows in his work. Amongst a hundred observations which he has published very few give rise to conclusive deductions. The facts scattered in the academic records (10), and in collections of individual case histories bearing on the nature and treatment of alienation, or on the organic lesions which are the effect or the cause, should be quoted, not to roll back the frontiers of medical knowledge but as material which can be used by a clever hand and which through their interconnections one with another or with other similar facts can be built into a solid whole.

Germany, England and France have seen men emerge who, strangers to medical principles, and only guided by sound judgment or some obscure tradition, have devoted themselves to the treatment of psychiatric patients. They have brought about the cure of a large number, either by playing for time, or forcing regular work on them, or by exercising gentleness or energetic discipline in a timely way. One can quote amongst others Willis (11) in England, Fowlen[2] (12) in Scotland, the Concierge of the psychiatric hospice of Amsterdam (13), Poution, Director of the psychiatric patients of the hospice of Manosque (14), Haslam, Apothecary at the Bethlehem Hospital in London (15), and finally M. Pussin, formerly Supervisor of the Bicêtre Hospice and now at the Hospice of the Salpêtrière (16), who through his zeal and skill has perhaps made himself superior to all the others I have just mentioned. The practice of constantly living in the midst of psychiatric patients, of studying their behaviour, their diverse characters, the objects of their pleasure or their dislikes, the advantage of following the course of their aberrations by day and night and in different seasons of the year, the art of controlling them and sparing them fits of anger and grumbling, the skill of adopting, at the right time, a tone of kindliness with them or an imposing air, and of subduing them by force when gentleness does not suffice, and, finally, continuous observation of all the phenomena of mental alienation, and the duties of supervision, must of necessity convey to intelligent and zealous men a great deal of knowledge and detailed insights which, unless

---

[2] *Pinel is referring to Thomas Fowler (he of Fowler's Solution) – Ed.*

he is specially interested, are most often missed by the doctor limited to passing visits. But, can men who are strangers to medical studies and devoid of preliminary knowledge of the history of human understanding put order and precision into their observations, or even rise to language suitable for expressing their ideas? Can they distinguish one kind of alienation from another and characterise it well by assembling a series of observed facts? Are they ever likely to link the experience of past centuries with the phenomena striking their eyes, or to restrain themselves within the limits of philosophical doubt in uncertain cases, or to adopt a firm and sure manner to direct their research, at least to set out a series of subjects in a systematic order?

It is important in medicine, as in the other sciences, to put great store by sound judgment, common sense and an inventive mind stripped of all other privilege. It matters little to know if a man has pursued the usual studies or fulfilled certain formalities, but merely whether he has fathomed some part of medical science or discovered some useful truth. Practicing medicine for nearly two years in the hospice at Bicêtre made me acutely aware of the need to apply these opinions so as to make some progress in the doctrine of mental alienation. The writings of the ancient and modern authors on this subject, together with my earlier observations, could not let me escape from a sort of confined circle. Should I ignore what seeing psychiatric patients over a large number of years, and the habit of reflecting and observing, had been able to teach one man (M. Pussin) who is gifted with a sense of what is right, very devoted to his duties and charged with the supervision of the psychiatric patients at the hospice? I abandoned the doctor's dogmatic tone. Frequent visits, sometimes lasting for several hours daily, helped me become familiar with the deviations, cries of rage and the excesses of the most violent maniacal patients. From then on I had repeated discussions with the man who best knew their previous condition and their delirious thoughts. I paid very close attention to treating the patient's pretentious self-importance tactfully[3]. I varied and often returned to questions on the same subject when the answers were unclear. I never offered any opposition to statements that were doubtful or unlikely, but made a note to examine the matter later so as to enlighten or correct him. I kept daily records on facts observed with no other concern than to build them up and keep them correct. This is the path I followed for close on two years to enrich medical understanding of mental disorders with all the insights gained from empiricism of sorts, or rather to complete the former and lead the other back to general principles that it lacked. Moreover, a separate infirmary housing a certain number of psychiatric and epileptic patients facilitated other research on the effects of medications and on the powerful influence of diet, which was varied depending on individual indispositions or *incidental* illnesses.

Thus the Bicêtre hospice, which was entrusted to my care as Chief Physician during Years II and III of the Republican Era, provided me with a free scope to continue research on insanity started in Paris several years earlier. Moreover, what better time than the storms of a revolution, always liable to exalt human passions to the highest degree, or rather to lead to insanity in all its forms! The supervision and in-house rules of the hospices for deranged patients was in fact under constant regulation and controlled with equal zeal and intelligence by one of the most capable men to assist me. But several circumstances combined to make

---

[3] *There is a possible ambiguity here – it could be interpreted as referring to M. Pussin's self-importance rather than that of the patients' – Ed.*

the strictly medical treatment very incomplete. The psychiatric patients had already been treated once or more often at the Hôtel-Dieu following methods in common use, and they were then taken to Bicêtre to bring about, or strengthen, the full return of their reason; something which could only bring uncertainty into my results. The use of iron chains to contain a large number of psychiatric patients was still going strong there – it was only abolished three years later. How then to distinguish the exasperation which followed this from the symptoms which were part of the illness? The faults of the location, the absence of provision there to divide the patients into separate sections depending on their degree of agitation or composure, the continual instability in the administration, the lack of baths and many other necessary things also posed new obstacles. The background case histories of phenomena peculiar to mental alienation were, therefore, in the hospice for psychiatric patients at Bicêtre, the principal objects of my research. I tried to determine the distinctive characteristics of the different species, the differences between continuous or intermittent insanity, the approach to take in mental treatment, the best methods of surveillance and best in-house rules for such a hospice and, lastly, a sound basis for a medical treatment based exclusively on observation and experience. A medical work published in France at the end of the eighteenth century should have a character different from a book written in earlier times. It should stand out for a certain boldness of ideas, a wise freedom of thought, and above all for the spirit of orderliness and research now pervading all areas of Natural History. It should no longer record particular opinions or the deviations of a vivid imagination but a frank and pure philanthropy, or rather the sincere desire to work towards the public good. I leave it to the enlightened reader to decide whether I have fulfilled this task.

NOTES TO INTRODUCTION

1. Celsus principally insists on the mental regime, and warns to conduct oneself according to the particular kind of insanity one has to treat. Cælius Aurelianus is no less precise and he recommends not aggravating the fury of psychiatric patients, either by too much compliance or by fresh aggravations. The latter author had appreciated the need for them to be managed by a leader capable of inspiring a feeling of mixed fear and esteem in them.

2. The articles *Hellebore* and *Helleborism,* which I inserted in the *Encyclopédie Méthodique par Ordre de Matières,* may be consulted for further details.

3. The following case history makes it regrettable that Galen was not especially interested in the study of mental alienation, since it takes exceptional wisdom to elucidate a hidden mental disorder. He is called to see a lady who was every night afflicted with insomnia and continuous agitation; he asks various questions to determine the root of the trouble, and far from answering him the lady turns away and covers herself with a veil as if to doze. Galen leaves, surmising that the despondency is connected with melancholia or some mysterious grief. The next day he carries out a subsequent examination but at this second visit the slave on duty says that his mistress cannot be seen. He again goes away, to return a third time, when the slave, dismissing him again, tells him not to torment his mistress any more since, on the second visit, she had got up to wash herself and take a little food. The doctor refrains from insisting, but comes back again the following day, and in private discussion with the slave learns that the complaint springs from a profound grief. At the very moment when he was focussed on the lady the name of the

strolling player Pylade, uttered by a person who had just come from a performance of the show, brought about a change in colour and expression of the face, and the pulse became irregular: something which did not happen either at the time or subsequently when the name of any other dancer was spoken. The object of the lady's passion was thereafter no longer in doubt. *(GAL. Book of Prognosis).*

4. 'For the most part an immense muscular strength, incredible ability to go without sleep, tolerance of going without food and of cold, dreadful mental images'.

5. *Battie's Treatise on Madness*, London, 1758. – *Th. Arnold's Observations on the nature,* etc, *of insanity,* 1783. – *Harper's Treatise on the real cause of insanity,* 1789, – *Pargeter's observations on maniac disorders,* 1792. – *Ferriar's medical histories and reflect.,* 1792.

6. *Faucet uber melancholie,* Leipzig, 1781. – *Auenbrugger von der stillen,* etc, 1783. – *Greding's vermischte,* etc, 1781. – *Zimmermann von D. Erfahs,* 1763. – *Weickard's Philosoph, arzt.* Leipzig, 1775.

7. *Annals of insanity comprising a variety of select cases in the different species of Lunacy, or Madness, etc,* 2nd edn, London, 1801.

8. *An inquiry into the nature and origin of mental derangement, etc,* London, 1798

9. *Della Pazzia en generale ed in spezie, Trattato Medico-Analitico; con una centuria di osservazioni di V. Chiarugi, D. M. Professor di Med. et Chiurg,* Florence, 1794.

10. Acad. Des Scienc., 1705. – Acad. Des Scienc. De Berlin, 1764, 1766. – *Transact. Philosoph, French Translation,* Paris, 1791. – *Act. Hafniensia,* tom. I, II. – *Disput. Ad Morb. Hist. Aut. Haller,* tom. 1. – *Med. Essays,* tom. 1V. – *Lond. Med. Journal,* 1785. – Gerard. Van-Swieten *Const. Epid. Ed. Stoll.* an. 1783, etc.

11. *Details of Dr. Willis's establishment for the cure of Psychiatric Patients,* Bibl. Brit.

12. *Dr. Larive's letter to the Editors of the Bibl. Britann, about a new Establishment for the cure Psychiatric Patients,* Bibl. Brit. tom. VIII. *(Ed. – 'Folwen really refers to Dr Fowler of the York Retreat which is of course actually in England, not Scotland)*

13. *Description de la Maison des fous d'Amsterdam,* par M. Thoulin. Décad. Philosoph. Year IV.

14. *Observations sur les Insensés par M. Mourre, Administateur du Département du Var,* 22 page Brochure.

15. *Observations on insanity, with practical remarks, on the disease, and an account of the morbid appearances on dissection,* by John Haslam, London, 1794.

16. *Observations made by M. Pussin on the Mad Patients of Bicêtre.* Year IV. (This is a manuscript of nine pages which has been entrusted to me). *(Ed. – an English translation of this manuscript has been published by Dora B. Weiner:* 'The Apprenticehip of Philippe Pinel: A New Document: Observations of Citizen Pussin on the Insane', *Am J Psychiat,* **139**(9), September 1979, 1128–1134).

GENERAL PLAN OF THE BOOK

1. The public's concept of medicine is not helped by exaggerated praise any more than by sarcasm or compliments directed at it. Anything can be excessively praised or denigrated. It is more important for humanity's sake to find out whether in the present state of the physical sciences one can get any closer to the truth in medicine by applying their principles and progress successfully, developing a sounder style through a thorough study of ancient and modern medicine, and by confining oneself over a long period of years to close observation of the course and features of illnesses. I intend to give a specific example of this in the *Treatise* which I am publishing on mental alienation.

2. I have deliberately picked the subject which is the most obscure and perhaps the most liable to eternal rambling if one indulges in the spirit of hypothesis. For what is more marvellous and yet more difficult to fathom than the function of human understanding with its progressive development, varying robustness, vulnerability to physical factors and its susceptibility to aberrations? It is even more difficult to consider the origins of the different faults, single or combined, which the perception of external objects, memory, imagination, judgement and sense of one's own existence can suffer. And can the least connection be seen between these various faults and the structure of the organ which seems to be its seat? So one must settle on a firm objective and proceed carefully, keeping strictly to observing facts, so as to come up with a general and really straightforward account of mental alienation. This is something which can only be achieved by bringing together a great number of individual observations, followed with the greatest care during the course and different stages of the illness from its beginning to its end. For these examples to be adopted, the distinctive symptoms and signs whose nature and progress are under study in individual cases first need to be studied in a large hospice. A rigorous critique must be applied, rejecting all those examples which are ambiguous or doubtful, and only accepting those which are clear to the senses, give no grounds for vague reasoning and are consistently seen in the different kinds of disturbances of reason. So the real foundation of the whole edifice is a preliminary and in-depth study of the many disturbances of understanding and the will which are manifest externally by changes in bodily habits, by actions and words likely to reveal the internal state, and by unequivocal abnormal physical signs (1).

Medico-Philosophical Treatise on Mental Alienation.
Philippe Pinel. Translated by G. Hickish, D. Healy and L.C. Charland.
© 2008 John Wiley & Sons, Ltd.

3. A further advantage arises from the simple gathering together of a great number of examples of mental alienation followed from their earliest beginnings through to their conclusion. This illness has, in some cases, a common origin and stems basically from an event or combination of similar events which must be regarded as its determinant cause. Amongst these must be numbered hereditary disposition, intense mental affections such as deep grief, thwarted love, extreme excitement over religious principles, or indeed profound immorality. The same effects can also be produced by physical causes such as a head injury, the consequences of another illness, the sudden arrest of a haemorrhage, or the repercussion of a skin eruption. A few of these causes are rare, others frequent. In some cases, the causes are wrapped in obscurity for family reasons, accidental oversights, or deliberate reticence. However, by comparing them with numerous histories of psychiatric patients nationally or abroad, recorded in the collections of observations or noted in hospices and private establishments, no uncertainty can remain over the general results which we have shown.

4. It is not a satire I am undertaking. I am describing the story of a real illness. So I must keep clear of everything understood in society by *delirium, eccentricity, loss of reason, or madness*, as well as all metaphysical discussion or hypothesis on the nature, generation, associations, or succession of intellectual or emotional functions (2). I keep strictly to observation, and this uncovers things it would have been difficult even to imagine. It shows that there can be selective faults in ideas obtained from external impressions, memory, imagination, judgement, the sense of one's own self, or the promptings of willpower, and that these faults assembled in greater or lesser numbers and with varying degrees of intensity give rise to an infinity of variations. It is essential to highlight these fundamental matters and to advocate a special study of them. We must observe the phenomena of alienation systematically, apply the analytical method to this illness with greater success, and advance our general understanding of it.

5. What a picture of confusion and disorder we get from a large collection of psychiatric patients, given continuously or intermittently to their various disturbances, and observed without any rule or methods! But with sustained attention and a close study of their individual symptoms, they can be classified in a general manner and distinguished by fundamental faults in understanding and freewill, without being derailed by a consideration of their innumerable variations. A more or less pronounced delirium over almost all subjects combined, in many psychiatric patients, with a state of agitation and fury, constitutes *maniacal insanity*. When the delusions are exclusive and limited to a particular series of subjects, with a form of stupor and vivid and profound affections, the state is named *melancholia*. Sometimes a general debility strikes the intellectual and affective functions, as in old age, and constitutes what is termed *dementia*. Finally, obliteration of reason with sudden automatic moments of anger is designated by the name of *imbecility*. These are the four kinds of mental derangement which the title of mental alienation denotes in a general manner.

6. It is generally so agreeable for a patient to be in the bosom of his family, and have the care and consolation of tender and compassionate affection, that it is painful for me to announce a sad truth, but I see from much repeated experience the absolute necessity of entrusting psychiatric patients to outside hands and isolating them from their relations. Confused and tumultuous ideas disturb them, arising from their surroundings. Their irascibility is ceaselessly provoked by imaginary objects. There are shouts and threats, and scenes of

disorder or acts of eccentricity. All this, together with the need for the judicious use of firm discipline and rigorous supervision over the staff, from whom rudeness and incompetence are equally to be guarded against, demands a collection of measures adapted to the particular nature of this illness. This can only be provided in establishments devoted to this. From such establishments precepts emerge that may vary with local dispositions, the distribution of the patients, the in-house service and the mental or physical regime put in place, depending on the character and variations of the alienation and its various periods of acuteness, decline and convalescence. This all presupposes profound knowledge of the course of the disorders and the most consummate experience.

7. The results of observation in medicine, or the history of illnesses in general, rarely give rise to division of opinions if they are thoroughly studied. But many vacillations and uncertainties are presented by the use of remedies which are often superfluous and yet more often harmful if they are not controlled with rare prudence and skill! Alienation offers a notable example of this. The ancients thought its seat was in the intestines and made use, above all, of drastic purgatives. Most modern physicians have attributed it to a rush of blood to the head, hence the prescription of forceful showers and repeated blood-lettings. Others have regarded the illness as nervous or spasmodic, leading them to insist on tranquillisers and sedatives. All have vaunted the favourable results and silently passed over the contrary cases, and this has only augmented the doubts and perplexities.

8. Those who think they can read through the complicated nature of our make-up, and manage to guess at the reparative means which the nature of their disorder calls for, are to be admired. I am less confident and more reserved than them. I first noticed in the Bicêtre hospice that insanity of recent onset could be cured by the forces of nature acting alone, provided one spared the patients from harmful factors and controlled the mental and physical care wisely. This became the first the object of my attention. In unruly cases I have made use of medicaments which are varied and adapted according to the circumstances. Should such an approach be adopted or should it be replaced by another one? The promising relationship which I obtained between the numbers of cures and admissions seemed reassuring. But so that there should be no remaining doubt, should similar research not be undertaken in public institutions and the findings recorded in the registers made available each year? One would then apply a calculation of probabilities to these results. A simple comparison would inevitably show which method was best and clear the way for all the ultimate progress to which this area of medicine is open.

9. It must not be forgotten that nature follows general rules in the course of illnesses, albeit with individual variations, and that true medical doctrine requires above all the faithful recording of symptoms, whether the event be favourable or the contrary. One must expect that, in insanity, some cases are beyond the resources of medicine, either because of physical disorders apparent in the anatomy, because of the chronicity of the alienation, or because of imprudent measures already adopted. So I have sought to determine, following the most repeated observation and experience, the cases which are by their nature incurable. Furthermore, preventing dangerous trials and errors, either of doubtful success or which are bound to fail, constitutes a real service to render to science and to the patients. It is also important to set the rules governing the hospice admission and discharge of psychiatric patients since these are still yet very indeterminate and lead to tiresome indecision.

10. The ardent devotees of the subtle theories of Darwin and Brown or other more recent authors will no doubt find that I am guilty of a grave omission, and that I should have engaged in their lofty speculations. I have only one answer to make to these reproaches: it is that I would hardly be able to cite these doctrines as other than examples of lapses of reason. To keep the peace, I have taken the wise course of passing silently by.

NOTES TO GENERAL PLAN

1. One sees that it is necessary to take as a guide in medicine the method which constantly succeeds in all areas of natural history. That is, one must start by looking carefully at each subject with no aim other than to store up material for the future. One must seek to avoid every illusion and prejudice and every opinion merely taken on word. This is precisely what I have done during a long succession of years with reference to alienation, not only in private establishments but again successively in the big hospices at Bicêtre and Salpêtrière.
2. Here I am speaking as a doctor, not a theologian. No unfavourable interpretation may be given to the silence I keep about everything which can come from an authority higher than human reason.

1

THE TRUE CAUSES OF
MENTAL ALIENATION

11. Details of the previous history presented to the doctor when taking over the care of a psychiatric patient can be precise, true and clearly stated, or quite inaccurate and ambiguous, and sometimes there is just no information available. Only the first kind of information is worth considering and the more details there are the fuller the emerging picture becomes. This can be further enhanced by observed supporting facts and by reliable written reports. Out of all this we have learnt that the origin of alienation sometimes stems from physical lesions, sometimes from an original predisposition, but most often from intense and frustrated affective states. Some of these causes are common and others very rare. It is very important to be acquainted with the former, as much to obtain a clear concept of alienation in general and its different species as to enable the development of a methodical treatment.

12. The effect of a physical impression or of an affective state depends just as much on the intensity of the determining cause as on the individual's sensitivity. The latter, moreover, shows great variations (1), depending on an inborn disposition, age, gender, climate, way of life and any preceding illnesses. Repeated observations have shown that this sensitivity is extreme at certain times of life in females, such as puberty, pregnancy, childbirth and at what is known as the change of life. So what trouble is not triggered off by lesser emotions? And is it surprising if, on the arrival of a female psychiatric patient in the hospice, the first hints obtained about her previous state so often indicate a likely cause of the illness?

13. Alienation so often derives its origin from intense or deeply frustrated passions that an English author (Chrigton[1]), announcing a work on mental derangement, confined himself almost entirely to describing the signs and particular characters of the different human passions, their varying degrees of intensity and their greater or lesser effects on the body (2). So medicine was destined partly to fulfil the opinions of the wise men of old, who in their

---

[1] *Pinel's spelling of Crichton – Ed.*

Medico-Philosophical Treatise on Mental Alienation.
Philippe Pinel. Translated by G. Hickish, D. Healy and L.C. Charland.
© 2008 John Wiley & Sons, Ltd.

subtle speculations on the passions looked upon them as illnesses of the soul. Whatever meaning one gives to this term, it is quite certain that they are the most frequent causes of this illness. Mental alienation has presented me with countless examples of this, either in the public and private establishments devoted to it, or in the many case histories, full of authentic details, on which I have been consulted.

I. INTRINSIC OR HEREDITARY ALIENATION

14. It would be difficult not to accept that some hereditary transmission of insanity occurs when one commonly sees, in several successive generations, some members of particular families affected with this illness. This is equally born out by public opinion, the administrative records regularly compiled by public or private establishments and the collections of observations published as widely in France as in England and Germany.

15. Hereditary alienation may be continuous or intermittent. A psychiatric patient, admitted a short time before to the Salpêtrière, and who has lost her mother in a state of dementia, herself experienced continuous insanity for which treatment was without success. Another woman, from a village near Paris, for several years spent summer in the hospice and winter with her family, her insanity being intermittent. The initial onset or alternating recurrences of attacks of intrinsic insanity sometimes come out of the blue, but at other times they follow an exciting cause. Sometimes an extreme vividness of imagination makes everything look rosy and builds up most fantastic pictures, and sometimes a touchiness of character can give rise to pusillanimous fears. Yet again, a natural weakness of understanding and progressive incoherence leads to the most bizarre mix of ideas.

16. One lady, whose mother, an aunt, a cousin and a sister had at different times experienced more or less prolonged attacks of maniacal insanity, had been extremely vivacious in her youth and was very intolerant. At the age of twenty-one, at the time of her marriage, she became touchy and full of the darkest suspicions, although without agitation and without any inconsistency in her ideas, during the first five years of a truly happy union. Towards the sixth year the serious illness of one of her children reduced her to despair and led to an overactive imagination, frequent scares arising from imaginary objects and a groundless jealousy that was both violent and exaggerated. Soon after that her maniacal insanity became evident with intense agitation, an inner sense of burning heat, continual insomnia, gesticulations and wild talk. After a duration of a few days, followed by an intermission of one month, her insanity returned.

17. A young man, whose mother had become insane, was exposed from the time he entered society to bitter frustrations and deep resentment. He became touchy and excessively irascible, his suspicions increased and he believed that he was being subjected to all kinds of persecutions. He even reached the point of thinking that he was being scoffed at in pamphlets, caricatures and theatre plays. His imagination was increasingly carried away and he became convinced that having been disgraced in the eyes of the public a dreadful plan had been made to kill him, and that his friends and relatives were involved in the same plot. His only recourse, he thought, was to take a resounding revenge on what he called traitors and monsters. It was in this state of heightened fury that he was seen going out

onto the street provoking the passers-by. So his imprisonment became necessary to prevent something disastrous happening.

18. Sometimes hereditary maniacal insanity may not develop until advanced age and its late explosion may be determined by other circumstances of life. A man, whose father declined into a state of dementia, occupied a public position with distinction until his fiftieth year. At that point, he developed an immoderate enthusiasm for sexual pleasures. His eyes became bright and animated, he visited places of debauchery, indulged in every excess and then returned to socialize with his friends to paint a picture of the charms of pure and spotless love. His distraction increased by degrees so that he had to be kept shut away, but his isolation further increased the ardour of his imagination. He painted fiery pictures of the pleasures he had tasted with what he called celestial beauties, going into ecstasy speaking of their graces and virtues, wanting to build a temple for love and thinking he had been elevated to the ranks of the gods. This was the prelude to a furious delirium.

19. The delirium of patients with a hereditary maniacal insanity may be of various degrees and may, as in the case of an accidental insanity, be marked by a complete subversion of reason. One of these psychiatric patients, whose mental and physical state I had to record, did not seem to receive any idea from impressions on his sensory organs, for all the replies he gave me were unrelated to my questions. He repeated, indistinctly and at random, the names of people he had formerly known. He had an inexhaustible loquacity, without showing any awareness of feelings of his own existence, his lodgings, nor his relations to the outside world. There was no trace of judgement and everything in his memory showed the most shapeless chaos.

II. INFLUENCE OF A DEPRAVED UPBRINGING ON LAPSES OF REASON

20. The education of children can be so misdirected, and the effects of this may combine so closely with an inherent weakness of understanding, that there can be doubt over what should be attributed to one of these causes rather than to the other.

21. It would be difficult to cite a more striking example of this kind than that of two young boys who were brothers and whose legal examination was entrusted to me. Orphans from a very tender age, they had been brought up, by a strange contrast, on the one hand, in the most effeminate softness by their governess and, on the other, with extreme harshness by a callous school teacher who was short-tempered and morose. Whether the fault of such schooling, or an inborn disposition, the understanding of these children remained stunted and their weakened body was vulnerable to various ills. This left no doubt, when puberty arrived, that they were suffering from a real dementia. They were both of normal stature for young men of twenty to twenty-two years when I examined them, but their feeble and deteriorated understanding brought them closer to the level of a child of three or four years: same gestures, same talk, same taste for childish games. While the speech of both was voluble, only the first syllables of words were audible, and they often became unintelligible. They usually, as if through a kind of automatic habit, finished their day with a touching scene. Cuddling in the corner of their room, they recalled with effusive emotion, and amidst sighs

and sobs, the sad loss of their parents suffered at a tender age. They spoke with gratitude of the care which their governess had lavished upon them, but only mentioned the odious name of their school teacher with a display of horror and curses.

22. There are, said La Bruyère, strange fathers whose whole life seems to be solely occupied in preparing reasons for their children to console themselves over their deaths. Do the public reformatories and establishments devoted to psychiatric patients not provide endless examples that can serve as commentaries on this practice? I am not speaking of open lessons on immorality given at a tender age, for some monstrosities are beyond the law and they must be covered with a veil in order to protect the honour of mankind. But how often is there bitter and angrily expressed scolding for the mildest errors, or even threats and blows, exasperating the spirit of youth, breaking all the bonds of blood and leading on to perverse tendencies or to precipitation into certifiable insanity! A young girl, always rejected and always treated with extreme harshness within the bosom of her family, had to cope with a sister who was cleverer than her at the art of making herself liked, and who became the constant subject of maternal tenderness. Unceasingly humiliated and overwhelmed with grief, she could not sleep and descended into a total loss of reason, and was taken to the Salpêtrière. When she had recovered completely, after treatment for several months, and was on the point of returning to her family, she lamented her sad destiny and her fear of a relapse with a touching sensitivity.

23. A violent and melancholic character can take on, from early youth, a cold reserve and a studied duplicity which could be mistaken for feebleness of understanding if one went by outside appearances. I was given the task not long ago of making a legal report on a seventeen year old young man who had been supervised from a tender age by a school teacher who was devout, pernickety and very bad tempered. He approached me with an air of defiance and suspicion shown by a downward glance and uncertain bearing. His mother put a few questions to him in vain. He balanced himself on the edge of his chair, only answering with a few disjointed words and no more, and seemed to be trying to escape. Was this a feebleness of understanding, or rather premeditated and forced silence? An initial interview did little to dispel my doubts and uncertainties, and I felt I still needed to defer my judgement. Further observations on his condition showed that this young man had a shrewd and deceitful mind, and that he was impatiently waiting for the time of his minority to come to an end so as to enjoy his fortune.

24. Is there less to be feared from the opposite extreme, an almost unconditional tenderness on the part of parents and unlimited kindness? It had been a principle never to thwart a young person with a haughty character and a lively imagination. One such woman had chosen a husband who was full of care and thoughtfulness in the first years of the marriage. When this enthusiasm, which she thought would continue indefinitely, eased off, suspicions and torments of jealousy developed which led in the end to an outburst of the most furious delirium. The habits of dissipation and pleasure seeking, the persistent reading of novels, and a society notable for the depravity of its customs and all the seductions of gallantry, have often led to the same outcome.

25. What a similarity there is between the art of managing psychiatric patients and that of raising young people! In each, great firmness is required, and not a harsh or repugnant

approach. A thoughtful and affectionate regard is needed, and not soft or servile compliance with every whim. By what fate is a rational attitude so rare that it can even be looked upon as a miracle?

III. EXTREME IRREGULARITIES IN LIFE STYLE LIKELY TO PRODUCE ALIENATION

26. Is not a series of eccentricities and extreme excesses in life style not often the prelude to manifest alienation?

27. A young man, distinguished by his talents and considerable knowledge of chemistry, had been meditating for some time on a discovery that, according to him, would lead him to a great fortune. His excited imagination made him shut himself in his laboratory for several days, and in order to increase his aptitude for work, and to ward off sleep and elevate himself to the demands of his task, he prepared stimulants of various sorts. A young female singer shared his quarters. He made repeated use of hard liquors. He also sniffed sweet smelling substances as well as potassium chlorate, and even went so far as to spray his laboratory frequently with what is known as Eau de Cologne. One may imagine how the combined action of all these measures, together with the heat of a kiln, was likely to excite his physical and mental faculties to the utmost. It was hardly surprising that towards the eighth day he succumbed to the most furious delirium. (The rest of his story may be seen in my *Nosography. volume III*).

28. Another young man who was well endowed successively applied himself during the different periods of his education to physics, chemistry and the fine arts. An exaggerated vanity dominated him, leading him to envisage a most brilliant future career. Nothing seemed better suited to achieve this end than a trip designed to educate himself in little known regions. The story of this journey, which would introduce his work to the world, must be remarkable in the novelty of its facts and in the typographical luxury and the elegance of the drawings. Recognised artists accompanied him everywhere. In order better to sustain the stresses of the day and the late nights he took excessive amounts of coffee. He stopped a few times during his scholarly excursions to set his collections in order or to write his notes, and took several days to compose an opinionated piece in a grossly overheated room. Still worried that his senses might not be sufficiently stimulated, he made abundant use of alcoholic liqueurs. Soon after, his raging imagination drove him to another excess. He wished to find out to what extent he could maintain abstinence. He ventured into scantily inhabited regions in a post chaise with a few trusted servants, only stopping to change horses, and for several days, as his sole nourishment, he took nothing but coffee and strong liqueurs, of which he had brought an ample supply. Rest abruptly followed movement. He stayed for a month lying on his bed, only getting up to take a hasty very frugal meal. His taste for the unconventional again drove him to try another experiment. He chose, for a stay, a town very well known to be unhealthy and to ward off noxious sensations he took strong doses of cinchona every day for a month. He returned to his normal home and, abandoned to his dreams, looked upon time spent in sleep as lost without return. Inspired by examples of many great men he went to bed very late and gave precise orders to be woken betimes,

and even forced to get out of his bed. A series of setbacks occurring at this time, and acute vexations, gave further shocks to his shaky mental state, and in the end a violent delirium erupted.

29. My advice has been sought several times about the extreme lability and variability of character of someone who from the tenderest age had been subject to skin disorders and irregular febrile movements. From the first development of reason she had been in the habit of reading with no order or discrimination. She busied herself in turn with novels, poetry, history and plays, which she alternately skimmed through as fast as a flash of lightning for whole days and a large part of the nights. Her monthly periods came on early and were often upset by significant domestic setbacks and recurring annoyances. She then developed an extreme irascibility, anger, violent cries and sometimes irregular convulsive movements. Fortune seemed to smile on her with a well-matched marriage, but she still showed the same vacillation of character and irresistible tendency to go from one extreme to the other. Sometimes, for several days, she was in a state of continuous agitation, rushing about and getting fatigued to the point of exhaustion. At other times she had a sombre moroseness, an overwhelming wish to retire, an apathetic drowsiness and she kept no order in the timing of her meals or choice of food. Some days passed without her taking any nourishment, while others were marked by an immoderate appetite which she did not hesitate to satisfy and which often led to digestive disorders and abuse of alcoholic liqueurs. Often in the same day, there might be a sudden change from cold apathy to outpourings of filial tenderness, enthusiasm for poetry and religious fanaticism. She also often treated the most important subjects like a game, while frivolities were treated with the most serious gravity and attention. Symptoms of hypochondria and various physical ills gave rise to unsuccessful treatment projects that were suggested by clever doctors, empiricists or wise women, and were in turn started, suspended or resumed in no pattern or order. Eventually this led to a clear onset of alienation of remarkable singularity. She spent six months of the year fidgeting, running about endlessly, giving birth to vain and illusionary projects, and the other six months were distinguished by deep stupor, sombre despair, and very strong impulses towards suicide.

IV. SPASMODIC PASSIONS LIABLE TO LEAD TO ALIENATION

30. The passions in general are a set of unknown variations in physical or mental sensitivity which we can only untangle and to which we can only allocate distinctive characters through external signs. However conflicting some of them may appear, like anger, fear, the sharpest pain or sudden joy, they are marked above all by various spasms of the muscles of the face, and in general are manifest through prominent features which outstanding poets, sculptors and painters have studied very deeply. The practiced eye of the anatomist can point out the muscles, which through isolated actions or their simultaneous or successive contractions, serve to express the passions of which I am speaking, just as they do for everything that stirs us.

31. The nature of the object that excites anger, as well as any related ideas and passions and varying degrees of sensitivity on the part of the subject, may lead to very different expressions of this passion. But when the passion is present in its simplest manifestation,

artists and keen observers are agreed in attributing the following traits to it: a red and inflamed face, or else a livid pallor, wild and sparkling pupils, raised eyebrows, wrinkled forehead, lips pressed against one another especially in the middle, a kind of smile of indignation and disdain, clenching of the jaws, sometimes with grinding of the teeth, and bulging of the veins in the neck and temples.

32. Repeated outbursts of anger are always harmful to judgement, as they impede its proper exercise. Extreme irascibility is sometimes the prelude to mental alienation or strongly predisposes to its development. It is an ominous sign in women, especially during their periods and following childbirth, as shown by frequent examples which I have recorded in the Salpêtrière hospice. If it becomes habitual, melancholic patients can end in a state of stupor and dementia. A very lively woman, commendable for her domestic virtues, was for a long time given to uncontrolled and excessive fits of anger for the slightest of reasons. The least event, the smallest delay in carrying out her orders or the merest mistake by the domestic staff or her children was followed by a violent rage and some tumultuous scene. This unfortunate tendency ran its course, leading to a complete loss of reason.

33. Feelings of horror, intense fear and the last stage of despair, although they cannot be regarded as synonymous, show a great similarity in the spasms of the facial muscles they elicit. The brow furrows from top to bottom, the eyebrows are lowered, the bright and shifting pupils contract and the nostrils swell, open and rise. The distress can sometimes be so profound that reason is lost. In different periods and within a short space of time three young girls who had become mentally unstable were admitted to the hospice. One was unhinged by the spectacle of a supposed ghost dressed in white with which some boys had confronted her at night, another by a violent clap of thunder at a particular stage of the month, and the third by the horror of a place of ill repute to which she had been lured.

V. DEBILITATING OR OPPRESSIVE PASSIONS

34. These passions, like chagrin, hatred, fear, regret, remorse, jealousy and envy, which are the seeds of so many disorders and ills in social life, also serve to enrich the fine arts, and seem to breathe in some of the masterpieces of leading painters and sculptors. They are susceptible to different degrees of strength and infinite nuances depending on combination with some other passion, individual sensitivity, associations they provoke or the intensity of the precipitating cause. They only degenerate into mental alienation by reaching a very high level of intensity, by sudden switches from one to another or when faced with powerful reverses. The outward features of deep chagrin are in general a feeling of languor, great reduction in muscular strength, loss of appetite, facial pallor, a sense of fullness and oppression, laboured breathing sometimes broken with sobs, greater or lesser drowsiness and finally a sombre stupor or a very violent delirium.

35. It will always be praiseworthy not to debase one's character and to remain level headed in prosperity as well as in ruin. But this counsel of wisdom, so often embellished with poetical spells, gains fresh weight from the concept of physical ills, and above all from the loss of reason that can result when it is forgotten. This is not the only example of the support medicine lends to morals. Melancholics are especially liable to indulge the feeling

of their pains to an excess. A lady of this character, who had just lost her father, rolled on the ground, tore out her hair, let out curses against all of nature and in her despair would have wished that the human race should be annihilated. Did her shouts and cries not make it clear she had arrived at the highest degree of delirium?

36. Reason can sometimes struggle with varied success against misfortune, only to eventually yield to profound and repeated feelings of bitter distress. A young woman, of feeble character but with an educated mind, was appalled by the sudden and unexpected loss of the family fortune and the death of her father. Her mother, overwhelmed by despair, lost her appetite, could not sleep and became deranged. To meet the cost of a residence which these events necessitated, the young girl gave up a capital worth eight hundred francs of income, found herself reduced to living by the work of her hands and saw the hope of a forthcoming marriage disappear. These accumulated disasters ended in absorbing all her intellectual functions and led to a kind of melancholic stupor which could only be cured by the most assiduous care and eight months' treatment in the hospice at Salpêtrière.

37. Within domestic situations humanity presents a perpetual contrast between vices and virtues. On one side one sees families thrive over a course of many years in the lap of order and concord, whilst on the other one sees many others, especially in the lower social classes, who offend by the repulsive picture of debauchery, arguments and shameful distress! Therein lays, according to my daily records, the most prolific source of mental alienation one has to treat in the hospices (3). Here, you have a working woman who sees the fruits of her labour and her finances vanish because of a husband addicted to all kinds of excess. There, you have another woman, careless or degraded who leads to the ruin of a hard working man. Elsewhere two spouses equally deserving of contempt are precipitated into joint ruin, and the alienation of one of them closely follows the depletion of their joint resources. I refrain from publicising examples of this kind to the wide world. Some are a credit to the human race, but many others make a disgusting picture and seem to be a disgrace to humanity.

38. It is sometimes the most cruel events which lead to despair and mental breakdown and, amongst examples of this kind, one may quote that of the farmer's daughter still in the hospice who saw her brothers and parents massacred during the Vendée uprising. Struck with terror and having lost her head she escaped from the carnage and ended up abandoned and bereft of all resources.

39. The development of certain principles, or contradictory ideas that gain a firm hold on the imagination, can produce internal conflicts and strong emotions which lead to a loss of reason. When she was twenty a young person who was brought up with strict moral maxims realised the imprudence of having taken a vow of chastity at the age of fourteen. She consented to being married after the most appropriate religious formalities to reassure her fearful conscience, but pious readings and melancholic meditations brought her daily scruples and remorse, and made her seek solitude. She was sometimes found melting in tears, and repeating amongst sighs and sobs, that *she is a poor soul and that she should never have got married.* She was, nevertheless, a tender wife and she successively became the mother to four children. Some vexations that occurred whilst breast-feeding the last one aggravated her condition and her scruples and melancholy seemed to increase every day. She developed palpitations and syncopal attacks, and in the end a furious delirium became evident.

40. The fatigues of war lasting through one or two campaigns, the very hard and tough life, the heat, the cold, the hunger and the snatches of sleep sometimes followed by several sleepless nights are all highly likely to contribute a male vigour to the body. Caesar himself made use of these tactics to overcome or strengthen a weak or damaged constitution. However, their sudden interruption and passage into an apathetic relaxation and quiet can debilitate both the mind and the body and cause all the activities of life to languish. It may produce an involuntary sadness, a kind of pusillanimity, and recurring anxieties against which there is no defence. A hypochondria gradually results which can escalate into a certified mania.

41. A most distinguished soldier, after fifty years of highly active service in the cavalry, switched in his last years to a contrasting situation and all the joys of an easy and comfortable life in a pleasant countryside. His organs of respiration and digestion soon showed the effects of this inactivity, besides being weakened through age, and there followed a periodic and very copious secretion of mucus. He developed different nervous afflictions such as spasms of the limbs, startled arousals from sleep, frightening dreams and sometimes an erratic hotness of the feet and hands. The disorder soon spread to involve his mental state. It began with him feeling strong emotions about the most trivial matters. For example, if he heard some illness mentioned he soon thought he himself was being affected. If somebody, in the circle of his close friends, spoke of a loss of reason, he believed he was also going mad and he retired to his room full of sombre reveries and worries. Everything became a subject of fear and alarm for him. If he entered a house, he was frightened that the floor might collapse and draw him into the ruins. He would fear to cross a bridge lest the command to fight and the call to honour were sounded. Is that not a condition of hypochondria ready to become a state of insanity?

42. A quick change from a very active life to a state of constant idleness can lead to various physical or mental symptoms, depending on a crowd of additional circumstances, but the result is similar. An Englishman, says Dr Perfect *(Annals of Insanity)*, who at the age of fifty-eight had acquired an immense fortune in commerce, decided to retire to the country and enjoy what is called *otium cum dignitate*[2] on his estate. Towards the fourth month of this happy change he began to feel despondency and a spasmodic contraction in the stomach region. He lost his appetite, had confused thoughts, his carotid pulse became irregular and turbulent, his abdomen appeared tightened and strained, and his head was painful, as was his left hypochondrium. From then on he experienced sensations of fleeting warmth, feverish thirst and indigestion. Strange conduct, words and actions full of eccentricity followed, with true melancholic delirium.

VI. CHEERFUL OR EFFUSIVE PASSIONS CONSIDERED AS CAPABLE OF DERANGING REASON

43. Painters and sculptors have conveyed with as much truth as energy the distinctive characteristics of these passions. They are manifest externally by a kind of radiance of the face and simultaneous contraction of particular muscles. I must only speak here of passions

---

[2] *'dignified retirement' – Ed.*

whose extreme intensity is likely to upset reason such as joy, pride, love, ecstatic rapture or devotion to religious objects. Similar affections, provided they are confined within certain limits, seem to add renewed impetus to the understanding and make its functions more lively and animated. But taken to the highest degree or frustrated by obstructions they may end up offering nothing but violent lapses, fleeting delirium, a state of stupor or real alienation.

44. An intense joy and unexpected prosperity can greatly weaken feeble minds and lead to a loss of reason but is this not because of successive upsetting shocks caused by major setbacks and deep distress? I was recently consulted about the condition of a talented man of lively character and great sensitivity, who had been weakened by an abuse of pleasures and had followed this with excessive studying. Then he became very rich through an inheritance, and believed he was called to play a major role in the world, and could achieve all sorts of honours and dignities. His expenses increased, as he embarked on constructing buildings in the countryside, and these became a major source of worry and annoyance. His irascibility became extreme. He thought of nothing but his properties and the supervision they required. His sleep was thereby disturbed and he even went so far as to get up at night to walk in the fields and enjoy the intoxicating spectacle of his new riches. His symptoms worsened and his mind became more disordered. Last winter brought him back to the city, his mind completely toppled and in a state of the most furious delirium.

45. Hope, which is just an anticipated joy produced by the thought of something good to come, is liable to stimulate the imagination and lead to the most powerful seduction, especially when it is directed towards objects of vanity and pride. This leads on to an increase in self-esteem and a deep conviction of deserving higher positions, especially in youth or mature age. Against this background, unexpected reversals or harmful incidents can cause sharp shocks and lead to manifest alienation. These examples are far from rare in private establishments for the treatment of mental illness.

46. It is quite common to find alienation associated with a presumptuous tone and inflated pride, solely during the attack and as a specific symptom. This same vice, carried from youth to an extreme and seemingly inherent in the constitution, can also grow gradually, get carried away and become the cause of true mania. A middle aged man of tall stature attracted attention by the harsh tone of his utterances and answers, no less than by his bursts of violent anger and his austere lifestyle. His countenance and the features of his face bore the imprint of haughtiness and the most touchy and morose mind. He displayed continual anxieties and had bitter reproaches or even abuse for everyone around. His rude misanthropy became worse through set-backs in his business and it was then that mania became apparent. He drew bills of exchange for exorbitant sums on his banker, as well as on other businesses with which he had no connection, and soon afterwards he was locked up on account of madness. He maintained the same pride in the place where he was detained and gave orders with all the arrogance of an Asian despot. He ended by believing he was the Chancellor of England, Duke of Batavia and a powerful monarch (Dr Perfect, *Annals of Insanity*).

47. Young women aged eighteen to twenty-two are often admitted to the mental hospice having lost their reason because of unforeseen obstacles to a marriage about to be contracted. Sometimes there is a violent and frantic delirium, on other occasions the most sombre

melancholy. It is not rare to see a state of stupor and a form of idiocy appear. Sometimes the spells of insanity are periodical and separated by lucid intervals. An extreme purity of feeling may characterise the first outbursts of love and this can lead to a loss of reason. A young working woman fell passionately in love with a man she often saw passing by her window, without ever having spoken to him. The single image of the loved one occupied her thoughts during her alienation and she showed such an antipathy to other men that she even struck her companions in misfortune if they were strong and of masculine appearance, looking upon them as disguised men. Another young woman whose marriage was about to be contracted was very offended, or rather outraged, by suggestions of an anticipated favour her intended made to her and she felt so profoundly mortified that her mind was deranged (4).

48. A young man was unable to obtain the hand of someone with whom he had fallen hopelessly in love. His offers were disdainfully rejected by her parents. He became taciturn, unresponsive to all pleasures and entertained only suspicions and sinister forebodings. He lost his temper over the most trivial things and fell alternately into a state of discouragement and utter perplexity. The company of his friends became more and more of a burden and he ended up in a state of a true melancholic delirium.

49. Sometimes it is ceaselessly renewed and concentrated agitations, and a kind of inner conflict between the inclinations of the heart and religious scruples, that bring on melancholic or maniacal delirium. A young girl of sixteen years, brought up with strict principles, was placed with a workman to learn embroidery, where she received for the first time the attentions of a young man of the same age. Finding herself exposed to all his advances, the pious feelings she owed to her education were strongly reawakened, so that she entered into an inner struggle with the affections of her heart. Melancholia followed with all its fears and perplexities, a loss of appetite and of sleep, and a furious delirium appeared. Taken to the hospice and given in turn to convulsive movements and all manner of mental abnormalities, she seemed to be assailed with the most incoherent thoughts. She often let out inarticulate sounds or broken sentences, speaking of *God and temptation*, and it was only with extreme difficulty that one could get her to take any food during the first month.

VII. A MELANCHOLIC CONSTITUTION, COMMON CAUSE OF THE MOST EXTREME DEVIATIONS AND MOST EXAGGERATED THOUGHTS

50. When the English are reproached for being sombre and melancholic, is this not a homage to their character? For one of these qualities seems to depend on the other. Moreover the conjectures which reading their novels usually generate can also be turned into unimpeachable testimony in their collections of observations in medicine which abound in examples of the most sombre and deep melancholy (5). The English doctor whom I have already mentioned (*Annals of Insanity*) has published many most remarkable cases. A thirty-year old woman this author quotes was plunged into the depths of despair by the death of one of her friends. She spent many nights and days without saying a single word or alternately shedding a torrent of tears and uttering very sharp cries. Her face was pale and swollen, she looked worn out and she made a few hardly audible inarticulate sounds. Another English

woman, led astray by fanaticism, had sunk into an apathetic indifference. The most sinister forebodings and ceaselessly returning fears brought the greatest confusion into her thoughts and life had become an insupportable burden. What a lugubrious picture this author recalls of a bilious poor soul who was found in a lonely place bathed in blood, with an enormous self-inflicted wound in the neck, his gaze wandering and ready to expire!

51. An over-exalted piety, considered from a purely medical point of view, can act with so much force on weak minds that the intellectual functions and other phenomena of life become disturbed and it becomes necessary to turn to physical and mental measures to restore them to a healthy state. This is an immediate conclusion from the facts observed in the hospices or other asylums devoted to the treatment of insanity. It is a source of ills of all kinds, all the more numerous as, depending on the particularities of character, additional thoughts to which they are susceptible and the complication or clash of other passions, it can give rise to the most violent commotions and a more or less complete loss of reason. The religions of the different peoples of the world can likewise provide examples.

52. It is perhaps prudent to pick examples elsewhere than from amongst ourselves of certain abuses which must be condemned. I confine myself to noting the influence which the fanatical sect of the Methodists or Puritans has on weak minds in England. Nothing equals the zeal of these sectarians for making proselytes and secretively propagating their sad exclusive doctrine. They only speak of a vengeful and terrible God, always ready to punish human weaknesses with eternal torment. An author, already mentioned, reports amongst other examples that of a very jolly man, given to the pleasures of the table, who was thrown into despondency and deepest melancholia by the discussions he had with a sombre and fanatical Methodist. Extreme anguish and progressive wasting away soon followed. He became touchy and pusillanimous, lost the ability to sleep and constantly sighing he descended into a manifest alienation with a strong tendency to suicide.

53. The same English author reports amongst other similar examples that of a man who was endowed with natural cheerfulness and lively imagination and was always ready for pleasure in moderation. A few encounters he had with a sombre and melancholic Methodist completely changed his ideas. He gave up all the most permissible pleasures, sank into solitude and thenceforth looked upon an eternity of punishment as an inevitable destiny. The lord of all beings was continually represented to him as vindictive, full of hatred and delighting in punishing his feeble creatures. These sombre thoughts led to a kind of despair and a marked leaning towards suicide. He developed a pale and livid colour, slept very little at night and continuously kept sighing. A few energetic remedies applied by Dr Perfect were successfully assisted by the very wise opinions of a superintendent endowed with a more enlightened piety, and with a more comforting doctrine, and a mental and physical regimen brought back a complete convalescence after two months of treatment.

54. Nothing is more common in the hospices than cases of alienation produced by over-exalted devotion, scruples carried to a destructive excess or religious terror. My daily records hold a crowd of details of this kind which I keep to myself. It is sometimes the memory of one or more confessions formerly made to a sworn priest which causes remorse or extreme perplexity. At other times it is a marriage contracted under republican documentation where there were fears of consequences after several years. Very fearful souls go as far

as reproaching themselves bitterly for reading novels in which they formerly delighted. Alternatively it is an irresistible tendency to laziness, with a love of spending, which throws one into distress and leads to an effort to find in extreme devotion a happy addition to the gifts of fortune. An extreme pride is sometimes combined with a great zeal for the religious practices. Take the case of the tailor's wife who spent part of the day in churches with well-dressed children, but who treated a very kind husband with the greatest disdain and insisted that he should wait on her on bended knee and see in her a privileged spirit showered with supernatural favours. Another well born wife, whose husband had fallen on hard times, thought she would find assured consolation first in long meditations and very fervent prayers, then in ecstatic raptures where she believed she rose up to a state of divinity. This was the prelude to an unequivocal alienation.

55. A gentle and affectionate piety and a lively imagination had characterised Mademoiselle . . . in her youth, and thus it was through very deep religious sentiments and by seeking solitude that she tried to console herself over the misfortunes and tragic death of her parents occurring during the disturbances of the Revolution. She faced new perplexities approaching the age of twenty-two years on account of many domestic cares and the countless details which a large fortune involves. There were other endlessly recurring worries, with court proceedings to pursue and the saddening prospect of a life given to celibacy, which disabilities seemed to make inevitable. Similar ideas were shrewdly suggested by her presumptive heirs and she sensed a kind of isolation in a world where she found only instability and frigid indifference. A deceitful man pretended to share her taste for meditation and retreat, and seemed to settle her uncertainties. To exert more power over this faint spirit, he mysteriously brought her together with a sect of visionaries and with the help of some occult ceremonies ended in persuading her that they were from now on united by indissoluble bonds of marriage and that she could enjoy all the rights that this title confers. This led to sudden rumours and heated complaints on the part of those close to her who feared they would be frustrated in their expectations. It is not difficult to imagine into what perplexities this victim of a great fortune found herself plunged, faced with violently conflicting pressures. She looked for fresh consolation in an affectionate piety, devotional practices, fasts, scourging, retreats and fervent prayers, but her imagination carried her away more and more, and insanity became manifest.

VIII. ON SOME PHYSICAL CAUSES OF MENTAL ALIENATION

56. It would be easy, but superfluous, to report particular examples of each of the physical causes likely to lead to mental alienation, since they are found in many collections of observations and the public or private establishments provide many examples. One must include, in the number of incidental causes, hypochondria produced by excesses of various kinds, the habit of drunkenness, the sudden obstruction of a discharge or the arrest of an internal haemorrhage, confinements, the change of life in women, the sequelae of different fevers, gout, imprudent suppression of scabs or some other skin complaint, a violent blow to the head and perhaps some defective conformation of the skull.

57. It is important, however, to recall an example of the extreme abuse of venereal pleasures which degenerated into a habit, for useful lessons about the passionate period can be learnt

from this. A young man with a strong constitution, and born of a very rich father, had become fully grown towards the eighteenth year of age. At this time of extreme effervescence of the senses he began to give way to his inclinations with all the impetuosity of an ardent character and the opportunities which a daily gathering of young girls working in a large factory gave him. He got into the habit of abandoning himself to unbridled and measureless pleasure, often at different hours of the day and night. At the age of twenty years he went on to other no less destructive excesses, those of intemperance and repeated frequenting of places of debauchery. Venereal diseases, in turn cured then contracted again, added to his exhaustion and were complicated by other skin diseases. Business matters required him to make frequent journeys in a post chaise by day and night in all seasons of the year. He repeatedly started mercury treatments and broke them off, then resumed them again with no order or control. From then on he displayed the most marked symptoms of a profound hypochondria, with laboured and incomplete digestion, very awkward flatulence, acid regurgitation and alternating constipation or diarrhoea. He had periodical sharp colicky pains, groundless fears, extreme pusillanimity and disgust for life, and he made several suicide attempts. He had a blind and childish belief in the effectiveness of medicaments and complete confidence in all kinds of empirical treatments. This added, by the age of twenty-five, to his complete incompetence for the pleasure he had excessively abused and led to a decline in reason which only got worse.

58. It is sometimes the opposite extreme, in other words desires that are keenly aroused but not satisfied, which can trigger a complete loss of reason. A mild melancholia and vague concerns, whose object was neither unrecognised nor concealed, distinguished a twenty-year old girl endowed with a strong constitution and marked sensitivity. Everything conspired to inflame her imagination, including assiduous reading of the most flirtatious novels, a kind of passion for all artistic productions of an erotic nature and the regular company of young people of both genders. Some of these charmed her with personal attractiveness and all the seduction of gallantry and others with dangerous examples and indiscrete confidences. The most refined coquetry became edified as a principle and a serious preoccupation. Her pride, flattered by small acts of thoughtfulness, caused her to regard these as an assured triumph: they became the endless topic of her conversation and her reveries until another new affair made her forget the last. A mistake seemed inevitable, or at least much to be feared, and the parents hastened to conclude a marriage based on certain proprieties. The chosen spouse was of a ripe age and, in spite of the advantages of his stature and robust complexion, perhaps less likely to satisfy than to trigger her desires. The young lady's melancholia degenerated into a sombre jealousy and she attributed to infidelities what was merely the effect of decline of the organs. A kind of wasting away followed, her features altered and an inexhaustible chatter began with a great disorder of thoughts, which was either a prelude to, or a manifest sign, of patent insanity.

59. My daily notes, as well as the authentic Collections of Observations, and facts recorded in the memoranda of the most celebrated scientific bodies, alike attest to the variety and multiplicity of the physical causes, all likely to produce mental alienation. One of the most common, in the hospices for psychiatric patients, has to do with the suppression or disorder of monthly periods, together with a very strong mental disturbance. I shall often have the opportunity, in the course of writing this work, to report particular relevant examples and I restrict myself here to the following. A thirty-year old woman, of weak and delicate

constitution, had long been subject to attacks of hysteria. She yielded to the advances of her lover, became pregnant and brought up her child with the greatest tenderness. A series of unhappy events followed. Her lover abandoned her, her child died and some time later a sum of money was stolen from her which she had in reserve and which was all she had in the world. She descended into deep mortification and her monthly periods, up till then regular, ceased. Her sleep became fleeting and troubled by dreams, she lost her appetite and soon after an attack of fury developed with complete loss of reason. In this condition she was taken to the hospice. (I will show in another chapter in this work the treatment which was followed and the success which was obtained.)

60. Another even more common cause of alienation, and of which there were endless examples in the hospice at Salpêtrière, had to do with the consequences of childbirth, which can give way to insanity in many varied forms. It would be superfluous to repeat particular examples of this kind and I will limit myself to remarking in general that at almost all stages of life women, through their extreme sensitivity and physical and mental disposition, are more exposed to mental breakdown and more or less complete loss of reason. At least this is the constant result of observations I have made in the hospice for psychiatric patients. What a lot of examples I have noted of idiocy and dementia at a tender age, be it at the time of breast feeding, or at the times of the first or second dentition, or following convulsions, often for the slightest causes! The effervescent time of puberty, that is to say from the fourteenth to the twenty-second years, seem to bring other dangers and new causes of a profound attack against the functions of understanding – such as the lively outbursts of an ardent temperament, the reading of novels, annoyance or indiscrete zeal on the part of parents, or unhappy love. Marriage, which appears to be a bulwark against these constantly increasing distresses to the mind, substitutes others of a different kind. These include accidents during pregnancy or childbirth, domestic vexations, unexpected reverses, mutual dissent or jealousy based on things which are either true or in fact just imaginary (6). I throw a veil over the change of life, which can only be painted along the saddest and most melancholic lines, if a noble character does not replace the reign of frivolous pleasures and the attractions of a dissipated life with pure enjoyment. A woman who was naturally inclined to sadness anticipated what is called the menopause with the greatest alarm. Her usual doctor, himself endowed with a melancholic nature, offered only scantily consoling words but a frivolous batch of medicaments. Her discouragement changed into despair. This led to endless recurring anxieties, insomnia and alternate fleeting delirium, together with a dry cough, thinness and spasmodic muscle contractions which made her worry that something was wrong with her chest. She developed frightening dreams and fell into a state of stupor and extreme despondency. She followed the advice of a clever doctor, who took a reassuring tone with her and tried to raise her courage. He prescribed a simple routine with varied physical exercise and recommended several objects of distraction. Calm returned, strength came back without any return of the delirium, but then uterine haemorrhages which recurred at different times also gave rise to new fears and an alternating loss of reason. This time, there were no rules or any plan of management. She saw different doctors and different empirical treatments were tried in turn. Several medicaments, taken in profusion, led to new symptoms and an increase in confusion (7). One single thought seemed to absorb all the faculties of understanding, which was that of an early end, and at this stage a mental alienation was confirmed.

61. Any consideration of the physical lesions which can cause alienation will be discussed elsewhere, when it comes to determining the principles of various treatments. It is less important to insist on particular examples of this sort if only because the same kinds of alienation, and varieties of alienation, can result from more or less intense psychological affections. The most constant observation shows in fact that maniacal insanity, idiocy, melancholia and dementia can equally well result from a blow to the head, suppression of haemorrhage, a retrocession of gout inwards etc, as they can from deep dismay or a strong and deeply frustrated passion. The varieties of maniacal insanity, relative to the different faults in understanding, the degrees of agitation or fury, or the object of the delirium, seem to be related to the intensity of the underlying cause or to individual disposition. The maniacal attacks of women generally consist of taciturnity alternating with inexhaustible chatter, fleeting anger, cries, curses and varied movements. Quite often a firm tone of voice from the guardian, a threatening glance, or the simple application of a straight jacket suffices to bring them to order. How different this is from the maniacal fury of a man, who behaves with a profound sense of the superiority of his strength, who attacks or resists with audacity, and who, without well concerted means of repression, could sometimes create the most tragic scenes!

NOTES TO FIRST SECTION

1. In private establishments more precise information can be gathered on the previous condition of psychiatric patients than in the hospices, where the patients treated come from the lower classes. Dr Esquirol, for instance, who directs one of these establishments, expresses himself in the following manner. 'Nearly all the psychiatric patients entrusted to my care', he says, 'have shown a few irregularities in their functions, their intellectual faculties and in their affections before becoming ill, and often since early infancy . . . Some had excessive pride, others were quick-tempered; some often sad, others ridiculously cheerful. A few have a distressing instability toward their education, while a few stubbornly apply themselves to whatever they are undertaking but without steadiness. Several are punctilious, pernickety, frightened, timid or indecisive. Almost all had had great activity of their intellectual and mental faculties which had redoubled some time before the attack. Most had had bad nerves; the women had had convulsions or hysterical spasms; the men had been subject to cramps, palpitations or palsies . . . With these original or acquired dispositions, it only needed a psychological affection to set off an outburst of fury or the overwhelming of melancholia'. (*Passions considered as Causes, symptoms etc of Mental Alienation.*)
2. One can hardly speak of human passions as illnesses of the soul without having immediately in mind Cicero's *Tusculan Disputations* and the other writings which this splendid genius has devoted to morals, drawing on all the experience of his mature years. What an appropriate time for philosophical studies – that of political storms and the tumultuous conflict of passions which led to so many misfortunes and ended up by shattering the Republic of ancient Rome!
3. It is especially during monthly periods, or else following childbirth, that emotions of all kinds are dangerous and it is this combination which makes alienation much more common in women than in men.
4. I cannot remember without a very painful feeling the example of a very beautiful young lady, brought to the hospice in a most violent state of delirium, having been seduced and

abandoned in a cowardly way by her lover in the ninth month of her pregnancy. Three months later her fury calmed down and there followed a gloomy stupor and an irresistible inclination to suicide. One morning she skilfully drew a lace round her neck and sank into her bed to deceive the guardian's supervision. She had almost suffocated and it was only through assiduous and prolonged care that she was restored to life. Hardly had she come round than she cast a wild look at those who had helped her and reproached them with threats for the odious service that had prolonged her deplorable existence.

5. Extensive correspondence and frequent communications of expert opinions have made me the repository of many similar facts, which it would be superfluous and indiscrete to make public. Many examples of melancholia are also available in the hospice and I only need to recall them to contrast these sad memories with an account of the methods used with more or less success to bring an end to these mental affections, which become all the more rebellious if one seeks to deal with them on supernatural grounds.

6. An English author reports an unusual example of the physical influence of the condition of the womb on the production of insanity. A young lady, hot from a long walk, was imprudent enough to drink a large volume of cold water and remain seated outside on damp ground. Next day, she had headache and backache, which were followed by shivers, anxiety and then great heat. Soon after, she complained of loss of memory, weakness and lassitude, and a state of delirium followed. The illness did not seem to respond to the remedies which were used, for at the usual time of menstruation the febrile symptoms returned and were followed by inexhaustible chattering, unusual gesticulations and a disturbance in the imagination which left no doubt that she had a patent alienation. It was only with great difficulty that the uterine vessels which had become contracted by the action of the cold were relaxed. Re-establishment of menstruation was soon followed by cure of the insanity.

7. The English work already mentioned *(Annals of Insanity)* contains similar examples. Observation XXXV which the author reports has strong strands of resemblance to the one I have just given, but it also shows differences marked by the symptoms of plethora which occurred – a dry cough and very disturbed sleep. In the latter case ophthalmia, headaches, great weakness and even a state of stupor also occurred.

2

PHYSICAL AND PSYCHOLOGICAL
ASPECTS OF MENTAL ALIENATION

62. The science of ideas no doubt can only have fallen in public favour when compared with the solid and rigorous progress of the physical and mathematical sciences. But although it may be far from outstanding in the precision and stability of its principles, should one just forget about it, neglect to make it more experimental and fail to appreciate how closely the study of the functions of human understanding is bound up with another subject which it is so important to fathom? I refer to the natural history and the various outcomes of mental alienation?

63. I can appreciate, in my mind, the immense gap separating analysis in the sense used by surveyors from the same term's application in medicine. But what name should one give to the art of splitting up a highly composite subject and carefully considering each of its parts separately? Are not the words *human understanding* and *will* generic and abstract terms which comprise between them different intellectual or emotional functions whose separate or combined aberrations produce different species of alienation, and whose true characters it is important to determine carefully?

64. It may be that my observations on alienation will have a fortunate influence on the principles of the science of ideas and turn this into a different direction. All metaphysical discussion about the nature of madness has been excluded and I have just laid emphasis on the historical aspect of the various faults of understanding and will, and the physical changes which correspond to them and show themselves externally through detectable signs such as disordered body movements, incoherencies and absurdities in speech, and strange and unusual gestures. The story of alienation then joins the ranks of the physical sciences and needs to be the subject of serious study, since treatment deprived of this foundation is reduced to dangerous trial and error or to blind empiricism.

65. How many examples can I cite of the turmoil and despair which the mental alienation of close relatives brings to families! What a fortunate combination of factors is required to

Medico-Philosophical Treatise on Mental Alienation.
Philippe Pinel. Translated by G. Hickish, D. Healy and L.C. Charland.
© 2008 John Wiley & Sons, Ltd.

bring it to a favourable conclusion even when it is actually curable! For medical treatment, in many cases, has strict limitations which it is as important to be aware of as it is to know about medicine's resources. Our failures can provide valuable lessons too.

66. A large collection of psychiatric patients alone can offer these lessons through all the reports they provide of the different lapses in reason and all the forms which the illness can take, and the range of conditions prior to its attacks, as well as seasonal variations and the sex of the patient. But a veil that is difficult to penetrate obscures these facts, and how can one really grasp them, distinguish their true character, or sort them out, if the various objects of this research are not agreed upon and if the art of observing them is unrecognised? Will it be possible to make an annual inventory and reach general conclusions if a systematic method is not followed? It is to ensure this progress and spread some light upon it that I put together here the result of my observations on the diverse disturbances in intellectual or affective functions which can be used to characterise the different species and varieties of mental alienation. I have considered these disturbances separately in order to learn how to appreciate them better and distinguish them by their special characters, even though many of them are combined and act as confounders.

67. The administration of an enlightened judge with austere manners is beyond praise and deserves the respectful attention of the Censors. Broadly speaking one can only admire the precautions taken to avoid mistakes in the legal examination of psychiatric patients. Nevertheless, there are many difficulties to be surmounted in certifying the true character and different degrees of their mental disorders! I have seen people who had reached a condition of complete convalescence for several months become irritated by the formalities of such an examination. They may adopt a quite uncharacteristic tone and speech and even deliberately talk incoherently, either out of spite or ill understood deceit. As a result they may unhesitatingly be declared incurable. When one wishes to interrogate psychiatric patients about their condition, they generally elude the questions they are asked, confining themselves to feigned reticence, or they give an answer quite the opposite to the truth. It is only by studying them for several months, in their conversation and their behaviour, gaining their confidence and thus getting them to pour out their souls, that one can succeed in unveiling their deepest thoughts as their illness subsides. Should one then wish to follow its precise course, as a doctor, it is necessary to familiarise oneself with the different subjects which are the subject of the present section.

I. DISORDERS OF PHYSICAL SENSITIVITY IN MENTAL ALIENATION

68. It is no doubt going too far to apply, like Dr Chrigton[1], the title of axioms to certain results of observations on physical irritability and sensitivity, since this term only seems appropriate for sciences of rigorous exactitude such as geometry. But this author's comments on the different sensations that the nerves of the internal organs such as the heart, the lungs, the intestines, the kidneys and the womb etc can appreciate are no less applicable in health than in disease. It is this sensation which conveys to us the feeling of comfortable digestion, breathing healthy air, well-being and vigour; as well of such opposite conditions as malaise,

---

[1] *Pinel's spelling of Crichton – Ed.*

debility or pain varied in undefined ways in different illnesses. I confine myself here to considerations relative to insanity.

69. The onset of maniacal insanity can sometimes be remarkably varied. It can bring convulsive movements or violent shaking of the body and limbs, a kind of disruption of the features of the face, with either a total loss of speech or else an extreme loquacity, piercing cries, anger and foaming at the mouth. The extreme intensity of the symptoms can sometimes be misleading, so that a malignant or ataxic fever can end up being taken as maniacal insanity. Not only can the same causes equally produce one or other of these illnesses, but they can have common features such as violent shaking, furious delirium, alternating stupor or nervous excitation. Both can cause a marked acceleration of the pulse, dryness of the tongue, pale and haggard face, light or interrupted sleep and total refusal of any food. So the distinction is difficult to make right from the start and it is often only by watching the illness for several days that one can settle one's doubts.

70. The amount of heat commonly developing in many bouts of maniacal insanity, sometimes inside the abdomen, at other times in the head, but most often throughout the body, is scarcely conceivable. It should be regarded as a form of torture for these psychiatric patients to remain lying on a feather bed or simply on plain mattresses, and it is hardly surprising if they prefer to spend the night stretched out on the floor, even on stone, as if to cool themselves down, and are very reluctant to lie anywhere else. In one such case, there was a blind insistence on keeping a maniacal patient in his bed day and night, using a straight jacket and strap, and I saw him with his eyes blazing and red in the face fighting against his bonds. I feared an impending attack of apoplexy if he was not allowed to get up for the day and if care was not taken to let him walk about in the open air. I always recall with an uncomfortable feeling the state of severe suffering of an unfortunate mentally deranged patient entrusted to my care during the storms of the Revolution, at the Bicêtre hospital. He conveyed to me, in a profoundly painful tone, the consuming fire he felt in his entrails despite the cooling drinks I had lavished on him. I was then without the means needed for the treatment of the insane and could not even have him take the repeated lukewarm baths which I now use at the psychiatric hospice so successfully.

71. Another unequivocal proof of this internal heat lies in the consistency and ease with which some psychiatric patients of either sex tolerate the most bitter and prolonged cold. In the month of Nivôse[2] of Year III, and during days when the thermometer indicated 10, 11 and down as far as 16 degrees below freezing, one mentally deranged patient at the Bicêtre hospice could not be bothered with his woollen blanket and stayed sitting on the frozen floor of his lodge. In the morning his door had hardly been opened when he was seen running about in his vest in the courtyards, taking a handful of ice or snow, putting it onto his chest and letting it melt with a sort of delight like someone trying to breath fresh air during a heat wave. But one has to be careful not to generalise too much. Many psychiatric patients who are less agitated and less violent, or have reached the stage of their attack where the illness is subsiding, show the greatest sensitivity to cold and in winter settle themselves down around the stoves. They even run the risk of their feet and hands freezing when the season is too harsh.

---

[2] *Nivôse – Fourth month of Republican calendar – Ed.*

72. A further remarkable feature of the nervous excitation peculiar to many maniacal patients is lack of sleep combined with a great increase in muscular strength. This long known phenomenon has rather too widely been applied to all the species of alienation and at all their stages. I have seen examples of the development of this strength which were prodigious, for the mightiest bonds gave way to the manic patient's efforts with an ease which was even more astonishing than the actual amount of resistance overcome. So how much more formidable he becomes with his audacity and the high opinion he has of the superiority of his strength! And what dangers those who approach him run if he grabs some handy article or murderous weapon! Hence various expedients and some tactics, which I will speak about later, designed to make his struggles ineffective and avoid tragedies. But this increased muscular power is not seen as the symptoms of the insanity subside or in some periodical episodes, where instead there is a state of stupor and the complication of the onset of apoplexy.

73. Can maniacal patients tolerate extremes of hunger and thirst as well as bitter cold? This question should also be settled by the facts. And is it not general knowledge that most bouts of maniacal insanity are distinguished by a series of irregular bouts of extraordinary hunger, and that a kind of fainting follows close on the lack of food? The example has been cited of a foreign hospital where a strict diet designed to make the mentally disturbed patient tired was one of the foundations of treatment. The influence of a warm climate and the way of life of those who live off the land in such countries might be linked with this precept, as long as its benefits are continuously monitored. However, nothing would be more harmful or destructive in our northern regions. Has a comparable experiment consequent upon the events of the Revolution not shown, at the Bicêtre hospice for the insane, that lack of food is only likely to aggravate and prolong maniacal insanity if not actually to be fatal (1)?

74. Instead of having a voracious appetite, deranged patients may feel full up, so that they turn against food and obstinately refuse to eat until their appetite comes back again. This reluctance to eat may be related to suspicions of an imaginary poison, or to an extreme dedication to religious principles, or to one of the antipathies common in maniacal patients. It has also often been observed that at the initial onset or the recurrence of maniacal insanity, when the patient has completely lost his reason and has no sense of his own existence, nor his needs, nor even where he is, he firmly shuts his mouth and clenches his teeth and may frustrate the best concerted efforts to get some kind of nourishment, even in liquid form, into him. The melancholic patient may also put up the same kind of extreme resistance. This is all the more difficult to overcome because it is based on an exclusive obsession which seems to dominate the mind completely and becomes set with inflexible determination. These patients also sometimes finally subside into marasmus and consumption, soon leading to their death.

75. An industrious kind hearted women tried to make up for the dissoluteness of her husband, who was given to gambling, drunkenness and utter debauchery, by working hard and behaving irreproachably. All her efforts were in vain. After a few years she and her children fell into the most distressing state. She was deeply despondent, full of bitterness and she tried in vain to find glimmers of hope through gentle and fond devotion. She could not sleep, became distraught and utter refusal of all food showed she was intent on self-destruction. It is in this state that she was taken to the Salpêtrière, where numerous testimonies of concern

and of esteem for her personal qualities were received from her former neighbours. She was determined to starve herself to death and it was only with extreme difficulty that she was sometimes made to take a little liquid nourishment with a baby's bottle. 'Enjoy what you've done', she said to her husband, who went to see her four days before she died; 'Now you've got what you wanted; I'm going to die'.

76. Some cases of idiocy can be so complete, and the state of stupor and insensitivity so pronounced, that such a patient does not have even the instinct of animals. A young girl of seven years appeared unresponsive either to threats or to caresses, and was unable to recognise the servant girl who brought her meals from all the others. She showed no pleasure at being given food, she watched it being taken way from her with indifference even when she was hungry, and did not seem to recognise anything as food, even when it was put in her mouth.

77. Another young girl looked at her dinner with pleasure when it was brought to her and ate it eagerly. If anyone pretended to take her food away, she cried out and even made threatening gestures, but once she had eaten enough she happily watched the rest of it being taken away with no thought for the future. I can also quote the example of a much more developed instinct in the case of a young idiot who can articulate her basic needs and who asks to drink and to eat. Once satisfied, she hangs onto the remaining food and gets annoyed if anyone tries to take it away from her. She even understands that money is a means of obtaining it and begs for this from strangers, and she gives the donations she has received to the servant girl as a sign of gratitude.

78. Should a veil be thrown over an unbridled passion, which is often no less likely to represent one of the distinctive features of alienation? This is, in either sex a physical turmoil in the reproductive organs, accompanied by quite lascivious gestures and obscene talk. It seems to stem from an inner inclination which only lasts as long as the illness. I have seen people whose behaviour is completely respectable indulge, during a given period of their maniacal state, in this unfortunate association with debauched women, and then once they have recovered go back to their former reserved and perfectly decent character. I have seen this disorder develop in severe cases as follows. First there is quite trivial cheerfulness, an alert look, voluptuous elegance of dress, anxious curiosity, trembling hands, dull pains in the womb, burning warmth in the breasts, roaming eyes and impatience. The episode then advances to babble full of lewd words and obscene talk, screams, provocative gestures and extremely lascivious body movements and all the frenetic anger and illusions of an erotic delirium. This impetuous ardour subsequently yields to an inevitable inhibition, and a gloomy peace and quiet, and a general lassitude, follows. At this stage the person may have become scrawny and this uterine frenzy leads to exhaustion, stupor and dementia. Afterwards, normal weight returns in stages. Sometimes the illness becomes periodical and life goes on with alternating states of erotic delirium and complete apathy.

79. A large hospice, like the Salpêtrière, offers numerous examples of a vice which is all too common amongst gatherings of sexually active people. I refer to masturbation, the unhappy habit of which has often been acquired before puberty, but which the most reserved and decent young girls can also experience as a result of the nervous excitement that distinguishes the maniacal state. This vice may be only short-lived and completely

disappear on convalescence, as I have often seen; but it may also continue and turn into a kind of chronic affection, and may be passed on as a kind of contagion to other psychiatric patients if strict supervision does not put an end to the malaise. The condition sometimes becomes so deep rooted that one sees patients fall into a kind of senseless stupor as a result of it, or into the last stage of exhaustion and actual consumption. Following any attempts to check this species of blind fury with a straight jacket, the resentful patient goes off and finds a thousand ways of circumventing the precautions taken. It is especially in winter that unfortunate consequences of this tendency are seen, since the scurvy then accompanying this state of wasting ends in being fatal.

80. It may well be assumed that another unnatural vice, which requires the participation of two equally debauched persons of the same sex, also takes place in the psychiatric hospices. These intimate liaisons are sometimes seen to develop as a result of depraved morals and are falsely veiled as natural friendliness. It is up to the supervisor always to be on guard and to prevent this spread of vices which can contaminate young people only recently admitted to the hospice with all the simplicity and naivety of innocence.

81. Related vices are among the greatest obstacles to the curing of maniacal insanity. Even when one has managed to dissipate the most violent symptoms, there can follow a more or less marked failing of reason or state of dementia. This, combined with a distaste for work and with other perverted tendencies, makes the people incapable of fulfilling an ordinary role in the community and confines them within the hospices for ever more. Every decency is then gone, vice is openly exposed and these unhappy victims of debauchery make disgusting comments and scoff at all the means of restraint one can use. There is nothing left but to confine them in separate lodges and let them immerse themselves in all the obscenities their befuddled imagination suggests to them, without contaminating everyone else with their example.

II. DISTURBANCES IN THE PERCEPTION OF EXTERNAL OBJECTS IN ALIENATION

82. The initial onset or the return of attacks of maniacal insanity can show great variation. But it is in the expression and features of the face that this development is clearly proclaimed, as the psychiatric patient shows his inner self to the outside world. Sometimes he keeps his head raised and his eyes lifted towards the sky, speaks in a low voice and stops and starts with an air of deep contemplation or ardent admiration. In some cases his face is red, his eyes sparkling and he indulges in inexhaustible talkativeness. On other occasions his face is pale and his features haggard, with an unsettled and wild look, as in the drunkenness resulting from an excess of liquor. Little by little spasm spreads to all the muscles of the face giving it more expression. The eyes become fixed and threatening, and the speech, tone of voice and gestures take on the character of anger or blind fury.

83. Efforts to convince a melancholic patient and distract him from an exclusive series of thoughts which obsess and dominate him are usually unsuccessful. He remains as if centred on himself and new impressions reaching his organs of sight or hearing seem not

to be transmitted to the seat of understanding. His look is wild, his countenance gloomy and quiet, and his face is pallid and all skin and bone. His thoughts of the future are full of sinister presages. He seeks solitude passionately and his sad thoughts and his extreme anguish give rise to deep sighs. He seems to be a stranger to everything around him, sees nothing, hears nothing, remains centred on the particular thoughts to which his memory keeps bringing him back and abandons himself to all the emotions to which they give rise.

84. A lifeless and expressionless physiognomy does not always indicate dementia or idiocy. I can cite the example of a seven-year old child, reduced to complete idiocy, who has rosy cheeks, black hair and eyebrows, extremely bright eyes and all the outward appearances of sound understanding. I have also sometimes noticed bright animated eyes and a smiling face, with an almost total absence of thought. Another young girl is the opposite: at her second dentition she had had repeated convulsions which caused her to lose the power of speech and functions of comprehension. Her face was expressionless and her eyes fixed without being directed towards any particular object. There is sometimes a lack of coordination between gaze and the sense of touch, which are not directed together towards an object whose interest appears to attract attention. An idiot I know first looks at a painted image or a solid object offered to him, but he puts his hand to it in a clumsy way as if the line of his vision is not directed towards it. His eyes themselves remain roving or move vaguely towards the brightest part of the room. The degree to which he can appreciate what he is being shown then can only be very obscure or none at all.

85. The functions of the sensory organs can be damaged by the various causes which have brought about the state of insanity, such as intemperance, excesses of work or study, or a state of hypochondria which has progressed to insanity, and all these faults can be associated with head pains, dizzy spells and vertigo. But in general the eyesight and hearing are extremely sensitive in maniacal insanity and the least sensory impression suffices to excite them. Experience shows that in the acute stage of this illness the patients must remain isolated in a darkened and quiet place until calm is re-established.

86. The sensitivity of hearing in particular appears blunt in certain cases of idiocy. As a result the patient cannot be roused from his stupor by sounds calculated to arouse the sense of surprise or of fear, or which relate to his primitive needs. But sometimes strange variations are seen and I saw a girl of seven years whose organ of hearing was very sensitive to the faintest sound, but she did not appear to distinguish articulated sounds or the different tones of voice which one could take with her, such as anger, threats or of affectionate kindness.

87. It seems that in many cases of idiocy or dementia everything is reduced to merely a physical impression on the sensory organs and that no actual perception gets through to the mind. One patient of this kind, whom I have often observed, has haggard eyes and keeps twisting her head in different directions. She gives no response to questions put to her, does not speak or at the most only utters a few insignificant monosyllables. She does not show, by any outward sign, either wishes, repugnance or anger, so she seems to be without passions and without thought, and is continuously restless, without purpose and without any immediate objective. Another young girl, in her sixteenth year, is like an infant. Her breasts and sexual organs are undeveloped. She remains on her bed all the time with her limbs flexed and her head resting on her chest. Her whole body in a continual state of unrest

and she repeats in a parrot fashioned way the word *mummy* without attaching any idea to this term and without appearing to understand anything of questions put to her about her mother. What will the end-result of this prolonged infancy be?

88. Maniacal insanity can show itself not by a total absence of any affective state or ideas, but by their rapid succession and their extreme instability. A young girl of twenty-two, who had become deranged as a result of an unhappy love affair, still retained her bright eyes and switched from one thought to another quite different one at the speed of lightning. Sometimes there were expressions of tenderness, full of propriety, then obscene words and a blatant incitement to the joys of love-making. A moment later she might be all puffed up with vanity, with a lofty and commanding air, soon thinking she is the Queen. With a proud and majestic step she would look at her hapless companions with disdain. Any advice or remonstrance was useless: she did not seem to hear anything and just followed the fleeting whims of the moment. Sometimes she might rush about, sing, cry out, dance, laugh or strike those around her with no intention of malice, abandoning herself to all these little eccentricities with a sort of childish instinct.

89. The thoughts of maniacal patients, although marked by their bizarre quality and sometimes extreme instability, take on the character which dementia gives, leaving aside their other distinctive differences. Some of these patients, in their agitated state, repeat the same word endlessly and seem to remain locked for whole months and even years in this confined sphere. On other occasions the patient changes the object of his attention on a daily basis, settling in the morning on a particular idea or set of ideas, which he repeats ceaselessly throughout the same day with gestures and movements corresponding to the dominant thought. In this case the sensations seem to constitute a physical impression. We notice then a kind of contrast compared with other maniacal patients who speak and answer correctly, and appear to reconcile the two opposite extremes of restlessness or fury and well-coordinated thoughts. Another quite common variety of maniacal insanity is that where the patient, in the middle of his wanderings and delirium, is liable to fix his attention on a subject and even write letters full of sense and reason. Then in other varieties, or in other periods of the same alienation, the most absurd talk and incoherent thoughts follow one another tumultuously, and finally disappear as fast as they arrive, leaving no trace. I was required last year to determine the state of alienation of a man who had reached the change of life and was in an inveterate state of maniacal insanity. I found him in a spacious garden where he was free to walk and all the questions I could put to him were frustrated because he just followed the thoughts bombarding his mind, as if he had heard nothing. Sometimes he murmured inarticulate sounds in a low voice. At others he stared – but at nothing in particular, or gave out piercing cries and seemed to be warding off an attack and making threats. It was noticeable that he generally becomes violent and angry when he is frustrated, but he looks after himself independently, is refined in his appearance and is straightforward in his behaviour.

90. The thoughts may be lively, clear or confused, depending upon the different periods of the maniacal insanity. Often after the first stages, when this illness is still at full strength and the patient retains the sense of his existence, his talk is characterised by striking thoughts and the cleverest and most surprising reproaches. He enjoys arguing with others and contradicting them and shrewdly notes everything incorrect or doubtful said to him. If he recounts some incident he expresses himself with animation and adopts an uncanny note of

inspiration and enthusiasm. As the effervescence settles down, the patient takes on a more composed tone and his ideas follow one another and are renewed more calmly, but with less sharpness and energy. His gestures are less expressive but more natural and true. He accepts contradictions more patiently, he is no longer so liable to become angry and reason gradually takes charge again. But if the insanity is complicated by the onset of apoplexy or threatens to degenerate into dementia, the thoughts appear to be confused. One object is often taken for another totally different one, and sometimes even the home where he is living is not distinguished from somewhere else. The smallest numerical calculation becomes embarrassing or very subject to error and the value of certain coins can only be appreciated, or their numbers counted, in a few very simple cases. Ideas of different periods of the patient's life are no less confused and there is a tendency to connect the earliest with those which are the most recent. The smallest sentences become shortened through involuntary omissions and one often has to guess what the patient is talking about or what the connection is which brought it up.

III. DISTURBANCES IN THOUGHT PROCESSES IN ALIENATION

91. The mind of a healthy man is generally capable of a very active function, namely concentrating attention solely on an object which is making a clear impression on the sensory organs, or on an object brought back by memory as an image. This attention may continue for a fixed time or be suspended and restored several times. It develops through training, clarifies ideas, makes the memory more reliable and conveys strength and accuracy to judgement. It also forms the solid foundation of our accumulated knowledge and of the production of works of genius. Association with a strong passion, such as love, ambition or hatred, conveys additional energy, and therein rests the motivation for all the great events which feature so vividly in the history of the human species.

92. At the height of maniacal insanity, when understanding is assailed by a rapid succession of the most incoherent and tumultuous thoughts, attention is completely destroyed, as is judgement and the inner sense of one's own existence. The patient, unable to recover, is unaware of all contact with the outside world. By his gestures and talk an order of thoughts, different from those which impressions on the sensory organs could generate, is evident. And these disordered and unconnected thoughts seem to form in an automatic way, come then instantly go, and follow their impetuous course like a torrent. I could mention as an example of this kind a man whose mental condition I was asked to record not long ago. I was able to ask him different questions, as did two of his relations of whom he had formerly been fond. But he merely pronounced, in no order or sequence, the words *tree, hat, sky* etc, turning his eyes elsewhere. He mumbled inarticulate sounds in a low voice, then suddenly raising his voice in a tone of anger, and turning his eyes up to the sky, he uttered piercing cries, then became calm again soon afterwards, continuing to speak in a quite incoherent way about imaginary objects.

93. Undoubtedly many examples can be quoted of a more or less major disturbance in the functions of the understanding which prevent maniacal patients from settling their attention on any given object. However, in many cases of maniacal insanity a few gaps in imagination do not prevent the patient from being able to link most of their thoughts together

and concentrating on some of them. They reason, discuss their interests, often beg to go back to their families and respond aptly when this is declined. Some are even sufficiently able to direct their attention, in the midst of their dreamlike wanderings, to write letters which are full of sense and reason to their close relatives or to the official authorities (2). I encouraged one of them, of a very cultivated mind, to write me a letter to arrive the following day, and this letter, written at a time when he was saying the most absurd things, was full of sense and reason. And it is known that one of the varieties of insanity, called *reasoning insanity (folie raisonnante)* in the hospices, is distinguished by the close coherence of the train of thought and precision of judgement. So the patient can read, write and reflect as if he enjoyed sound reason, but is, however, liable to commit the gravest acts of violence. I have seen some of them tear up everything they could get hold of, such as their clothes or the blankets on their bed: a kind of blind fury.

94. Another excess to combat, and indeed one of the particular attributes of mental alienation, is the concentration of the mind of melancholic patients, fixated night and day on a specific object. It cannot be deflected, because it is continuously associated with some deep passion such as anger, hatred, wounded pride, wish for revenge, profound chagrin, an extreme distaste for life or indeed an irresistible tendency to suicide. A similar mental concentration, which cannot be stopped or redirected at will, appears to be purely passive and can arise from regrets felt over something good that is thought to have been lost, over the personal persecution of which one thinks one is the victim, over a state of distress which only exists in the mind or over any other imaginary idea. Focussed delusions can also spring quite often from religious terrors, thoughts of a vengeful and inexorable God, and the everlasting punishment one believes one has earned. Hence the extreme difficulty of dissipating these dismal delusions and gaining, through counselling, the confidence of the melancholic patient. He is always ready to set the unvarying will of the Supreme Being against the vain talk of men.

95. A sensitive man may experience wide variations depending upon the development of his understanding and sweeping changes depending on the vagaries of the atmospheric conditions, the seasons, the climate, the way of life, psychological affections and most illnesses. But one of the constant features of dementia and idiocy is to render the man quite incapable of this active function, and contribute powerfully to the state of negativity which he would have bemoaned if he was capable of knowing his own self.

96. A young man, whose mental state I was required to certify, had reached his fourteenth year and since his earliest age was very easily distracted. Impressions on his sensory organs occur normally if one manages to hold his attention, but he only retains these impressions momentarily and it is only by their frequent repetition that ideas can be inculcated into him. Things which seem extraordinary to him are best engraved in his memory and it was only with great difficulty that he was taught to read and write.

97. Some highly spirited maniacal patients can still retain their freedom of thought and the ability to fix their attention on a given object. Even those who are quite restless and prone to rambling may attentively consider objects which appeal to them and fleetingly show all that distinguishes a sound mind. But in general, extreme mobility leads a maniacal patient to switch quickly from one subject to another, often quite incoherently, and the remission of

the illness is indicated by a more pronounced ability to reflect in a consistent manner upon all that it is important for him to know, or even to undertake regular work. It is then that convalescence progresses rapidly. In this case, are the same principles not to be followed as in the education of children? Sometimes excellent minds seem quite impervious to successful development because of the clumsiness of their teachers, the harshness of their principles or their disheartening approach. It is noticeable in the hospices that the psychiatric patients who had in their youth developed a taste for culture readily resume their former habit as their illness subsides and are able to turn their attention to sedentary work. This work merely incurs the distaste of other country women used to hard work and heavy agricultural tasks. Furthermore, the latter remain apathetic and inactive, progressing at a slow pace towards the desired end of convalescence, or they may indeed become incurable. But, what obstacles there are to the restoration of reason to rich women, devoted to frivolous tastes since their youth, and incapable of applying themselves to the culture of fine arts or to the physical sciences!

IV. DISTURBANCES IN MEMORY AND THE PRINCIPLE OF ASSOCIATION OF IDEAS IN ALIENATION

98. I am not going to consider here either extreme vividness of the memory or states in which it languishes for different physical and mental causes and in various illnesses. I am only going to comment that earlier ideas can return to the understanding in two quite different ways. On the one hand, through a kind of inner influence, without the assistance of the free will, and sometimes in spite of efforts to dismiss them. On the other hand, through a strictly active power, the mind can bring back some earlier thoughts through their various connections or their association with other objects appreciated and present in the memory. This brings us back to the principle of the association of ideas, generally agreed by all the authors who have concerned themselves with the workings of human understanding (3).

99. Associations of strange ideas can occur in alienation which can give rise to serious mistakes or quite childish delusions. The exclusive object of one melancholic lady's delusions is the Devil, whilst otherwise, in every other respect, her understanding is quite sane. She would scold her servants for having been to a marionette show, on the pretext that the Devil intervenes in this popular amusement. She had some furniture delivered from along the Seine; but when it arrived at her home she refused to accept it, and forced her husband to sell it as bewitched, on the pretext that it had passed under the Chatou Bridge, which people said had been built by the Devil. The story went round that there were once witches in Louviers, and from then on the lady forbade her husband from having anything to do with the inhabitants of that town. If in a gathering where she was present the name of the Devil was mentioned, she became flustered, turned red and pale in turn, and for her it was a sign of the most sinister portent.

100. A sixty-year-old lady, following prolonged spiritual dispute, dropped into a kind of strange melancholia, which involved associating the idea of witchcraft with everything she saw or heard. She thought that all her gold or silver, whether she received it or gave it away, was imitation and valueless, that all the food she took was too spicy, that everybody was

plotting to deceive her and that everything anybody promised her or told her was untrue. In brief, she thought everything in this base world was but duplicity and lies.

101. In many psychiatric patients, all coherence or association of ideas seems to be destroyed in the most severe degree of insanity. They pass rapidly from one idea to another, which are sometimes far-removed, and their talk often shows unexpected and very strange contradictions or a confused assembly clearly corresponding to the disorder of their thoughts. One maniacal patient I was watching who was unaware of my presence kept repeating the words *sword, sun, hat* etc. He responded volubly and angrily to a speaker he thought he could see up in the air, let out piercing cries, spoke in a low voice, lost his temper, laughed, sang and all in all showed the most versatile and incoherent instability. This feature is indeed shared by many psychiatric patients seen every day in the hospices.

102. Memory, like all other functions of the mind, seems to be suspended during the outbreak of some attacks of maniacal insanity and it is only when the attack subsides that it seems to come into free play again. The patient no longer retains any memory of his delirium or his eccentric behaviour and he cannot conceive of having stayed as long in hospital as the records show. A young girl had been brought up in the house of one of her uncles of whom she was very fond, and he told her of plans for a marriage which seemed very much one of convenience. It being the time of her monthly period, she was so upset by this and felt so mentally shaken that she shrieked: *'But I think I shall go mad'*. The chagrin soon led to a state of stupor and alienation and she was taken to the psychiatric hospice at Salpêtrière. She seemed to have completely lost her power of speech and stayed squatting in a corner of her lodge for some of the day, not seeming to know where she was or having any real sense of her own self. The success of her treatment became increasingly in doubt during the course of the year, at the end of which her reason gradually began to return. This patient had forgotten about her previous condition so completely that she maintained that she had only been in the hospital for six weeks – the time of the clearing of her delirium (4).

103. One must not conceal the fact that sometimes psychiatric patients retain their memory of everything that has happened during their fiery agitation. They show the deepest regret during their lucid intervals and after they are fully recovered, and they avoid meeting those who have seen them in that state, as if anyone could blame them for the unwitting results of an illness. A young patient one morning had a bout of maniacal delirium, to the extent of tearing up everything she could get her hands on and violently attacking everybody who went near her. She had to be put in a straight jacket. This method of control immediately calmed her fury down, but she retained such a bitter memory of her previous outbursts that she showed the deepest repentance for it and felt she had deserved the severest punishment.

104. One cannot moreover marvel too much at the ways memory can undergo changes during any bout of maniacal insanity and the extent to which it then may become stronger or weaker. A young man who had been precipitated into this condition by too much study seemed to retain all his shrewdness and used it very successfully to get to the bottom of his delusions. Former thoughts then returned very vividly, to the point of greatly obscuring perceptions of present objects. He seemed to be living in a different world from others and added that it would be impossible for him to understand them as long as he remained subjected through his illness to this new order of things (5). In similar cases, memory of the

past seems to come back clearly and what had been forgotten in periods of calm returns in vivid and very lively colours, as I have seen many times in public and private establishments devoted to the treatment of mental alienation.

105. A type of alienation and delirium which follows an attack of apoplexy nearly always leads to a substantial reduction if not complete loss of memory. This disturbance may also be restricted to the terms which express ideas. A lawyer for whom my advice was asked had forgotten, following an attack of apoplexy, his own name and also his wife's, children's and his friends' names, whilst otherwise his speech was quite fluent. He could neither read nor write, yet he appeared to remember things which had formerly made an impression on his senses and which were relevant to his profession of lawyer. He was seen pointing with his fingers to files containing deeds or contracts which were missing and showing, by other signs, that he retained the former chain of his ideas.

106. Idiocy also causes a marked obliteration of memory and I can quote for this the example of a young man of sixteen years whose sensory organs receive impressions of external objects, but who cannot retain any ideas about them so that the moment afterwards everything is forgotten. Nothing seems to attract his attention except what is related to his basic needs. If someone annoys or threatens him, he cries out and goes away trembling, but he comes back at once and seems to have forgotten everything. He responds to simple questions in the same tone as they are put to him, but he cannot compare two ideas with one another because of his memory defect. If food is offered to him when he is hungry, he appears unable to make any choice and prefers whatever is nearest at hand.

V. DISTURBANCES OF JUDGEMENT IN PSYCHIATRIC PATIENTS

107. 'After sound judgement', said La Bruyère, 'what is rarest in the world is diamonds and pearls'. This sad truth, which applies every day to events in civil life, is no less noticeable in the fields of science and letters, because their pure source is so often contaminated by a bizarre mixture of fiction, childish sallies of imagination, conceits, false ideas or inflated pretensions. But here I must restrict myself to considerations of anomalies in judgement in relation to a state of illness.

108. At the start, or even during the course of a maniacal state, one often sees such a major disturbance or such an ill-assorted succession of gestures, ideas, words, facial expressions and psychological affections, that there is a complete image of a total disruption of judgement as of other intellectual functions. Sometimes in this extreme stage of delirium, especially among women, there are also convulsive movements of the muscles of the face, grimaces, heated anger or even at intervals piercing shrieks or loud screams. That is the scene often to be beheld in public and private establishments devoted to psychiatric patients.

109. Mistaken judgement can also occur in a state of calm and the appearances of consistent reasoning and lead to an inexact or even ridiculous link between widely separated ideas. A patient of this kind, whose treatment I had in hand, and who lived in a house within view of

the dome of the Val-de-Grace, maintained that this edifice had to be transported to the garden of the Tuileries and that two men would be sufficient for this operation. He thought he could see an appropriate relationship between the strength of two men and the resistance offered by this enormous mass. However much one used examples to try to draw his attention to the huge disproportion involved, roughly calculating the weight of each of the stones of this vast building, he continued to judge that the enterprise was possible and even proposed to take on the job himself. Eccentric behaviour of other kinds soon followed. The same patient thought he was the proprietor of all the forests in France and in this capacity signed money orders for several hundred millions to be drawn on the public exchequer. His ideas became increasingly exalted and he ended up believing he was the most powerful ruler in Europe.

110. Psychiatric hospices are never short of an example of maniacal insanity characterised by eccentricities, or even fury, with a kind of judgement preserved in its full integrity if one is to go simply by what the patient says. He may give perfectly correct and precise answers to questions from bystanders and no incoherence in their thought is perceptible. He may read and write letters as if his understanding is completely sound. Yet, in stark contrast, he pulls his clothes to pieces, sometimes tears up the blankets or straw of his bed and always concocts some plausible reason to justify his odd behaviour and fits of anger. This type of madness is so often encountered that it has been given the common name of *reasoning insanity (folie raisonnante)*.

111. Strong application and commitment, as well as profoundly entrenched combinations of ideas, seem to be the characteristic feature of the melancholic patient. This would ensure that his judgements had the rare quality of soundness and stability if he was not influenced all the time by a mental disturbance which dominates him and makes him single minded and always liable to go beyond the limits. A man with a cultivated mind and gifted with a good memory had made a diligent study of Condillac's works. He became so imbued with them that he thought he had found the kernel or nugget of all the other sciences and asserted that all the other books on history, physics, chemistry and even mathematics should be burnt as useless. His imagination became more and more carried away and he thought he was the envoy from the Almighty sent to spread this doctrine and make it known throughout the world. He expected, like all great men, to be persecuted. One day when he was threatened with being transferred to a psychiatric home he seemed to enjoy it, for this was for him a moment of triumph: 'All the better!', he said, smiling, 'Now my enemies are frightened of me, and are stepping up their acts of hatred and vengeance as my principles spread throughout the Earth'.

112. The nature of an alienation which resembles a mixture of reason and eccentricity, and of discernment and true delirium: features which appear mutually exclusive, is difficult to imagine. One psychiatric patient, whose breakdown goes back seven years, understood his condition perfectly well and judged this himself as sanely as if he was a detached outsider. He wanted to take the necessary steps to make a recovery, but on the other hand he was convinced that he was incurable. If one pointed out the inconsistency in his thoughts and talk, he agreed in good faith, but replied that this tendency dominates him so strongly that he cannot escape. He added that he did not guarantee the soundness of the judgements he made but that it was not within his power to put them right. His understanding was much more altered in another respect. He believed he was above common rules and that if he made up his

mind to get closer to other men in his behaviour he would have to start by doing something extraordinary, and that this would lead to bad and even terrible consequences for him. He believed, for example, that if he blew his nose, his nose would remain in his handkerchief, and if he tried to shave himself, he would not be able to avoid cutting his throat, and that if he walked, his legs would break as if they were made of glass. He sometimes confined himself for several days to strict fasting, under the pretext that any food he took would inevitably choke him. What can one think of such a sustained and strange aberration of judgement?

113. The faculty of making judgements, one author has subtly stated, is the same thing in the psychiatric patient as in the man endowed with sound understanding. This is so in the case of a musician from the Island of Nootka compared with a pupil at the Conservatoire. The faculty which draws ideas together by their points of real or apparent conformity is the same in both but they have different perceptions and their judgements are different. When a patient judges that government of the world is in his hands, that the seasons obey his command, that he can dry up the Ganges River at will etc, he makes these judgements because the perceptions presented to his mind force him to draw such conclusions. The errors of judgement only result from material on which this faculty is working. If the facts are insufficient in number, or their examination too brief, then unsound and incorrect judgements result, and what a lot of examples of this one sees every day in civil society! Is not the man gifted with the soundest understanding subject to these aberrations of judgement if he talks of things he doesn't know enough about, or expresses his opinion over a matter which needs, to reach a conclusion, more facts than he possesses? False and illusory perceptions sometimes dominate patients' understanding so powerfully that they are driven by an irresistible force to form a judgement consistent with what they inwardly feel, and which may also stem from a sudden change in their physical state. It is sometimes through energetic restraint that one manages to expose discrepancies in judgement. A young girl, who had been tipped into maniacal insanity as a result of excessive devotion, was in a state of eccentricity and extreme fury. She issued the most imperious orders, and at the least resistance to her wishes she invoked the fires of heaven to punish the guilty parties. She was agitated, threatening, cursing violently and everything annoyed her and incurred her wrath. She was taken to a lodge and put in a straight jacket to control her. A few hours later, the hospice director came to visit her and had a joke with her over her claim to be able to bring down the fires of heaven – she who would not even know how to get a garment off which is too tight for her. Since that evening she became much calmer and from then on her treatment encountered no further obstacles.

114. As maniacal insanity increases, or threatens to end in dementia, a deterioration in judgement is seen stemming from deteriorating memory and a sudden forgetfulness for ideas which have just come into the head and the words needed to express them. The answers to questions which have just been put are repeated again and again *ad nauseam*. There is an endless chain of worries and anxieties over domestic matters if the patient goes home to their family too soon. Odd articles in her hands are scattered around and dropped and picked up again with no idea where they have been left. Timing is muddled, there is only a vague idea of distance and far-away things are associated with others right under one's eyes. Earlier events which may even have nothing to do with the matter being considered come to mind, sometimes distorted or completely changed, with cheerful or sad

associations. Words expressing them keep being repeated with outbursts of laughter or tears or doleful sounds, till fresh impressions on the sensory organs drive these parasitic ideas away. How feeble and indecisive judgement becomes in this chaos! How can objects be compared with one another and their points of conformity be truly grasped? This aberration of judgement is also shown by the muddling of epithets associated with proper nouns in a disorderly and undiscerning manner, always with much exaggerated expressions.

115. It is sometimes very difficult, in dementia or idiocy, to distinguish the signs of poor judgement from those of the capacity to imitate. I do not wish to renew here a discussion which arose at the time over the subject of the so-called Savage of the Aveyron. The zeal which went into cultivating his mental faculties certainly deserves the greatest praise. However far removed he was from being deaf and dumb, it was no less important to take every care to develop his feeble understanding. But is the potential scope which the power of imitation can have in very handicapped children fully recognised? One young idiot I often watched had a very pronounced and quite irresistible tendency to imitate everything she saw happening around her. She automatically repeated any words she heard and accurately imitated the motions and actions of others quite unabashed. Another similar patient slavishly carried out everything she was told to do with no consideration as to whether this was sensible or crazy. She jumped, laughed or cried to order and pulled any faces suggested to her, obeying a child just as readily as a big strong man. A child with very limited understanding who has wandered for some time in the woods and hamlets was first able, driven by hunger, to survive on wild food. He then gradually got used to more refined dishes, finally going from having acorns and raw potatoes to having chestnuts, cooked vegetables or even meat, But no particularly favourable inferences should be drawn from this as to his understanding or social manners.

VI. EMOTIONS AND OTHER AFFECTIVE STATES TYPICAL OF PSYCHIATRIC PATIENTS

116. He who regarded anger as a fury or a fleeting maniacal insanity *(ira furor brevis est)* has expressed a very true thought, the soundness of which one appreciates all the more having had the benefit of observing and comparing a large number of attacks of maniacal insanity and seeing that they commonly show themselves in the shape of a more or less fiery fit of anger. It is more these emotions of an irascible nature, rather than disturbed ideas or strange singularities of judgement, that make up these attacks. Furthermore, the term *maniacal insanity* as synonymous with *fury* is found in the writings of Aretaeus and of Cælius Aurelianus, who excelled in the art of observation. One must just correct the excessive application they give to this term, in as much as attacks are sometimes seen without fury, but almost never without some change or perversion of mental qualities. A man, who had become maniacal through the events of the Revolution, roughly pushed away a child whom he had always cherished tenderly as his attack came on. I have also seen a young man, very attached to his father, offend or even seek to strike him during his periodic attacks. I could also cite many examples of mentally ill patients of either sex, known moreover for strict probity during their calm intervals, but who were remarkable during their attacks for an irresistible tendency to steal and swindle. Another insane patient,

of a peaceful and gentle nature, seemed to be inspired by the demon of malice during his attacks, when he entered upon a continual state of evil activity. He shut up his companions in their lodges, provoked them, hit them and aroused quarrels and brawls amongst everyone nearby. Another example of this kind worth mentioning is that of a man suffering from an inveterate periodic maniacal insanity. His attacks usually lasted for eight to ten hours each month and seemed to show a complete contrast to his normal self. In his lucid intervals his face was calm, his manner gentle and reserved, he answered questions respectfully and accurately. His behaviour was urbane and very correct, and he had the wish to please everyone, together with an ardent will to be cured of his illness. But on the return of an attack, indicated especially by a certain redness of his face, pronounced heat in the head and strong thirst, he paced about, his tone of voice became masculine and dominant, his bearing impudent and he felt a strong temptation to provoke those who got near him, to get them agitated and to fight quite outrageously with them.

117. Examples of maniacal insanity with fury, but without delusions or any inconsistency in thoughts, are far from rare in either women or men. They show how much aberrations of the will can be distinct from those of the understanding, although they often go together. One cannot think without horror of the frightening power these involuntary tendencies can seize. I once saw a maniacal patient in the Bicêtre hospice whose symptoms might appear puzzling according to the concepts which Locke and Condillac have used to explain psychiatric behaviour. His maniacal insanity was periodic and his attacks recurred regularly after intervals of calm lasting several months. Their onset came with a burning heat felt within the abdomen, then in the chest and finally in the face. Then there followed flushing of the cheeks, flashing eyes and marked dilatation of the veins and arteries of the head. Finally, a deranged fury led him with irresistible determination to seize any object or offensive weapon with which to assail the first person coming in view. He said he had a continuous kind of inner struggle between the fierce impulse of a destructive instinct and the deep horror the thought of a heinous crime made him feel. There was no sign of any lapse in memory, imagination or judgement. He confessed to me, during his close confinement, that his inclination to commit a murder was completely enforced and involuntary, and that his wife, in spite of his tenderness for her, had been on the point of being a victim of it and he only just had time to warn her to run away. Lucid intervals brought back the same melancholic reflections and expressions of remorse, and he had conceived such a disgust for life that he had several times sought to put a final end to it. 'What reason', he said, 'would I have to cut the hospice superintendent's throat, when he has treated us so kindly? However, in my moments of fury, I only want to jump on him, like on everyone else, and stick a dagger into his chest. It is a miserable and irresistible urge, which reduces me to despair, and has made me try to commit suicide'.

118. The capacity for affectivity, like the functions of understanding, seem to be completely suspended in some attacks of maniacal insanity and this kind of apathetic stupor can show all the features of short-lived idiocy – a fixed and expressionless look, automatic immobility, no speech, no expressive gesture and complete indifference to any kind of food. In other cases, the patient retains some spark of unsteady reason. With a look of surprise, he takes a detached and worried view of everything around him, lets out occasional semi-articulate sounds or groans and shows an inner restlessness always on the point of exploding in some act of fury. In a further variety of attacks of maniacal insanity we can note a continual ebb

and flow of sad or happy affects and ideas, threatening gestures or an air of benevolence. The facial features then unravel successively, as if in a mobile tableau, showing fleeting passions, hope, terror, hatred and lust for vengeance, in flashes that disappear as quickly without trace. This variety of insanity, considered in all its breadth, also includes cases of inexhaustible babble, extreme volubility, incoherent speech, with irregular and unexpected returns of very strong and short-tempered emotions. Finally, nothing is more hideous than the spectacle of some patients who seem to be overcome by a kind of blind rage, who pour out sharp yells, outrageous or obscene language and all kinds of oaths and curses, with flashing eyes, frothing at the mouth and the most bloodthirsty urges.

119. Perhaps one should admire the unfortunate wealth the English have of vigorous language calculated to express the extreme perplexities, dejection and despair of melancholic patients in their medical texts, let alone in their novels and poetry (6). This exclusive delirium, always associated with a strong concentrated passion and a craving for solitude, is common in the psychiatric hospice. Many of these melancholic patients walk about sadly in their courtyards, sunken in deep reverie. Some stay alone, squatting in isolated places, while others suffer inner conflicts between the leanings of the heart and fear of the torments of another life. Yet others hope for nothing else but an early death by completely abstaining from any food or by some tragic event resulting in suicide. The following example seems very noteworthy to me. A mother with five children to care for and steeped in deep misery went very reluctantly, during a bitter winter, to ask for aid which the Government was having distributed to the poor of the parishes. The priest in charge of this relief work roughly pushed her away, making out that it she had committed a crime by limiting herself, during the Revolution, to a civil baptism for her children rather than having presented them to the Church. He showered her with reproaches and in his misguided zeal predicted the worst misfortunes for her and her family. This woman was dismayed at this and reduced to despair. She made her way home as if lost and told her husband that they were going to be put imprisoned and executed. She was unable to sleep, fell into a kind of stupor and showed a repugnance for any kind of food. In this state she was taken to the Salpêtrière and it was only after four months' treatment, which will be detailed elsewhere, that her reason was restored.

VII. DISTURBANCES OF THE IMAGINATION IN MENTAL ALIENATION

120. I set aside the question relating to the position that imagination should occupy in the hierarchy of the functions of understanding (7) and I look upon it as the complement of all the others, since it seems to have available at its disposal previous perceptions, memory, judgement and affective states with which to make up more or less consistent pictures, in novels, as well as in ethical works, the fine arts and the sciences. I leave the charge of picking out the discrepancies of this function, which may be contrary to the principles of strict taste, and corrupt them, to the critics. My aim must only be to make these discrepancies known in relation to mental alienation, and clarified through examples and the results of repeated observations. It is through these illusions that current objects are disfigured or embellished and sometimes seem to be completely changed. Absent objects are also sometimes represented in such vivid colours that an intimate conviction of their actual presence results, often giving rise to very mistaken and strange judgements.

121. A patient who had been calm for several months was suddenly seized with an attack of maniacal insanity when out on a walk. His eyes start to sparkle as if out of their orbits. His face, the top of his neck and chest were scarlet red. He thought he could see the sun four paces away and he said he could feel intense bubbling in his head. He himself asked to be locked in his lodge right away because he could no longer master his fury. During his attack he continued to rush about, think the sun was close by, speak with extreme volubility and show nothing but disorder and confusion in his ideas.

122. Nothing is more common in the hospice than the nocturnal or diurnal visions suffered by some women afflicted with religious melancholia. One of them believed that in the night she saw the Holy Virgin descending into her lodge in the form of tongues of flame. She asked for an altar to be erected to receive the sovereign of the heavens, who came to talk with her and comfort her in her sorrows, with due dignity. Another woman, of a cultivated mind, whom the happenings of the Revolution had plunged into deep grief and a maniacal delirium, continuously went for walks in the hospital garden, advanced solemnly with her eyes turned to the sky, and believed she saw Jesus Christ with all the celestial hosts walking in procession on high, intoning canticles accompanied by melodious sounds. She walked forwards herself in a solemn step to follow the procession and pointed it out, plainly convinced that it was real and actually impacting upon her senses, and became violently angry with those who tried to persuade her otherwise. This is not reminiscence; it is intuitive knowledge, a true inward fascination whose effect is analogous to that which can be excited by a vivid impression on the organ of sight.

123. The example is much quoted of the madman of Pyree in Athens, who delighted in seeing ships coming into the port which he believed belonged to him. Nothing however is more common than this kind of illusion, which leads one to think one possesses hidden property or even treasures. And besides, where in the world do people not dream about honours, dignities and riches? A woman deprived of most of her assets by the events of the Revolution completely lost her reason and was sent to the psychiatric hospice. First she gave way to an inexhaustible babble, and in the extreme of her delirium she addressed disjointed words to quite inanimate objects and let out noisy cries and shouts. She thought she was the granddaughter of Louis the Fourteenth and claimed her rights to the throne. Her imagination soon seemed to achieve her wishes. It was she who had, in her imagination, the tax revenues at her disposal and the army in her pay. If a stranger came into the hospice she thought this was in her honour and it was, she said, on her orders alone that it had been possible to introduce him. Her companions in misfortune were, for her, marquises and duchesses who walked behind her and she ordered them about with a tone of supreme authority.

124. Attacks of maniacal insanity sometimes seem to carry the imagination to the highest level of elaboration and richness, and give rise to a torrent of words which are often strange and incoherent, yet at other times to conversation which is grammatically correct and dictated by good taste. The most salient thoughts, and the most ingenious and surprising linkages, give the patient a supernatural air of inspiration and enthusiasm. Memory of the past seems to unroll easily in front of them, and what he has forgotten in his intervals of calm then come back to his mind in the most vivid and animated colours. I once stopped, when I was a doctor at the hospice at Bicêtre, in front of the lodge of an educated man who during his attack expounded on the events of the Revolution with all the force, dignity and purity of

language which one could have expected from the most highly educated man of soundest judgement. At all other times during his long intervals of calm this was a normal man. This exaltation, when associated with the fanciful idea of supreme power or participation in the divine realm, elevates the insane patient's intense pleasure to the most exquisite delight and a kind of enchantment and happy rapture. A psychiatric patient confined in a boarding house in Paris, who believed during his attacks that he was the prophet Mohamed, at these times adopted the commanding attitude and tone of the Almighty. His features were radiant and his bearing full of majesty. One day when the cannon was fired in Paris in the Revolution he persuaded himself that it was in his honour. He made everyone around him be quiet, could no longer contain his delight and I would have been tempted, had I not been kept back for other reasons, to see there the truest picture of the supernatural inspiration of the ancient prophets.

125. Some things seem so extraordinary that they have to be backed up by the most authentic evidence not to be dismissed in doubt. I refer to the poetic enthusiasm said to have characterised some attacks of maniacal insanity, even though the verses recited cannot be regarded as any kind of reminiscence. I myself heard a maniacal patient gracefully and discerningly recite a fairly long series of verses from Horace and Virgil which had long gone from his memory because after his education he had spent twenty years in the American colonies, concentrating on making his fortune. It was solely the disturbances caused by the Revolution which had produced his breakdown. But the English author I have already mentioned attests that a young person of delicate constitution and subject to nervous afflictions became alienated, and during her delirium she easily expressed herself in very harmonious English verse, even though previously she had never shown any inclination towards poetry. Van Swieten also reports another example of a woman who, during her attacks of insanity, showed a rare faculty for versification, despite the fact that she had previously been engaged in manual work and her mind had never been enriched with culture.

126. Imagination – this function of the mind which is so difficult to confine within sensible bounds, sometimes even by the man gifted with the soundest reason, and which so often gives rise in civil life to so many mad, ridiculous, or deplorable scenes – could this not be the richest source of the illusions, discrepancies and eccentric opinions that mental alienation exhibits? It draws together or confuses the divers partial sensations which memory recalls, builds up pictures from them which are more or less coherent, true or false, happy or sad and in keeping with real or strange and fantastic things, and sometimes presents the most monstrous and melancholic whole. A woman hearing the alarm bell sounding when it was time to get up, during the first year of the Revolution, became flustered, worried and fell into a most gloomy delirium. She became very frightened, thought she was close to a torture machine and let out lamentable cries. She kept asking to see her children or her close relatives, who she maintained had been put to the assassins' swords or reduced to the cruellest straits. She could scarcely bring them back to mind and could not recognise them when they were brought to her. For a few days of this sad delirium, her imagination prevailed over the genuine evidence of her senses and over the obvious and much repeated impressions made on her receptive organs.

127. It would be tempting to treat the fantastic ideas of hypochondriacs as vain fiction or fables, if they were not vouched for by the common consent of all ancient and modern

observers, and if examples were not recurring every day with increasing frequency. Does everything preceding or accompanying them not indicate that the primary seat of this illness is in the abdominal viscera, whence it seems to be transferred, by a kind or radiation, to the nervous system, especially the brain, although some deep obscurity clouds the nature of this physical affection? Several years before hypochondria passes on to a state of alienation, there are disorders in the digestion of food, spasmodic contractions of the abdominal muscles, embarrassing flatulence, faulty perceptions, the strangest affective states, and sometimes an inner conviction that there is a real live animal inside the abdomen, or of actual possession by the Devil. There are various other symptoms depending on the progress of the illness, such as irregular alternate feelings of coldness or warmth, blackouts, vertigo, short-lived episodes of deafness and ringing in the ears. In the mind there may be exhaustion, recurring anxieties, pusillanimous terrors and pernickety concentration on everything experienced internally or thought to be experienced. There are some who think their legs are made of glass or wax, others who believe their heart, the principle organ of the circulation, has been removed. Some are clearly convinced that they have ceased to exist, and a few amongst them imagine they have been changed into wild bests or into monsters (8). I leave off subsequent details of these deplorable testimonies of human misery, which I just consider here in relation to mental alienation.

128. Melancholia may spring from a natural disposition which becomes stronger with age, and which various circumstances in life may aggravate, but people are also seen of a cheerful character, full of vivacity, who because of genuine grief sink into gloomy moroseness, seek solitude and lose their appetite and sleep They get more and more suspicious, and end up thinking they are surrounded with traps and plots hatched with the darkest perfidy. Some of these melancholic patients in the hospice are so convinced in their imagination by the idea of persecution directed against them by invisible enemies that they suffer from constant anxiety. At night they even believe they can hear the muffled sounds of secretive conspiracies, of which they constantly dread becoming the victims. One of them, who had once heard electricity being talked about, and who had read a few articles about this branch of physics, thought that her enemies, determined to get rid of her, could have disastrous effects on her from great distances, and she thought she could see electric currents in the air which threatened her with dire danger. Other women bring in supernatural beings which a poor imagination seems to conjure up, attributing totally sinister intentions to them. One woman about twenty-five years old, with a strong constitution and married to a weak and delicate man, became subject to violent hysterical affections and to nocturnal visions which were bound to alarm her. She was completely convinced that a beggar she had turned away one day and who had threatened to put a spell on her had indeed carried out this disastrous intention. She imagined she was possessed by the Devil who, according to her, took on various forms and sometimes emitted bird songs, and at other times mournful sounds and piercing cries which gave her a sudden fright. She laid in her bed for several months, deaf to all the advice which anyone could give her and to the consolations of friendship. The local parish priest, an enlightened man with a gentle but persuasive character, influenced her spirits and persuaded her to get out of bed, resume her domestic chores and even dig her garden and go outside to carry out other healthy exercise. This had the most successful effect and resulted in a cure which lasted for three years. But then the good priest came to die and he was replaced by a superstitious and narrow-minded former monk. The latter gave complete credence to the patient's visions, let there be no doubt that she was indeed

possessed by the Devil, carried out repeated exorcisms and kept her in close confinement. The consequences of these absurd prejudices are not difficult to foresee.

129. One cannot close one's eyes to the extreme difficulty of dispersing prestigious influence of this kind which stems from over-exalted devotion or from fanaticism, and on this point my observations over many years agree with those I made on the psychiatric patients at Bicêtre and those which have been published in England. How is it possible to restore to sane thinking a patient puffed up with pride, who thinks solely about his destinies on high, believes he is a privileged being, a messenger from the Almighty, a prophet or even a divine? What words can counterbalance the effect of mystic visions and revelations, on the truth of which the patient is indignant that anyone could have any doubt? One such patient, whose attacks I carefully studied in the hospice at Bicêtre, believed he could see devils in different forms everywhere. One day, when a group of nosy parkers had come to visit the hospital, he leapt into the middle of them in fury, as if attacking a legion of demons. Another, with a gentle character, constantly invoked his guardian angel, or even some of the apostles, and took no pleasure except in scourging, fasting and prayer. However, as he had to live by the labour of his hands, how could he then provide for the needs of his family? I sometimes liked to talk about religious devotion to a patient who, like the old disciples of Zoroaster, worshipped the sun, religiously prostrating himself before this celestial body as it rose and dedicating his actions, pleasures and penances to it all day. He can be compared with another much more dangerous maniacal patient who was normally calm during the day, but who during the night believed he was surrounded all the time by ghosts and phantoms who conversed in turn with good and wicked angels. Depending upon whether the character of his visions was beneficent or dangerous, he proceeded either to kindly deeds or acts of barbaric cruelty. The following case history will show to what atrocious excesses such an alienation can lead.

130. A missionary, as a result of his lurid declarations and the frightening image of the torments of the next life, so shook the imagination of a naïve wine grower that he believed he was condemned to eternal flames and that he could only prevent his family from suffering the same fate by what is called *blood baptism* or martyrdom. First he tried to murder his wife, who only just managed to escape from his hands. Soon afterwards his frenzied arm turned on two little infants and he barbarously sacrificed them in cold blood in order to secure eternal life for them. He was summonsed to Court and during his trial proceedings he cut the throat of a criminal who was in the cell with him, again with a view to carrying out an expiatory deed. With his alienation certified, he was condemned to be detained for the rest of his life in the lodges at the Bicêtre. The isolation of prolonged detention, which is always liable to fire the imagination, and the thought of having escaped death despite the verdict he assumed had been reached by the judges, aggravated his delusions and led him to think he was all-powerful, or as he put it that he was the *fourth member of the Trinity*, that his special mission was to save the world by blood baptism, and that all the potentates in the world together would not know how to make an attempt on his life. His illness was, moreover, only partial, as in all cases of melancholia, and was specifically limited to everything related to religion. On every other subject he seemed to enjoy the soundest reason. More than ten years passed in strict seclusion, and sustained appearances of calm and tranquillity led to his being allowed the freedom of going into the hospice courtyards with the other convalescent

patients. Four years on trial like this seemed reassuring, when suddenly his sanguinary ideas recurred as a cult-object, and one Christmas Eve he conceived the atrocious plot of making an expiatory sacrifice of everybody at hand. He found a cobbler's knife, waited for the superintendent (M. Pusssin) to come round, gave him a slash from behind which fortunately slid over his ribs, cut the throat of two patients who were beside him, and would have carried on with homicides if someone had not promptly come to take charge and stop the disastrous consequences of his frantic rage.

VIII. CHARACTER CHANGES IN ALIENATION

131. Extreme agitation, alteration in facial features, disorderly thoughts and continuous or intermittent fits of fury, if they develop suddenly and for the first time, are manifest signs of alienation and leave no doubt as to the exact date of its onset, besides pointing back to the usual causes which can produce it. But in other cases the condition develops gradually and can even escape an experienced observer unless closely and continuously watched for several days. The agitation and fits may be attributed to heightened vivacity and a sense of exasperation, produced by substantial annoyances or chagrins. Fleeting errors in reason can be related to the same cause. And it is all the more easy to be mistaken when one normally lives close to the person and does not recognise the slight changes which can build up over a long period, without any abrupt or violent transition. A very enlightened man who came to find out about the condition of his wife who was alienated and being treated at the Salpêtrière hospice, believed in good faith that the lapse of her reason only went back about six months at the time of an acute and furious delirium. He accepted however that the cause of this illness dated from the very stormy times of the Revolution, when he had himself caused the loss of nearly all his fortune in order to enable some emigrants to leave the country. His wife had been deeply upset by this. He was asked several questions and he recognised that this woman had then undergone a complete change in her personality and character. Her natural gentleness and modesty had given place to extreme harshness in speech and manners. Her former parsimony was no longer in evidence and all the money she received for the ordinary necessities of life was instantly being dissipated. She sometimes disappeared for several days for no apparent reason whereas before she was spoken of as a model of attachment to her family and of a quiet and focussed life. Direct answers to similar questions revealed that the illness went back more than fifteen years, and that it had become chronic, with no hope of cure. One cannot look upon this unfortunate victim of the Revolution without tenderness, now given to all the fits of a furious delirium, and hardly retaining the sense of her own existence.

132. Indulgence in vice, as in drunkenness, unlimited and unselective womanising, disorderly conduct or apathetic lack of concern can gradually degrade reason and result in a certified alienation, as numerous examples seen in the hospices show. These perverted tendencies seem to become stronger with increasing age. A prolonged seclusion can lead to a more regular routine and more or less durable re-establishment or, alternatively, just to a complete void and an incurable state of dementia. But in all the asylums devoted to psychiatric patients people of either sex are seen who are commendable for their sober and industrious lives, completely irreproachable manners and most delicate sentiments, but

who sink through some recognised physical or mental cause into a complete loss of reason. They develop vices which constitute a striking contrast with their basic character during the course of their alienation, before finally returning, when they are better, to their normal happy disposition. How many men there are, quite sober in their remissions of periodic maniacal insanity, who give way to an irresistible urge for drunkenness when they relapse! And how many others there are, who under the same circumstances, cannot stop themselves from stealing and carrying out all sorts of swindles whereas in their lucid intervals they are said to be models of austere propriety! And also do we not see gentle and benevolent characters changing, following alienation, into turbulent, quarrelsome and sometimes completely unsociable spirits? I have quoted elsewhere examples of young people, brought up strictly, and further deserving public esteem, who sink into alienation and offend modesty by the indelicacy of their talk and the indecency of their gestures. On their recovery, everything returns to normal and they are then so many models of righteous manners and all the candour of innocence (9).

133. The observant eye can follow the gradual slow development of the physical and mental changes which precede the more intense symptoms of maniacal insanity. An individual of either sex of a happy nature plunges following a known cause into gloomy moroseness. They become subject to vain fears, speak harshly, are abrupt in their manners, strange in their conduct and show deep sentiments of aversion or hatred towards people who may be strangers to them or of whom they are fond. This gives way to violent fits and they slip into a state of stupor, cannot sleep and show a pronounced alteration in the features of the face. One is rightly alarmed and fears another outburst of violent symptoms of insanity. Indeed the disturbance soon appears to reach its height with continuous restlessness, cursing, profuse volubility, piercing cries and disordered and disjointed words. There may be repeated furious and insolent behaviour, or in some instances recurring weakness and faint-hearted fear, a dreamy detached air, wild look or obstinate reticence broken up by fits of frenzied anger. Thoughts may be clear, and judgment sound, in the middle of this agitated restlessness, and the mental character may be altered or changed to the opposite of the previous state. The change may be such that the powerful longing an individual has for life may be completely destroyed, or rather converted into a kind of blind rage leading to suicide, as countless examples show.

134. Maniacal insanity of recent onset, however complete the disruption of reason, may continue for a longer or shorter time depending upon the nature of the underlying cause or the principles of treatment adopted. But generally there is a period marked by the greatest intensity of symptoms, and their gradual easing off indicates its decline. The same discrepancies and perverse tendencies continue but to a much reduced degree, and it is only when complete convalescence has been reached that calm is restored and the mental state returns to its original state. The key issue then is to allow reason to become consolidated, avoiding premature discharge from the hospice and preventing any relapse. But whatever discernment and whatever practice one may have acquired for recognising this favourable point, uncertainty may remain when one has not obtained precise knowledge of the person's character prior to their state of insanity. A woman aged twenty-four years with a strong constitution developed maniacal insanity following her confinements and had been brought to the hospice in a very violent state. She smashed everything she got hold of and she had to

have a straight jacket applied and be detained in her lodge to avoid any accidents. More than three months passed in this extreme agitation, with a few intervals of calm. There was no longer anything to fear from her as the illness subsided, but there was still marked briskness in her movements, petulance, playful cheerfulness, a certain jumping about and outbursts of immoderate laughter, which lasted most of the fine weather. Then there followed a kind of stupor towards the end of October and a few internal stimulants were resorted to. Gloomy silence continued through the winter with a particular leaning for meditation, which made me fear that the illness was not over. But I was whole-heartedly reassured by the parents on learning that this was what she was normally like and that she had in fact resumed her normal character. So her discharge was agreed.

NOTES TO SECOND SECTION

1. Before the revolution the normal ration of bread for each psychiatric patient in the Bicêtre hospital was only one and a half pounds; the distribution was in the morning, and it was consumed right away, and part of the day passed in a kind of half starved delirium. In 1792, this ration was increased to two pounds and distribution was made in the morning, at midday and in the evening with a carefully prepared soup. This is no doubt the reason for the difference in mortality noted on making an accurate summary of the registers. Out of one hundred and ten patients admitted to the hospital in 1784, fifty-seven died; that is, more than a half. The ratio was 93 out of 151 in 1788. On the contrary, during Years II and III of the Republican period, only one eighth of the total number died.

2. A silversmith who had the eccentricity of thinking he had been given a different head was also infatuated over the pipe-dream of perpetual motion. He was given the use of his tools, which his family had made a point of sending him, and he set to work with the greatest determination. It comes as no surprise that the planned discovery did not materialise; but some very ingenious devices resulted, implying elaborate mental interconnections.

3. Perceptions formed at the same time, and others which follow them in regular order, can constitute a natural association of ideas and are often brought together in the mind. But we also have the ability to detach one or more perceptions or ideas from those which were associated with them, and we find another place for them in a new combination which will be all the more solidly established because this association will be based on a great number of links. This is what is called abstracting and is the foundation of the different methods in common use in natural history and, consequently, in medicine. The word *abstraction* in this case is far from indicating a primitive function of the understanding, as English and French authors have imagined, since it is a necessary sequence of the principle of the association of ideas.

4. It is common knowledge that a lady had the same mental turmoil after twenty-seven years of imprisonment and insanity. Her delirium and fury were continuous during this stretch of time, to the point of tearing her clothes, staying naked and scribbling the most disgusting obscenities. At the end of her delirium she seemed to come out from a deep dream and asked for news of the two very young children she had before her alienation, and she could not conceive that they had been married for several years.

5. A psychiatric patient, cured by Dr Willis in England, himself put the story of the episodes he had experienced as follows: 'I always waited', he said, 'impatiently for the onset of agitation which lasted ten or twelve hours, more or less, because while it lasted I enjoyed a kind of bliss. Everything seemed easy to me, nothing stopped me either in theory or in practice; my memory suddenly acquired a remarkable perfection; I recalled long passages from Latin authors: I normally have difficulty in remembering rhymes but then I wrote in verse as quickly as in prose. I was cunning and even malicious, full of all sorts of expediencies . . .' *(Bibliothèque Britannique)*.

6. Dr Perfect, speaking about a lady who was overcome with fanatical ideas, put it as follows: 'Her ideas in general were confused, gloomy and distressed; her apprehensions without foundation and her life so burthensome that had she not been prevented, she would actually have committed suicide. . . .On her features were strongly imposed a pale and settled melancholy; her eyes looked wild and staring, and her nights were watchful and restless; she discoursed on religion in a strange, timorous, despondent and incoherent manner . . .'

   The same author said, speaking of another melancholic patient: 'A gentleman of fortune, habitually intemperate in his way of life . . . became suddenly low spirited, with great distress and anxiety of mind; every trifling occurrence was considered by him as an object of intense trouble and inquietude; he was disgusted with almost everything and everybody . . . and in a short time his mind was sunk into the lowest abyss of melancholy and dejection.'

7. I will refrain from adding new obscurities to those still remaining to be clarified in medicine, and I must carefully distance from my considerations all the philosophical theories still contested on the nature, linkage and successive generation of the functions of human understanding. It is more prudent to stick to the results of rigorous observation of the faults with which these different functions can be afflicted, and learn to distinguish them by sensitive signs.

8. It is very difficult to conceive of the maniacal hypochondria known under the name of lycanthropy, or the inmost conviction of being transformed into a wolf, and the irresistible inclination to take up its habits. Several examples are to be found in the various collections of observations and a doctor in Nancy has just communicated a new one to the Society of the School of Medicine. Towards the autumn of Year XII a mason descended into a deep sadness and the gloomiest misanthropy without any obvious cause. He had fantastic visions at night and in the morning he escaped furtively into isolated places. On the tenth day of the illness he refused all food; but two days later he descended voraciously on the food offered to him, let out howls like a wolf and several times went into a kind of fury with a will to bite. On the fourteenth day as night approached, he again escaped into the fields where he once more let out howls which subsided with repeated drenching in cold water. This remarkable illness appeared to end up on the eighteenth day with a violent attack of fever which lasted about twenty four hours; complete recovery seems to have followed, brought about solely by the resources of nature.

9. There are a large number of similar examples in the collections of observations published in England by Dr Perfect. A titled Lady he refers to, aged twenty-four years, full of vitality and gifted with rare talents, developed attacks of hysteria following irregular menstruation and ended in a state of certified maniacal insanity. Her words and actions,

which previously radiated nothing but reason and decency, were marked by strangeness, incoherence and eccentricity. She was subject to frequent and extreme anxiety; her appetite was so perverted that she put everything coming to her hands into her mouth and she was so voracious that she swallowed all her food without chewing. She often let out bursts of immoderate laughter, abruptly switching to involuntary tears or even howls, cries, and all the excesses of a furious delirium.

3

DISTINGUISHING THE DIFFERENT
SPECIES OF ALIENATION

135. Does the ability to have an object fixed in one's memory and have a clear idea of it not depend upon taking care to circumscribe it within precise limits and avoid unrelated issues? How can what should rightly be understood by mental alienation be defined, avoiding any confusion if, as some nosologists have done, one includes the various disorders of the senses such as sight, hearing, taste, touch and smell which arise from other illnesses? Hypochondria can gradually degenerate into mental alienation but considered on its own it is quite different, constitutes an extensive group and can give rise to some remarkable quirks of the imagination. Likewise there are many primarily nervous disorders known under the names of somnambulism, vertigo, oddness, antipathy, nostalgia, nocturnal terrors, and frenetic desires for the pleasures of love-making called, depending on the sex, womanising or nymphomania.

136. The welcome influence which the study of other sciences has latterly had on medicine no longer allows the blanket name of madness to be given to alienation. Madness covers a wide realm and embraces all the mistakes and failings of which the human race is suspect, and which thanks to mankind's weakness and depravity knows no limits. So should the entire mistaken and inaccurate ideas one can have of things, all the outstanding errors of imagination and judgement, and everything which excites and provokes unrealistic desires, not be included under this heading? This would then be setting oneself up as the supreme censor of peoples' private and public lives, taking into account history, morality, politics and even the physical sciences whose domain has so often been contaminated by dazzling niceties and dreams.

137. An English nosologist (Cullen) has made some sound remarks about the distinctive character of delirium with mental alienation which he considers consists of errors of judgement, mistaken perceptions of external objects, unusual association of ideas and more or less violent unprovoked affective states. But are the useless explanations and groundless theories he puts forward purporting to demonstrate the mechanisms giving rise to the observed

Medico-Philosophical Treatise on Mental Alienation.
Philippe Pinel. Translated by G. Hickish, D. Healy and L.C. Charland.
© 2008 John Wiley & Sons, Ltd.

facts not contrary to the serious and cautious progress a faithful historian of the symptoms of illnesses ought to be making? How could he think that a few subtle opinions on the movement of blood in the brain, and the different degrees of a supposed *excitation* and *collapse* of that organ, would suffice to fathom the deep mysteries of the seat of thought and the derangements to which it is susceptible? I am far from anxious to go wandering into these uncharted territories and restrict myself to a simple exposition of the results of the most continual and repeated observation.

138. Is the distinction between the three species of insanity accepted by Cullen, the first mental, the second physical and the third obscure, based on basic differences, and are their external signs clearly characterised? Are there clear differences between the symptoms of each of these species, or really do they merely differ in their greater or lesser intensity, their length of duration or other accessory variations? One has to deplore the fact that the fate of the human race is so often the victim of superficial studies undertaken in medicine, and the slovenliness with which such studies apply the methods of classification adopted by the Naturalists. To establish this classification on a sound basis, should particular objects not be considered with the closest attention first, then a large number of observed facts be gathered together and separated into several bundles depending on their many points of conformity and striking similarities? It is through following an opposite course that so many arbitrary subdivisions have been created in medicine, ending in setting the doctors one against another, and leaving public opinion bewildered as to their principles.

139. Another medical author who has become famous in England, and is full of ingenious ideas, has based a classification of illnesses along the strangest lines. He just considers insanity in relation to the affective states it can produce. He distinguishes that which is associated with agreeable thoughts and no agitation or build-up of muscular force, that which leads the patient to take violent steps to get what he wants or get rid of what he dislikes, and that which is associated with a state of torpor and an irresistible tendency to despair. It has been easy for this author to gather together some surprising anecdotes about the monothematic delirium of melancholic patients (1) in daily life or in various medical works, and amuse the reader whilst sacrificing truth for convenience and forgetting about the fundamental characteristics of insanity and its true distinction as a species. He even looks upon straightforward vices and the failings seen all the time within the bosom of society, such as sentimental love, selfishness, arrogance of birth, ambition for fame, dwelling on sadness, the dismay of women on losing their beauty and the fear of death etc, as alienation. Is this not like converting our most flourishing cities into Petites-Maisons[1] houses for the insane?

140. Amidst these swings of opinion over the fundamental characteristics of alienation and its division into species, there is a general conformity which results from oft repeated observations on the real notions of alienation, and the distinction between insanity with fury, tranquil insanity and melancholic delirium with dejection and inclination to despair. Dr Chrigton[2] also drew up three species of insanity included in the first group of mental

---

[1] *Petites-Maisons was an old asylum in Paris – Ed.*
[2] *An inquiry into the nature and origin of mental derangement etc*, by Chrigton, London, 1798. (Pinel is referring to Alexander Crichton – Ed.)

illnesses. But he looks upon illusions *(hallucinations)* consisting of false perceptions of external objects with no other derangement of mental faculties as in hypochondria as a second group of mental illnesses. He puts demonomania or the conviction of being in direct communication with evil spirits, vertigo and somnambulism in the same group. Then he makes a third group named dementia *(amentia)* in which he includes particular faults in the different functions of understanding. This author has come the closest in recent times to an accurate division of mental illnesses, but he includes several ill-assorted things, among them symptoms specific to maniacal insanity and melancholia such as the vertigos and belief of communicating with the Devil. The specific failures of the mental faculties are also symptoms of various species of alienation which must be considered according to their varieties and different phases, and I have looked upon them (Second Section) as distinctive characters which will serve to make them known and to track their course faithfully.

141. The diversity of the terms used by the ancient Greek physicians to express the nuances and different degrees of feverish delirium is a testament to the close study they made of this cerebral illness. But can they be applied with equal success to quite different species of alienation, and would anyone appreciate their particular significance sufficiently to make use of them to make progress in this area of medicine? What mistrust vague and uncertain methods used in observing mentally deranged patients must engender! And is medicine not up till now showing the effects of the natural tendency people have of making fun of their crazy ideas, and making a sort of buffoonery of them rather than a serious study? So time is wasted over the oddness of their talk and their sombre or cheery humoured witticisms, making a joke of it, rather than directing attention towards the discrepancies of their perceptions, the fluidity of their ideas, the disturbances of their memory, the figments of their wild imagination or the frenetic ardour of their passions. Furthermore, unless their reason is completely upturned, mentally unstable patients attempt to frustrate anyone who has tried to examine them too closely. They can be very underhand or coldly reserved to stop anyone getting through to them and it is often difficult to get an accurate idea of their real situation and the distinctive characters of their delirium. It takes several attempts, in different skilfully handled interviews, using a good-natured and straightforward approach, before one can penetrate their deepest thoughts, clarify one's doubts and get rid of apparent contradictions by way of making comparisons. The principles followed in public or private establishments for looking after them can also induce thoughts or emotions which are foreign to them. If treated haughtily and with misplaced harshness, they become short-tempered and full of hatred and violence. They can only be helped back to their normal affective state by treating them in a gentle, benevolent way, and it is only then that the actual story of their breakdown can be studied as an illness. That is also how both maniacal insanity and melancholia can be followed in their various steady states and through their unexpected changes, and it is only when this is done that it is possible to get to know their characteristic signs. So is it surprising if observations hitherto made on psychiatric patients have generally been incomplete and scarcely fit to serve as sound basis for a consistent classification of mental alienation into its several different species?

142. The general reform introduced in the public establishments and in particular those for psychiatric patients, and the simplicity of methods and the good order brought into their management as a result, now make it possible to embrace the whole gamut of maniacal

insanity. One can look at it through its three successive stages of extremely severe symptoms, improvement and convalescence without disturbing or even actually reversing their progress. This makes it possible to multiply the numbers of observations of points of similarity and dissimilarity, and based on these we can progress to abstract ideas and broad terms for expressing the different kinds of mental alienation. Any superficial theory is far removed from these actual cases and stress is only laid on symptoms manifested to the senses by external signs, such as words, unusual gestures, the expression of certain strange angry emotions and different changes in the physical condition. So why not bring the approach used in all branches of natural history into this field of medicine as it is elsewhere? Are the distinctive traits of mental alienation, at least of some kinds, not the same in all the precise observations collected in different eras? And from this should it not be concluded that all the other facts gathered in the future will fall into the divisions which will have been adopted? Moreover, this is what patients of either sex admitted to the hospices confirm every day.

143. It is easy to recognise that the division of alienation into its different species has up till now been based on arbitrary collections of small numbers of observations which were often incomplete and imprecise, rather than being founded on counts of large numbers of facts, gathered methodically over a long succession of years in public establishments for insane patients of either sex. Strict and unvarying order in the department, and in the management of these patients, must ensure that the progress of the symptoms is not disturbed or derailed during their course. It must also make it possible to follow carefully all the graded phases of the alienation from its extreme intensity through its decline and into convalescence. The historical recording of this data must be subjected to a sound and consistent method, and the observer must have especially stressed the distinctive characters of alienation arising from the different faults in understanding and will (Second Section). He must be warned that the secondary varieties of this illness, arising from the diversity of the causes, the greater or lesser severity of the symptoms, the differences of the objects of the delirium or the particular nature of the affective state, cannot constitute specific characters. Some symptoms which appear diametrically opposed may exist in the same patient under different circumstances and at different stages of the mental alienation. This is enough to indicate the principles I have followed in this classification in order to make it accurate and complete.

144. I had previously communicated the result of my research on alienation in one particular establishment to the Society of Medicine, but I was too well aware of the inadequacy of these observations to go on to generalisations regarding its subdivision into species. The same plans were resumed more effectively and with more extensive resources during the first year of the Revolution, on my appointment as Physician to the Bicêtre Hospice, where before my eyes I continually had the spectacle of over two hundred mentally deranged patients who were entrusted to my care. Several years later I wrote up the results of my copious observations and I thought I could establish a sound division of alienation into its different species, drawing together all the case histories of my own and those of other authors and dividing them up into separate groups according to the extent of their similarities (2). Thus more or less severe general delirium, with greater or less agitation, irascibility or tendency to fury, was designated intermittent or chronic *maniacal insanity*. I kept the name *melancholic delirium* for that which was centred solely on a single subject or series of subjects, with despondency, moroseness and greater or lesser tendency to despair, particularly

when it reaches the point of becoming incompatible with social responsibilities. A particular deficiency in the operation of understanding and actions of the free will, which shows all the features of senile daydreaming, has been denoted by the name *dementia*. Lastly, more or less marked stupidity, with a very limited range of ideas and lack of character, constitutes what I call idiocy.

I. MANIACAL INSANITY OR GENERAL DELIRIUM

The Specific Characteristics of Maniacal Insanity

145. Maniacal insanity, the commonest form of alienation, is distinguished by nervous excitation or extreme agitation which sometimes develops into fury, and by a more or less pronounced general delirium, sometimes associated with the wildest judgement or even a complete disruption of all the functions of understanding. It also has its own precursory signs, but may develop out of the blue or come on insidiously, and it has its various periods of intensity, decline and of convalescence provided its progress is not derailed. It may have the features of an acute illness; but equally may become long drawn out like a chronic illness, in which case it may be continuous or periodic. Anything existing in the mind or body, and even vain figments of the imagination, may become the object of its particular delirium. It is important, using a few examples, to see to it that its innumerable varieties are appreciated, in order to grasp its specific characteristics properly.

146. The preceding account of the causes of maniacal insanity (First Section) shows that there is no immediate connection between its progress and intensity of its symptoms and its particular cause, because very different causes can lead to the same types in some cases, and the same cause can give rise to very different cases of maniacal insanity. The intensity of the attacks again is independent of the triggering cause and seems to spring from individual constitution or rather to different degrees of bodily and mental sensitivity, typified commonly enough by hair colour. Patients of either sex with blond hair are more liable to develop day-dreaming and a state bordering on dementia than to throw fits of fury, and in wards for either sex it is repeatedly noted that patients with brown hair retain a general character of moderation and gentleness in their insanity, and their affective state only develops in a measured and restrained manner. Robust men with dark hair, by contrast, conserve the impetuosity of their leanings in their distracted states and seem to be driven by an irresistible fury. It is enough to say that people of either sex with a vivid imagination who are very sensitive, and those who are prone to deep, powerful passions, all have a disposition not far removed from maniacal insanity if sound, active and strong reasoning has not found a way of counterbalancing this impetuous ardour. This is a sad reflection, but invariably true and something to be born in mind with regard to unfortunate deranged patients. I must no doubt make exceptions, and recognise that in the hospices there are sometimes unhappy victims of debauchery, loose living and very depraved morals. But generally speaking I can only pay a brilliant testimony to the pure virtues and strict principles which recovery often reveals. Nowhere, except in novels, have I seen spouses more deserving to be cherished, more tender fathers or mothers, more passionate lovers and people more devoted to their work than most of our insane patients once they have been happily restored to the stage of convalescence.

147. The preludes to the onset or recurrence of attacks of maniacal insanity can be very varied (First Section), but generally speaking it seems that the primary seat of this alienation is in the region of the stomach and intestines, and that it is from this centre that the disturbance of understanding spreads like a kind of radiation (3).

148. In this part of the body there is often a feeling of constriction, a voracious appetite or a rejection of food, stubborn constipation and intestinal burning calling for cooling drinks. Then agitation follows, with vague worries, panic attacks and continuous insomnia. Soon afterwards disorder and turmoil of thoughts become outwardly apparent, with unusual gestures, peculiarities in the countenance and movements of the body which cannot but be vividly striking to an observer's eye. The patient sometimes keeps his head raised and turns his eyes up to the sky, speaks in a low voice or shouts and screams for no obvious reason, and walks about then stops in turn, with an air of ardent admiration or kind of deep contemplation. In some deranged patients there are superficial bouts of jolly humour or bursts of immoderate laughter. And sometimes, as if Nature enjoyed contrasts, there is sombre taciturnity, involuntary floods of tears or even concentrated sadness and deep anguish. In some cases sudden redness of the eyes and exuberant talkativeness are forewarning signs of the next outburst of maniacal insanity and the urgent need for close seclusion. After long periods of calm, one deranged patient first spoke volubly, let out frequent bursts of laughter then shed a torrent of tears. Experience had shown the necessity of confining him quickly as his attacks had been very violent. Ecstatic visions at night are often preludes to attacks of manic devotion. And sometimes an erotic maniacal insanity bursts out dramatically in enchanting dreams and the alleged apparition of the object of love featured in ravishing beauty, but it can also take the form of a sweet dream, or simply show extremely confused ideas and completely disrupted reason.

149. A fundamental truth which was unrecognised until recent times and which the most repeated observation alone could confirm, is that maniacal insanity resulting from an accidental cause closely resembles other acute illnesses in its progress. It has its successive periods of extreme intensity, decline, and convalescence, as long as nothing interferes with the salutary efforts of Nature and that these are supported with simple measures and thorough surveillance. Here I must recall the observations on one of the first cases of this kind I made several years ago to clarify this delicate point of internal pathology. These observations have been endlessly repeated since in all cases of maniacal insanity that have resulted from a triggering set of circumstances. The determining circumstances in this case have been indicated in paragraph 27 in the First Section as follows:

150. *First Period. 4th day.* Pale face, fixed eyes, loud voice, confused thoughts, delirium the object of which is a so-called discovery made in chemistry. *One single idea,* he said, *must replace all the others... I am God, I am Father of the Universe...* Reddened face, fury imprinted on his features, sparkling eyes, shower of injuries on those who go near him, threats to kill everybody. *(He is restrained in a straight-jacket, and he consumes a large quantity of acidified or emulsified drinks).* Alternating shouting and swearing or dropping into a coma. Similar picture the following days. *12th day.* Much agitation during the night, false perceptions; the patient thinks he can see cats, dogs and wolves around him; at times a kind of fleeting tetany; eruptions of blisters on the back and chest. *15th day.* The blisters, full of clear fluid, burst the day after: sleep for the first time. After this day, reduction in the

tetanic convulsive movements which had previously occurred. *(Frequent oxycrat lotions to the head, which is shaved and uncovered; clean garments called for because of vomited fluid).* The *24th day*, a few lucid moments, but mostly a state of delirium, false perceptions, a kind of fury which keeps leading him to break everything or tear it up in his distraction. He speaks in turn of mysteries, conspiracies, the philosopher's stone, he draws hieroglyphics on the walls, he has a devouring hunger, drying up of his blisters . . . *(Second period). 35th day.* He asks with interest about news of his parents and one of his compatriots, speaks about his friends; but shows incoherence in his thoughts soon afterwards. *46th day.* Short walk in the garden as on the following days. *52nd day.* Stubbornness about sitting in the sun, which is bad for him: then red face, eyes fixed or rolling, threatening look, muscular spasms in the limbs, trunk and face, has a kind of fleeting fainting fit. These incidents recur on exposure to the rays of the sun, which calls for increased surveillance. More regular and less dark stools, fleeting recurrences of delirium but with longer lucid intervals. *57th day.* Ride in a carriage for several hours *(convalescence)*, complete return of reason; wish to return to his old way of life when understanding is fully recovered: something which implies the inner appreciation of his true condition. Muscular spasms less frequent. *76th day.* Salivation which daily becomes more copious and goes on for a fortnight; desire of the convalescent patient to see his lover again, who had carefully been kept away. *80th day.* He went back into the outside world and was married one and a half months after his discharge; since then his reason has been completely sound, despite the excessive heat of the following summer, the inevitable worries of an ill-matched marriage and many business matters.

151. It was only in Year X that I appreciated the great advantage of writing up the individual case histories of maniacal insanity following the preceding plan, and of indicating their successive stages, so as to show their progress, not least to come to sound treatment principles, which are always uncertain and shaky if the beneficial influence of Nature is not recognised and facilitated. But the contradiction reigning between this simple and encouraging way of looking at maniacal insanity and the violent and disruptive methods hallowed by routine called for scrupulous examination. It was only prudent to reach a decision after many repeated experimental results in a large collection of psychiatric patients. To make this research more consistent and sound, and create orderliness in the establishment, the patients in the Salpêtrière were allocated to three types of department, depending on whether they were at the full blown stage of the illness, its decline or convalescence (4). I thought then that it was advisable to suspend judgement and I continued to record the individual case histories of maniacal insanity. I did not stress the striking and often laughable oddities of maniacal patients in their delirium in a light-hearted way and with a kind of self-satisfaction like most authors do. Instead, I made comments on the specific or combined faults in understanding, thereby getting to the true character of maniacal insanity considered in its different stages. Then one sees how many constant factors can complicate this kind of alienation and make treatment difficult.

152. Maniacal insanity can present, even in its simple state, in very varied forms, depending on its different stages, the faults of one or more functions of understanding, the degree of agitation and violence of the affective state, whether cheerful or sad, calm or hot-tempered, with periodic returns of attacks or a sustained state. This is the broad spectrum shown in a large assembly of psychiatric patients. Other secondary varieties arise from the influence of

the seasons, the orderliness maintained in the hospice, the judicious dispersion of the patients into different departments or their confused cramming together in the same place, the harsh and repressive manners of the attendants or the gentle and benevolent methods employed. External appearances are liable to be misleading as well, and cases of maniacal insanity with external similarities may be very different depending on their recent or long-standing status, their physical or mental causes, age, or the treatment methods already applied. Consequently a cure may be difficult to achieve and is sometimes impossible. Differences of another kind may stem from the complication of maniacal insanity with other illnesses, gradual wasting away, acute fever, scurvy, gout, hypochondria, arrest of haemorrhage or the repercussions of a skin disease, hysteria or various other physical traumas. So it may be seen how superfluous it would be, and how interminably long it would take, to try to base a general account of maniacal insanity on individual case histories. I thought I should take a more direct route, and greatly simplify this objective, by drawing together the distinctive characteristics of this species of alienation as described in the second section of this volume.

153. The first phase of maniacal insanity is easily distinguished from every other species of alienation, and from every other kind of illness, by various disturbances of sensitivity present to a greater or lesser degree, by the occasionally excessive development of internal heat (paragraph 70) and a remarkable ability to tolerate bitter cold. There is an inability to sleep (paragraph 72), alternating states of exaggerated appetite followed by rejection of food and sometimes an utter determination to eat nothing and starve to death (paragraph 75), and there may be either a loss or an excess of libido (paragraphs 78, 79). At the time of its onset, or the return of attacks, maniacal insanity is associated with unusual changes in the colour or features of the face (paragraph 82), sometimes with extreme sensitivity of the sensory organs, especially sight or hearing (paragraph 85), and by a rapid succession and great vacillation of affective states and of ideas. Other varieties show either a ready capacity or a complete inability to maintain attention on a given subject (paragraph 92). Another remarkable variation in the state of maniacal patients is in the preservation of coherence of certain ideas combined with other obvious discrepancies of reason (paragraph 93). Memory may be simply suspended during attacks of maniacal insanity (paragraph 106) or its integrity may be fully preserved. It is the same with judgement; but then spirited quick-tempered passions, as well as other physical or mental disturbances, leave no uncertainty about the lapse (paragraph 110). In the end severe turmoil in the ideas, complete obliteration of judgement, and strange ill-assorted emotions with no motive or order, betray complete disruption of mental faculties (paragraph 118). When maniacal insanity declines and symptoms gradually become less intense and begin to clear away, it again has distinctive characteristics (paragraph 90) and its harbinger signs of a gradual return to reason continue to show themselves until convalescence is complete. But this delicate passage and the particular precepts derived from them will be especially called for in the application of supervision regulations which a hospice for psychiatric patients requires from the superintendent, as well as in the physician's list of duties and the great reserve he must apply in his testimonies when the convalescent patient is ready to return to the outside world.

154. Maniacal insanity may be so deep-rooted or may be dependent on a physical or mental underlying cause so that nothing can prevent its course or the indefinite continuation of the symptoms at the same level. But its gradual amelioration may also be the effect of some happily applied measure and depend on the dexterity used in inculcating different ideas from

those which are dominant. A twenty-seven year old lady of very sensible character came to experience profound vexation and out of the blue her periods stopped. The two events were accompanied by a light delirium, but in the third month there was great disorder in her ideas and the patient's utter conviction that certain perverted inclinations which were overcoming her could only be put down to suggestions from the Devil. From then on she believed she was possessed and went into several houses crying out loudly to be *exorcised*, and endlessly repeated the words *Devil, exorcism, seven Angels of the Apocalypse* etc. Her face was red, her voice loud, her eyes flashing and distracted, and she attributed a spasmodic choking she felt in her throat to the efforts of the malign spirit to strangle her. Rosaries and mystic pictures were hanging round her neck to drive away the evils which were threatening her, and in this condition she was taken to the Salpêtrière. The superintendent of the hospice, when this patient was admitted, spoke to her in a firm and forceful tone. He assured her that the Devil would never dare to come into this asylum which she had come to live in. He took her under his wing and got her to put on clothes which, he told her, had the power of destroying every kind of spell. Her rosaries and pictures were carefully removed from her sight and she was exhorted to feel that she was completely safe. The patient put up no resistance, went to bed and slept peacefully. The next morning, on the tenth day of her maniacal delirium, all that remained was a sort of surprise in her head. She no longer understood how she could have thought she was possessed and realised her mistake. On the eleventh day she slept peacefully for part of the night, but had some diarrhoea. On the fourteenth day she had a little insomnia, thirst and was sweating. Taking tepid baths helped her monthly periods to return, which happened on the twenty-eighth day. Since then, melancholic and sad ideas and intermittent recurrences of fleeting delirium gradually ceased, but it was not till the third month that reason was fully re-established. For safety's sake it was felt that her discharge should not be allowed until after two months of convalescence.

Is an Episode of Periodic Maniacal Insanity a Form of Chronic Maniacal Insanity?

155. An attack of periodic maniacal insanity may be regarded as a true form of chronic maniacal insanity if one leaves aside the length of time it lasts, and it is only possible to give a more exact idea of one by recalling all the circumstances of the other. The character is the same regardless of the remote cause or the kinds of acts of eccentricity or fury, regardless of whether there are disorders of one or more functions of understanding and regardless of the extraordinary number of objects towards which the delirium is directed. Either of these maniacal insanities may be the fruit of everything the passions have in the way of excessive vehemence and anger, all the most vivid and fieriest things to which enthusiasm can give birth, and everything wild and fabulous that fantasy and love of the supernatural can suggest. Sometimes there is a cheerful and jolly delirium which comes out in lively and incoherent witticisms and remarks full of exuberant stupidity, and sometimes there is inflation with enormous pride which simply deludes itself with the pompous ceremony of dignities and glories.

156. I have seen some patients rambling at their ease over a crowd of objects present in their imagination, waving, ranting and shouting all the time and seeming to see and hear nothing of what is going on around them. Others, given to a kind of glamour, see things with shapes

and colours which their imagination attributes, like that patient who took every gathering of several people as a legion of demons and wanted to get out of his lodge to batter them to death. Another patient tore everything to shreds, his clothes and even the straw on his bed which he thought was a heap of twisted snakes. Delirium can sometimes continue in a furious state for a long succession of years. At other times it continues with the episodes of fury only returning periodically or because of some fortuitous cause. Advancing age most often finally brings about a state of calm, but again sometimes the attacks of fury then become more frequent, and this is an ominous sign.

Can Maniacal Insanity with Delirium Always be Cured?

157. One of the most fatal prejudices for humanity, and one which is perhaps the deplorable cause of the state of abandon in which psychiatric patients are left almost everywhere, is to look upon the illness as incurable and put it down to an organic lesion in the brain or some other part of the head. I can confirm that amongst the greatest amount of data which I have gathered on delirious maniacal insanity which had become incurable or had come to an end through some other fatal illness, all the results of autopsies on the corpse, set against the symptoms which had developed, show that this alienation generally is purely caused by nerves and is not the result of any organic abnormality in the substance of the brain, as I will show in the Fifth Section. On the contrary, everything indicates strong nervous excitation or a fresh development of vital energy in these patients. Their continuous agitation, their sometimes furious cries, their tendency to acts of violence, their obstinate sleeplessness, animated expression, desire for the pleasures of love-making, their exuberance, quick retorts, and I know not what sense of superiority in their own strength and their mental faculties, all give rise to a new order of ideas which are independent of impressions on the senses, to new emotions with no real cause and to all kinds of deceptions and illusions. It is somewhat surprising that expectant medicine, that is, mental and physical care, is sometimes enough to lead to a complete cure, as I will show elsewhere when speaking of treatment.

Can Maniacal Insanity Exist Without a Disturbance in Understanding?

158. One may rightly admire the writings of Locke yet at the same time agree that his notions about maniacal insanity are very lacking when he looks upon it as inseparable from delirium! I thought along the lines of this author myself when I resumed my research on this illness at Bicêtre, and was not a little surprised to see several patients who never showed any disturbance of understanding, and were dominated by a kind of instinct of fury, as if only their affective faculties had been damaged.

An Example of a Kind of Maniacal Attack Without Delirium (*Manie Sans Délire*)

159. An education which is either poorly supervised, or not supervised at all, or indeed a character which is perverted and beyond discipline, may both give the first hints of this

kind of alienation, as the following case history shows. A single child brought up by a weak and indulgent mother got into the habit of indulging in whims and hot-headed and wild impulses. The impetuosity of his inclinations increased and became strengthened as he got older. Money squandered on him seemed to remove any obstacle to his getting what he wanted. If anyone stood up to him he became exasperated, attacked them fiercely, tried to get his way by force and spent all his time in quarrels and brawls. If any animal such as a dog, a sheep or a horse upset him he had them killed right away. If he went to some gathering or fair he lost his temper, delivered and received punches, and departed covered in blood. On the other hand he was full of common sense when calm, and when he reached adult age he became the owner of a large residence. He governed over it in a correct manner, fulfilled other responsibilities in society and got a name for charity towards the poor. Injuries, legal actions and financial compensations had been the only consequence of his unfortunate addiction to brawls, but a notorious incident put an end to his violent behaviour. He got angry one day with a lady who swore at him and he threw her down a well. Legal investigations proceeded before the Courts and on the evidence of a host of witnesses who recalled his quick-tempered distracted states, he was sentenced to imprisonment in the hospice for mental patients at Bicêtre.

Maniacal Insanity Without Delirium (*Manie Sans Délire*) Marked by Blind Fury

160. I can make the ultimate degree of development of this species of alienation appreciated by means of an example. A man who was previously engaged in a mechanical job, and later detained at Bicêtre, had attacks of fury at irregular intervals which were marked with the following symptoms. First, there was a feeling of burning fieriness in the intestines, with intense thirst and stubborn constipation. This heat gradually spread to the chest, the neck and the face, giving this a more animated look. On reaching the temples it became even more active and produced strong rapid pulsations in the arteries there as if they were going to burst. Finally, the nervous affection reached the brain and then the patient was overcome by an irresistible bloodthirsty lust, and if he could get hold of some sharp weapon he would go on in a sort of rage and make ready to attack the first person coming into view. However, in other respects he enjoyed the free exercise of his reason, even during the attacks. He answered questions straight away and let no incoherence in his ideas escape. He even profoundly appreciated the horror of his situation and was full of remorse, as if he should blame himself for this deadly inclination. Before his confinement at Bicêtre this attack of fury came over him one day in his house. He immediately warned his wife, of whom he was very fond, and he just had time to call out to her to flee quickly away to escape from a violent death. At Bicêtre he had the same attacks of a periodical fury and the same automatic tendency to carry out atrocities which were sometimes directed against the superintendent, whom he never ceased to praise for his compassion and gentleness. This inner conflict resulting from a sound reason opposed to a bloodthirsty cruelty sometimes reduced him to despair and he often tried to put an end to this unbearable struggle through death. One day he came to seize the hospice cobbler's leather knife and gave himself deep wounds in the right side of his chest and his arm, which were followed by heavy haemorrhage. Close confinement and a straight jacket put an end to his run of suicidal attempts.

Another Example of Maniacal Insanity Without Delirium

161. Maniacal insanity without delirium[3] (*manie sans délire*) was at the root of an extraordinary scene at a period in the Revolution which one would like to see expunged from the history books. At the time of the prison massacres the brigands worked their way in amongst deranged patients in the psychiatric hospice at Bicêtre on the pretext of liberating sane patients admitted under the old regime who had been mixed with the common patients. They went, armed, from lodge to lodge, interviewing the detainees and passing on to the next one provided alienation was in evidence. But one of the recluses, bound in chains, attracted their attention as a result of speech which was full of sense and reason, and bitter complaints. Was it not heinous that he was being held in irons and was mixed up with all these deranged patients? He challenged the idea that anyone could reproach him for the least act of eccentricity. It was, he added, a most appalling injustice. He beseeched these newcomers to put an end to such oppression and make themselves his liberators. From then, mutterings of violence and shouted curses against the hospice superintendent broke out amongst this armed mob. He was forced to come out and give an account of his actions, while all the sabres were pointed at his chest. He was accused of perpetrating the most blatant humiliations and he was immediately silenced when he tried to justify himself. He had wanted, in vain, to point out his own experience, citing other similar examples of deranged patients with no delirium who could yet be formidable on account of a blind fury. This was greeted with abuse and had it not been for the courage of his wife, who physically protected him with her body, he would have fallen pierced with stabs. The order was given to set the patient free and he was led away in triumph to shouts of *Long Live the Republic!* The spectacle of so many armed men, with their noisy and confused shouting and faces flushed with wine fumes, rekindled the patient's fury. With a firm arm he grabbed the sabre of a bystander and slashed to right and left, setting blood to flow. If someone had not managed to overcome him quickly, this time he would have avenged outraged humanity. The barbaric horde led him back to his lodge and appeared to submit, somewhat red-faced, to the voice of justice and experience.

II. MELANCHOLIA, OR SELECTIVE DELIRIUM

Popular Meaning of the Term Melancholia

162. A dreamy taciturn manner, touchy, and suspicions, with a desire to be left alone, such are the features which serve to typify certain men in the community, and nothing is more hideous than this picture when it is associated with the notion of the abuse of power, depravity of behaviour and a bloodthirsty streak as was the case with Tiberius and Louis XI (5). The life stories of men who are famous in politics, the sciences and the fine arts have revealed melancholic people with a contradictory character, in as much as they are endowed with a keen enthusiasm for the masterpieces of the human spirit, for profound thoughts and for everything that is great and magnanimous. There are again melancholic folks on a lower plain who liven up and enchant society with their warm and concentrated

---

[3] I have quoted other examples of insanity without delirium in the First Section on periodical insanity (IV).

affection and all the reactions of a strong and passionate spirit, who are also only too clever at tormenting themselves and all those who go near them with their umbrages and fanciful suspicions (6).

Melancholia Regarded as Mental Alienation

163. Mentally disturbed patients of this species are sometimes dominated by a single idea which they keep endlessly going back to in their conversation and which seems to absorb all their faculties. On other occasions they stay locked in complete silence for years without giving away the secret of their thoughts. Some give no hint of any gloom and seem to be endowed with the soundest judgement, until some unforeseen circumstance causes their delirium to burst out in a flash. A superintendent came one day to Bicêtre to discharge the patients who were considered cured. He asked one former wine grower some questions, and he showed no discrepancies or inconsistencies in his replies. The legal certificate confirming his condition was drawn up and as is customary it was given to him to sign. The Magistrate's surprise may be imagined when he saw that he had signed his name as *Christ*, and then embarked upon the kind of daydreaming this idea suggested to him! An object of fear or terror can set up persistent dismay and lead to withering away and to death. I saw two Austrian soldiers who had been made prisoners of war, and were completely convinced that they were going to be guillotined, succumb like this in the Bicêtre sick bay. A certain sourness of character, or primitive misanthropy, leads some patients to stay isolated at the back of their lodges and lose their temper furiously with anyone who comes to disturb their solitude. If one of these becomes obsessed with religious ideas and persuades himself that he is called by Heaven to carry out some expiatory deed, he may commit the gravest crimes in cold blood. Here I can add an example similar to the one I gave in a preceding article. A former monk whose reason had been lost as a result of devotion thought one night that in a dream he had seen the Virgin surrounded with a choir of blessed spirits and had received the express command to put a man he treated as a disbeliever to death. This homicidal deed would have been put into effect if it had not been avoided by close confinement.

Two Opposite Forms Which Melancholic Delirium May Take

164. Nothing is more inexplicable, and at the same time nothing is more striking, than the two opposite forms which melancholia can take. Sometimes there is inflation with pride and the fanciful idea of possessing immense riches or boundless power, while at other times there may be faint-hearted despondency, deep dismay or even despair. The psychiatric hospices often provide examples of these two extremes. The steward of a grand lord lost his fortune in the Revolution and spent many months in prisons continuously in fear of being tortured. His reason went and he was transferred as insane to the Bicêtre, where he ended up thinking he was King of France. A Jurist, dismayed to find himself robbed of a dearly loved only son through some incident, gave way to deep grief, lost his reason and soon afterwards thought he had been transformed into the King of Corsica. For a long time I had in the Bicêtre sick infirmary an inhabitant of Versailles who had been ruined in the Revolution and soon afterwards was given to the illusion that he was the ruler of the world. On the other hand

what a lot of examples there are of deep and focussed sadness which is unchanging in its object and which ends in delirium! A weak timid man said a few reckless words during Year II of the Revolution. He was suspected of being a Royalist and his life was threatened. He was utterly perplexed, could not sleep and stopped doing any work. He was then admitted to the Bicêtre as insane and remained so completely convinced by the idea of a sinister death that he kept provoking the execution of the supposed decree which had been laid against him, and nothing we tried could bring him to himself again. It is not without emotion that I have seen demented patients, casualties of a sensitive tender nature, repeating day and night the cherished name of a wife or son who had been taken away through premature death and whose image was always in front of them. A young man who was distraught by an unhappy love affair was so overwhelmed by the illusion that every strange woman coming into the hospice was his former lover that he called her *Marie Adeleine* and kept talking to her in a most passionate way.

Can Melancholia Degenerate, After a Few Years, into Maniacal Insanity?

165. Melancholia often remains static for several years, without any change in the object of delirium or alteration in its mental and physical features. Patients of this species detained in the Bicêtre hospice have been observed for twelve, fifteen, twenty or even thirty years, during which they are still given to the original ideas which distinguished their breakdown and are still dragged along by the slow evolution of a monotonous existence consisting of eating, sleeping, withdrawing from the outside world and only living with their ghosts and fantasies. Some, with a more labile character, go on to a confirmed state of maniacal insanity just through seeing or hearing furious or crazy patients. After several years others undergo a kind of inner revolution for no known reason and the object of their delirium changes or takes on a new form. A patient of this species, confined under my care for twelve years and already of a good age, for the first eight years had as a delirium just the fanciful idea of a supposed poisoning with which he believed he was threatened. During that time there was no lapse in conduct and no other sign of alienation. He was even extremely reserved in what he said, convinced that his parents wanted to ban him and get hold of his belongings. The idea of a presumed poison made him very nervous and he only dared to eat surreptitiously in the kitchen of his lodgings. Towards the eighth year of his seclusion his original delirium changed in character. First he thought he had become the greatest of potentates, then the equal of the Creator and sovereign of the whole world: this idea was his supreme delight.

Variety of Melancholia Leading to Suicide

166. 'The English', says Montesquieu, 'kill themselves for no imaginable reason; they kill themselves in the very bosom of happiness. This action, amongst the Romans, was the result of education; it stemmed from their way of thinking and their customs: with the English it is the effect of an illness, and arises from the bodily physical state . . . ' The kind of tendency to suicide to which the author of *The Spirit of the Laws* refers, and which is independent of the very powerful motives to kill oneself such as loss of honour or of fortune, is not

an illness peculiar to England. Numerous examples are seen in France in the hospices. I have published elsewhere some examples of this type in a periodical journal[4], and I confine myself to mentioning one of these cases in brief.

167. A young man of twenty-two years was destined by his parents for the Church (this was before the Revolution), but when he declined they left him to himself. He moved from one precarious means of existence to another, but he seemed at last to find peace and calm in a home where he was loved. However, it was then that his imagination was assailed with very sad and melancholy ideas, weariness of life and various thoughts about ways of killing oneself. One day he was thinking of throwing himself from the top of the house, but his courage failed him and the plan was deferred. A few days later a firearm seemed more suitable for delivering himself of life's burden; but at the last minute there were still fainthearted fears and recurring perplexities. One of his friends, to whom he had spoken of his sinister plans, came to tell me about it and joined with me in doing all we could. But begging, pressing invitations and friendly remonstrance were all in vain and the will for self destruction followed the unhappy young man all the time. He shied away from a family where he was showered with evidence of attachment and affection. It was no good thinking about a distant voyage and a change of climate, for the state of his pocket seemed to put that out of the question. This would need to be made up for, as a powerful diversionary objective, by hard and sustained manual work. The young melancholic patient, full of the horror of his situation, accepted my opinions completely, changed his situation, went to Port-au-Bled and mixed in with the other workmen, only distinguishing himself from them by a greater zeal to deserve his pay. He could only manage two days of this exhausting work and another expedient had to be tried. He went as an unskilled worker to a master mason in the Paris area and was all the more welcome because at intervals he could make himself useful with the education of an only son. What kind of life could be better and healthier for a melancholic person than the alternatives of labouring with his hands and studying at a desk! A healthy diet, comfortable accommodation and all the consideration he received on account of his misfortune seemed to aggravate rather than calm his deadly inclinations. After fifteen days he went back to his old friend to tell him, with tears in his eyes, of the inner struggle he was having and the awful dislike for life which was driving him irresistibly to suicide. The reproaches he received filled him with grief, he withdrew in a state of consternation and despair, and there was no doubt he was going to throw himself into the Seine as the final stage of an existence which had become unbearable.

168. A melancholic frame of mind may persist in a more or less marked form without becoming a certifiable illness, but then it can cause alarm not only because of a determination to shirk social responsibilities, but also by an irresistible urge to impose privations on oneself which can become deadly, or even to commit atrocious crimes in cold blood, following involuntary ideas which have come into one's head. A melancholic person sometimes utterly refuses the food he needs to maintain his strength and stay alive (paragraphs 74, 75). In some cases he goes round an exclusive string of ideas which haunt and dominate him (paragraph 83). Sometimes his mind is fixed, night and day, on a circumscribed object (paragraph 94) from which he cannot be deflected. His imagination is so vivid that it makes him see wonders in the most simple and least likely things (paragraph 99). This is an abundant

---

[4] La Médecine éclairée par les Sciences physiques

source of mistakes and illusions (paragraph 100). He is liable to work diligently but on the contrary is liable to grasp false connections between things because of some fixed mental disorder dominating him (paragraph 111). What a lot of strong and angry emotions there are to drive him beyond the limit and make him see some things under false and borrowed colours! These emotions can even push him into extreme excesses and the most atrocious crimes (paragraph 118), as well as making him capable of deeds which are most generous and magnanimous!

169. A young lady with rich parents, who had had an excellent education, found herself with no resources as a result of their death and she threw herself completely into fervent devotion in the hopes of gaining the favour of Providence. The only way which seemed open to her was that of marrying a rich man, and so there were prayers, fasts and mortification, all resorted to in order to gain this favour from Heaven. The overexcitement progressed in bounds and a true melancholic delirium followed to the point of completely refusing any food whatever. Five days of total fasting had already passed by the time of her admission to the Salpêtrière. Showers were resorted to as a means of restoring control; she agreed to take a little nourishment but only wanted to eat bread. Gradually she was persuaded to take something more substantial. She then set about undertaking some work and her convalescence was complete towards the third month of her stay at the Salpêtrière. Generally speaking a remarkable gradation is noticeable in the mental disorders of young melancholic patients with a passionate temperament. They can lapse into the most elevated piety, direct fervent prayers to the heavens to fight against natural urges and emerge triumphant from this difficult struggle. Often, the opposite happens, and the flames of love seem to come back with renewed strength. One single route is open to them to get everything right: the hope of a fortunate marriage. With what fervent ardour do they not solicit this new benefaction of Providence! What a lot of prayers, and austere fasts! But more often than not the imagination only gets wilder and wilder, sleep becomes impossible and a true state of maniacal melancholy is established.

170. The ideas of melancholic patients with delirium are often so tenacious, and seem to be so deeply engraved in their memory, that they are constantly present, and any measures which could be tried become ineffective. The patient then gladly abandons herself to crazy ideas which she looks upon as well-founded, without having any doubt about their veracity. However, if one succeeds in shaking her with reasons to the contrary and manages to gain her confidence, or rather if one has already inspired in her the wish to come out of her state, she first becomes deeply perplexed. This tumultuous upheaval of ideas, struggling with one another within a frail understanding, is quite chaotic. Any choice between them remains impossible. There is no more rest, no more calm and no more sleep, and troubles may endlessly burden the mind. A young melancholic patient had been criticised for her relationship with a man she could not hope to marry but of whom she was very fond. Thoughtlessly, she was bitterly reproached for following the longings of her heart. Her anxiety and agitation became intense, and it was then that she kept seeking to have meetings with the superintendent of the hospice to confide in him about her torment and grief, and insistently ask him to sustain her courage. The superintendent was too clever not to see a decline of her symptoms in these confidences, and the opportunity of dispelling her illusions. Little by little all the doubts were resolved and two months later the convalescence was complete.

III. DEMENTIA, OR ABOLITION OF THOUGHT

The Most Salient Features of Dementia Sometimes Observed Amongst the General Public

171. The frivolity and crazy lack of attention, the endlessly repeated wild improprieties and strange absent-mindedness which make up the character of Ménalque in La Bruyère's work are far from being one of those imaginary pictures which only exist in novels. Amongst the general public the observant doctor will sometimes see this early stage of dementia, full-blown forms of which are to be found in the hospices. A man who had been brought up with the prejudices of the old nobility, and who was barely fifty years old, was rapidly heading for this kind of mental disorganisation before the Revolution. There was nothing like his instability and the aberrations of his childish effervescence. He fiddled about all the time in his house, chattered, shouted, got angry over the most trivial things, tormented the servants with pernickety instructions and his family with fecklessness and sudden divergences which a moment later he remembered nothing whatever about. In turn he talked with great fickleness about the court, his wig, his horses and his gardens without waiting for any reply and hardly giving time to follow his incoherent jumbled up ideas. A very religious lady, who shared her destiny with him because of their social rank, became deeply affected by hopeless hypochondria as a result of this union.

172. Is it within the capability of medicine to restore reason which has become distracted as a result of exhaustion and extreme abuse of pleasures, and is this not a form of accelerated dementia?

Ideas Which are Inconsistent with One Another, and Unrelated to Outside Objects

173. Unruly and uncontrollable instability, a succession of ideas which is rapid and almost instantaneous and seems to be born and to proliferate in the understanding without any stimulus having been applied to the senses, a constant and absurd ebb and flow of imaginary objects which shake, change and obliterate one another with no break and no interconnection, the same incoherent but calm combination of mental disorders, feelings of happiness, sadness and anger, which arise fortuitously and disappear in the same way without leaving a trace and having no connection with impressions of outside objects: all these are the fundamental characteristics of the dementia I am discussing. A keenly patriotic though not very enlightened man, who was one of the famous Danton's most ardent admirers, found himself present at the sitting of the Convention where the indictment decree against this Deputy was passed. He went away in a kind of consternation and despair and remained at home for several days abandoned to very sinister and melancholic ideas: 'What? Danton a traitor?' he kept repeating, 'There is nobody to be trusted any longer. And the Republic is lost'. He no longer had any appetite and could not sleep and soon he was completely alienated. He underwent the treatment in common use at the Hôtel-Dieu and was taken to the Bicêtre. I looked after him for several months in the infirmary at this hospice, where he was overcome with a kind of gentle daydreaming, confused and continuous chatter and quite incongruous

talk. He spoke in turn of daggers, sabres, dismasted ships, green meadows, his wife, his hat etc, he only thought about eating when food was put into his mouth and he was completely reduced to a mechanical existence.

174. The different degrees of disturbance in memory, although very alike, can also have very big differences if they are carefully examined and compared with one another. A young man of fifteen years, who in a stormy period in the Revolution was witness to his father's violent death, was so affected by this that he lost the power of speech and, almost completely, the use of his reason. However, he felt sensations appropriate to the objects which gave rise to them, and even appeared to grasp some connection between sensations that had a direct bearing on his needs, and retained memory of them for some time. He recognised the nurse responsible for looking after him and asked him for something to eat by making particular gestures. If he received some kindness from somebody, he showed some thoughtfulness towards them, and on the other hand he avoided those who had treated him badly or threatened him. He compared things that were presented to him with one another, and between two pieces of bread which were offered to him he took the bigger one without feeling its weight. He could tell an adult from a child and obeyed one whilst holding out against the other; but his judgement seemed absent for the greatest number of objects which were foreign to his needs and he did not seem to have any idea of propriety or decency.

Example to Clarify the Difference Between Dementia and Maniacal Insanity

175. One could not understand dementia better than by comparing it with maniacal insanity with delirium, so as to really grasp their differences. In maniacal insanity, the perception of objects, imagination and memory may be damaged, but the faculty of judgement, or the association of ideas, often survives. The maniacal patient, for example, who thinks he is Mohammed, and fits in everything he does and says with this idea, is indeed making a judgement, but he associates two ideas without any foundation: in other words, that judgement is false. And as far as this goes, what would become of most men if their mistaken judgements were a certificate for incarceration in the Petites-Maisons asylum? On the other hand, in dementia there is no judgement whatever, be it true or false. Ideas are as if insulated, and emerge one after the other but are not linked at all, and the faculty of thinking is abolished. As an example I can again quote a patient I have often had under my care. There was never a picture of more striking chaos than his movements, ideas, talk and the confused and short-lived outbursts of his mental afflictions. He would come up to me, look at me and shower me with exuberant and inconsequential verbosity. A moment later he would have turned away towards someone else whom he deafened with his eternal and disjointed babble. His eyes shone and he seemed to be threatening, but he was as incapable of a fit of anger as of a positive thread of ideas. His emotions were limited to quick bursts of childish effervescence which subsided and vanished in the wink of an eye. If he went into a room, he would soon displace and upturn all the furniture. He would seize a table or chair, lift it up and shake it, and carry it somewhere else without showing any plan or direct intention. Hardly had one turned one's eyes than he was already far away in an adjoining passage where his capricious instability was again in evidence. He stammered a few words, moved some stones and pulled up some grass which he soon threw away to get

some more. He walked backwards and forwards, continuously fidgeted, with no memory of his previous state, his friends or his close relatives. He just rested for a few moments at night, only stopped at the sight of something to eat which he then consumed, and he seemed to be driven by a perpetual unrolling of ideas and disjointed mental afflictions which disappeared and sank into oblivion as soon as they were formed.

176. The facts which have just been reported, together with other features of dementia taken from the previous section, provide sound specific characteristics which can be expressed in the following manner. When dementia is full-blown it shows a quick succession or an uninterrupted alternation of isolated ideas and faint and disparate emotions, disorganised movements and successive eccentric actions. There is complete loss of memory for everything going before, an abolition of the facility to perceive objects through impressions received by the senses, an abolition of judgement, constant activity with no object or intention and no inner feeling of one's existence.

IV. IDIOCY, OR OBLITERATION OF THE INTELLECTUAL AND EMOTIONAL FACULTIES

Deficiencies in the French Language for Expressing the Different Degrees of Alienation

177. The author of French Synonyms tried hard to discern the slight differences between what is called in society *lunatic, eccentric, unreasonable, idiot, imbecile* etc, but he only indicated the ultimate term on the scale grading reason, prudence, perception and the mind etc and he is a long way away from achieving precise notions about the different kinds of alienation. Idiocy, which he defines as a defect in knowledge, is in the hospice environment nothing else but a more or less complete abolition, be it of the functions of understanding or of the affections of the heart. It may arise from various causes such as abuse of stimulating pleasures, taking narcotic drinks, head injuries, frantic fear or deep and unadulterated chagrin, forced and randomly directed study, tumours inside the head, one or more attacks of apoplexy, or the misuse of too many blood-lettings in the treatment of other kinds of insanity. Most idiots have no speech or they are limited to muttering a few inarticulate sounds. Their face is expressionless, their senses dulled, their movements automatic and there may be a constant state of stupor. A kind of insuperable inertia makes up their character. For a long time I had under my care at the Bicêtre a twenty-eight year old sculptor who had previously become exhausted from excesses of intemperance and the pleasures of the flesh. Most of the time he was immobile and taciturn, but at intervals he let out a sort of inane and stupid laugh. There was no expression in his face, no memory of his previous life, he never had any appetite and it was only the approach of food that set his organs of mastication in play. He continually lay down and ended up by sinking into a hectic fever which became fatal.

178. Idiots make up a very numerous species in the hospices and their condition often arises from an over-energetic treatment to which they have been subjected elsewhere. Those who are congenital sometimes have a malformation of their skull, about which I will speak in the final section when making anatomical observations on the conformation of the skull.

179. One of the most unusual and extraordinary cases I have ever observed is that of an eleven year old young idiot, the illustration of whose skull I have had engraved. From the shape of her head, her tastes and her way of life she came near to the instinct of a sheep. For the two and a half months she stayed at the Salpêtrière she showed a distaste for meat, but ate vegetarian food such as pears, apples, salad and bread hungrily, as well as pancakes which were a speciality of her region and which her mother sometimes brought for her. She only drank water and showed, in her own way, definite recognition for all the attention the servant girl lavished on her. These displays of sensitivity were limited to saying these two things: *Baa! my aunt!*, for she could not utter any other words and seemed to be completely dumb for the simple lack of ideas, since her tongue was otherwise fully mobile. She also had a way of alternately extending and flexing her head whilst pressing it against the same servant girl's stomach, like a sheep, to express her gratitude. She carried on in the same way in her little quarrels with other children of her own age, whom she tried to strike with the top of her tilted head. With a blind instinct which was animal-like she was unable to restrain her behaviour when angry, and her outbursts at the slightest provocation, and sometimes for no reason at all, went as far as convulsions. One could never get her to sit on a chair to take a rest or have her meals, and she slept with her body rolled up and stretched out on the ground like a sheep. Her whole back, loins and shoulders were covered in a kind of soft blackish hair one and a half to two inches long which was like wool in its fineness: this was a disagreeable aspect. And some circus tumblers who had heard about the condition of this young idiot had suggested to her mother that she should let them put her on display in the neighbouring fairs and markets as a rare object of curiosity. She refused to do this in spite of being very poor. Through being away from them this young idiot ended by falling into a progressive state of languor and died after two and a half months in the Salpêtrière hospice. I have carefully preserved her skull, which is remarkable for its dimensions and shape.

Form of Idiotism Produced by Strong and Unexpected Affections

180. Some people of extreme sensitivity can be so severely shaken by a sharp sudden emotion that all their mental functions are suspended or obliterated by it. Excessive happiness, like a deep fear, can also lead to this inexplicable phenomenon. An artilleryman, during the second year of the Republic, proposed the idea of a newly invented canon of dreadful effectiveness to the Committee for Public Security. A trial of this was ordered for a certain day at Meudon, and Robespierre wrote a letter to the inventor which was so encouraging that on reading it he froze to the spot and was shortly sent to the Bicêtre in a complete state of idiocy. At the same time, two young conscripts left for the army and in a bloody encounter one of them was killed by a gunshot beside his brother, who then froze like a statue at this spectacle. A few days later he was returned in this state to his family home. His arrival had the same effect on a third son of the same family – the news of the death of one of his brothers, and the mental breakdown of the other, threw him into such consternation and stupor that nothing better illustrated the frozen immobility of terror which so many ancient and modern poets have depicted (7). I have had these two unfortunate brothers under my care for a long time in the infirmary at Bicêtre; and what was even more heart-breaking, I have seen their father come to cry over these sad remnants of his former family.

Idiocy, a Species of Alienation Common in the Hospices and Sometimes Cured by an Attack of Maniacal Insanity

181. It is unfortunate that the species of alienation which is generally the most incurable should be so common in the hospices. Formerly it constituted a quarter of the total number of those who have lost their senses at Bicêtre, and it may be that the cause for this is easy to point to. This hospice was regarded as a place of refuge and recovery for those who had elsewhere been subjected to over-energetic treatment with blood-letting, baths and showers. Many arrived in a state of weakness, lifelessness and stupor, to the extent that several succumbed within a few days of their arrival. Some regained their intellectual faculties following the gradual restoration of their strength. Others suffered relapses in seasons of hot weather. Some, especially the young, after remaining for several months, or even for whole years, in complete idiocy, developed an attack of maniacal insanity which lasted twenty, twenty-five or thirty days, and was succeeded by a restoration of their reason as though by some sort of inner reaction. I have already indicated that there may be similar effects in periodic maniacal insanity but it is important to make another case known in full detail. A young soldier of twenty-two was struck with terror by the din of the artillery in a bloody encounter in which he took part soon after joining the army. His reason was shattered and elsewhere he was subjected to treatment with the usual method of blood-lettings, baths and showers. At the last blood-letting, the bandage became untied, he lost a large amount of blood and he sank into a prolonged syncope. He was restored to life with tonics and restoratives but he remained in a state of languor which left everything to be feared and, not wishing to watch him perish before their eyes, his parents sent him to Bicêtre. His father, visiting him several days later, thought he was in despair and let him have some money to help matters. At the end of a month warning signs developed of an attack of maniacal insanity: constipation, redness of the face and volubility. He came out of his state of inertia and stupor, walked about inside the hospice, and then embarked upon a thousand wild and animated eccentricities. The attack lasted for eighteen days. Calm returned with the gradual reestablishment of reason and the young man, having spent several more months in the hospice to ensure full convalescence, was returned full of sense and reason to the bosom of his family. Sometimes young females have also experienced this transformation of the illness, and I have noted a few examples of this in the Salpêtrière hospice, but after the forty or forty-fifth year it is very rare to have this salutary reaction.

Principal Features of the Physical and Mental Character of the Swiss Cretins

182. The largest group of incurable mentally deranged patients is undoubtedly the idiots, who, compared with one another, show varying degrees of stupidity depending on whether the idiocy is more or less complete. This state of degeneration and loss is carried much further in the cretins of Switzerland. They show signs of what is ultimately to become of them from their infancy. Sometimes (8) there is a goitre the size of a walnut from their first years. Generally speaking there is puffiness of the face, disproportionately large hands and head, little sensitivity to different atmospheric changes, constant state of stupor and drowsiness, difficulty in suckling because of a weakness of instinct even for basic needs, and very late and incomplete development of the facility to articulate sounds, since they only

learn to pronounce vowels, without any consonants. As their body grows there is always heaviness and stupid clumsiness in their movements; and there is even a lack or absence of intelligence at the age of ten or twelve years, for the little cretins of this age do not know how to raise food to their mouth or to chew it and it has to be pushed down their throat. In adolescence there is always a weak, heavy and tottering step, if one succeeds in getting them to move. There is never any laughter, always dazed stubbornness and an annoying and rebellious character which only maternal tenderness can cope with. There is disproportion of the head, which is small compared with the rest of the body, flattening at the top and temples, and a slightly prominent occipital tuberosity. The eyes are small, sometimes deep-set and at others protuberant, with a staring, stunned look. The chest is hollow, the fingers thin and long with not very prominent joints; the soles of the feet are broad and sometimes curved, and the foot is most often out-turned or in-turned. Puberty comes late, but there is a large development of the reproductive organs, and hence a lewd lustiness and strong inclination for masturbation. Only at this stage does the cretin begin to walk about, but again his range is very limited, and only stimulated by the desire to get some food, warm himself by the fireside or enjoy the sunshine. His pallet is another deadline for his long and difficult journeys and he makes his way there staggering, with his arms hanging down and his trunk unsteady. On the way he goes straight ahead and he does not know how to avoid any obstacles or dangers. He would not know how to go by a different route from the one he knows. When he has reached his full height, usually thirteen to sixteen decimetres, the cretin's skin becomes swarthy, his sensitivity continues to be obtuse and he is indifferent to cold or warmth, or even to blows and wounds. He is usually deaf and dumb, and the most pungent and repellent odours hardly affect him. I knew one cretin who avidly ate raw onions, and even coal, which shows how much the organ of taste is coarse or little developed. I say nothing about sight and touch, which are the organs of discrimination and understanding, and whose functions must be very restricted or crude. Their affective faculties again seem non-existent and there is often no trace of recognition for kind acts done for them. They hardly show any awareness at the sight of their parents, and register neither sorrow nor pleasure over anything related to their everyday needs. Such, says Fodéré, is the physical and mental way of living of the cretins throughout the prolonged course of their disorder, for being reduced to a sort of vegetable and automatic existence they reach advanced old age without any difficulty.

General Remarks About the Different Kinds of Alienation

183. The well-known natural history of the different species of alienation undoubtedly casts much light on the way of managing its treatment. It may be that it will also serve to enlighten jurisprudence in doubtful cases referred for decision by the Courts. But in the present state of our knowledge it is the jurisprudence in relation to the different lapses of reason that seems least advanced to me. What a lot of different disturbances there are which one or more functions of understanding may suffer, without the individual being any less capable of carrying out transactions and undertaking engagements in civil life! What can the judges think when listening to a man, arguing soundly, who is affected by what in the hospices is known as reasoning insanity, and who at the same time is tearing his clothes and breaking everything up? A young man who just had the insanity of wearing women's clothes gave rise to a big court action and the will that he had made was annulled. Sanctimonious melancholia, which consists in spending part of one's time in churches, may

be of no significance to a rich person, but can be intolerable in a working man's wife upon whom all the running of the household rests, and then it is a form of distraction of reason which can gradually lead to a certified alienation. I know people who live in the heart of society and who have an irresistible urge to commit suicide. And it is this same urge which causes several people affected by it to be detained although they do not show any other signs of mental distraction. How often people who only have a single simple deficiency of the functions of understanding end up dropping into a confirmed maniacal insanity when their tendency to become overexcited or mad about something is skilfully exploited! And what a lot of drawbacks must come about from this, if the courts grant to a presumptive heir the entire control of the individual and the freedom to get around them by accomplices who carry out his wishes!

184. The different types of alienation which have just been discussed do not remain invariably the same during their course. That is to say that an alienation allocated to one of these types may undergo a kind of transformation, and then come to be classified as another type. Thus we see melancholic become maniacal patients, and some maniacal patients fall into dementia or idiocy, and sometimes even idiots, through some incidental cause, go through a passing attack of maniacal insanity and then recover their reason completely. Maniacal insanity finally may be complicated by other nervous illnesses such as hysteria, hypochondria, epilepsy or a tendency to apoplexy etc. But to avoid confusion, should we not consider things in their original simplicity?

NOTES TO THIRD SECTION

1. Darwin (*Zoonomia, or the laws, of organic Life,* London, 1796) designates *paupertatis amor* as a species of insanity, and quotes the example of a miserly parsimonious surgeon who having inherited an annuity of nearly one hundred thousand pounds became insane over the fear of poverty. He moaned every day over the destitution which meant he was going to die in prison or in a public home for the poor.
2. A collection of nearly eight hundred mentally deranged patients, either submitted to treatment or else regarded as incurable, which I had before me at the Salpêtrière, put the classification method I had adopted to a further trial. And since the first edition of my work on Insanity I have never seen a single case of alienation which could not be allocated naturally to one of the species I have just indicated. I have only recognised that maniacal insanity without delirium was not a species but rather a variety, for even when these patients are reasoning soundly, they give other evidence of aberration in their actions and show other characteristics peculiar to maniacal patients.
3. Close examination of the precursory signs of maniacal insanity provides striking evidence of the extensive influence which *La Caze* and *Bordeu* have attributed to the epigastric forces, and which *Buffon* has painted so well in his Natural History. Indeed the whole abdominal region seems to be involved in this sympathetic connection.
4. M. Esquirol, one of my former pupils, has used the same method in a private establishment which he set up for the treatment of patients of either sex, and about which I will give an account later in this volume.
5. Sombre taciturnity, harsh and ungracious gravity, the grim changeability of a character which is full of sourness and fits of anger, the pursuit of solitude, sidelong glances and

the bashful predicament of a deceitful soul, all betray the melancholic disposition of Louis XI since his youth. There are features of striking similarity between this Prince and Tiberius. There is no distinction between them in the art of war, which during the tumultuous coming of age and for the rest of their lives was passed in imposing but ineffective preparations, carefully contrived waiting periods, illusive plans for military ventures and negotiations which were full of shrewdness and perfidy. Before coming to the throne each of them voluntarily exiled themselves from the Court and went to spend several years in the oblivion and inactivity of private life, one on the Isle of Rhodes and the other in solitude in Belgium. What utter falsehoods, what indecisiveness, and what ambiguous responses there were in Tiberius's behaviour on the death of Augustus. And had not Louis XI for the whole of his life been the very epitome of the most perfidious and subtle politics? Beset with their brooding suspicions, sinister omens and terrors which were constantly recurring towards the end of life, they went on to conceal their disgusting tyranny, one in the Plessis-les-Tours chateau and the other on the Isle of Capri. This was a period of atrocities no less than one of feeble but unrestrained debauchery.

6. It is not uncommon amongst the public to find strongly pronounced changes in melancholy which have descended into insanity. A very educated and uniquely gifted lady acceded to the conventions of her social class and married a neighbour who was in a state of dementia. The desire to please her own family and her superior calibre led her to tolerate this awful union courageously for a long time, but every day there was some new development which needed her supervision and which saddened her, with her imbecilic husband's childish fits of anger, threats and assaults on the domestic staff and totally inconsistent behaviour. Outside, and when in company, there was disjointed and incoherent talk and sometimes absent-minded eccentricity and nonsense. The physical and moral upbringing of two children, whom she cherished tenderly, and the amount of care she gave them alone brightened her sad and insipid existence with moments of happiness, but it failed to arrest the progress of her melancholy. Every day her imagination gave birth to new matters for distrust and fear. Certain untoward events happening on particular days of the week, especially Friday, persuaded her that this was an unlucky day and she ended up not daring to leave her room that day. If the month began on a Friday, this was then a matter for fainthearted fear for this long string of days. Then gradually Thursday, being the day before Friday, became equally alarming for her. If she was in company and heard one of these days mentioned she went pale and wan, and spoke with distress and confusion as if she was confronted with something disastrous. It was a few months before the Revolution that I was asked for my advice about this melancholic derangement. I applied some simple remedies, with the mental steps this situation called for; but the events of 1789, and soon afterwards family set-backs and emigration, put the progress of the illness out of my mind, and I surmise that a new chain of ideas, a change of climate and perhaps falling on hard times have driven the clouds of melancholy away.

7. Strong and unanticipated affections also sometimes lead in young females to a state of idiocy, especially if they happen at the time of a monthly period, which is consequently suddenly stopped.

8. *Traité du Goître et du Crétinisme* by F.E. Fodéré, former Physician to the Civil and Military Hospitals, Paris, Year VIII.

4

IN-HOUSE MANAGEMENT, AND RULES TO BE FOLLOWED, IN ESTABLISHMENTS FOR THE MENTALLY ILL

185. Distinguished travellers curious to visit the Salpêtrière hospice for the mentally ill, on witnessing the orderliness and calm prevailing there, have sometimes exclaimed on looking around *'But where are the patients?'* These foreigners did not realise that they were expressing the most encouraging praise for this establishment, or that their question touched on a major difference between it and other hospices. In them, the unfortunate patients, crammed together any old way, with no choice, are exasperated by the coarse uncouthness of the staff. They are subjected to the futile whims and arbitrary commands of an incompetent or uncaring chief, and are in a permanent state of agitation, giving vent to nothing but complaints, curses and tumultuous shouts.

186. A hospice for the mentally ill will ideally combine the benefits of its setting with those of an extensive site, and spacious and convenient premises. It lacks something fundamental if owing to its internal layout different kinds of patients cannot be kept apart. Those who are most disturbed or raging need to be kept away from those who are peaceful, or their communication with one another prevented. This is essential in order to avoid relapses and it helps with carrying out all the internal regulations and supervision, but it also helps to avoid unforeseen anomalies in the sequence and collection of symptoms which the doctor has to watch and describe. Above all it is important that the patients should be controlled, in keeping with humane principles and the results of enlightened experience, and that their outbursts should be firmly curbed. At the same time each patient should enjoy the degree of freedom which is compatible with his personal safety and that of others. Finally, whenever this is possible the superintendent should become the confidant of their troubles and concerns. Methodical distribution of the hospice patients into different departments immediately reveals the measures to be taken for feeding them, keeping them clean, and also for their mental and physical care. The requirements of each of them are then

Medico-Philosophical Treatise on Mental Alienation.
Philippe Pinel. Translated by G. Hickish, D. Healy and L.C. Charland.
© 2008 John Wiley & Sons, Ltd.

calculated and anticipated, the different disturbances of understanding are appreciated for their distinguishing characters, and events are observed and compared and combined with other similar events, and thereby converted into sound experimental evidence. It is from the same source that the observant doctor can derive the fundamental rules of treatment, and learn to recognise the species of alienation which respond the most or least readily to the passage of time and to active management, and those which constitute the greatest obstacles to a cure or may be regarded as incurable. These are those disorders, in short, which urgently call for the use of particular medications, even in the eyes of those judicious and enlightened souls who do not wish to overrate their effects yet do not close their eyes to the benefits of medications. The details which I am going to communicate regarding the internal organisation and running of the hospice will show to what extent the plan, whose fundamental basis has just been set out, has been achieved.

I. GENERAL PLAN AND INTERNAL ARRANGEMENT OF THE HOSPICE FOR THE MENTALLY ILL

187. It is easy to give a brief idea of the whole, and the separate parts, of the Salpêtrière hospice, which have enabled a judicious distribution of the patients. In the centre is a square courtyard with a fountain in the middle and a double row of lime trees along each side about forty-six metres in length. It is made up beyond by a line of small surrounding lodges which open onto this courtyard; and it is in these pleasant premises that the melancholic women are accommodated, each in a separate lodge. The same goes for two other courtyards which are oblong and about six metres wide, formed by double rows of adjoining lodges, parallel with the side of the central courtyard and facing west, and for another courtyard parallel to the south side of the central courtyard. Three other fenced courtyards formed by double rows of adjoining lodges lie to the east. It is in these three oblong fenced courtyards that the patients most likely to spread disorder within the hospice are accommodated. In one of them are idiots who are liable to go into lodges indiscriminately grabbing anything they find, as well as other patients who are irresistibly tempted to steal and disruptive people liable to spread discord everywhere. The second division is reserved for more or less agitated or furious patients whose condition is deep-rooted and looked upon as being incurable. The third division confines patients with fury of recent onset and those with variably longstanding maniacal insanity but for whom there is a reasonably well-founded hope of successful treatment. In the latter case, strict confinement within their lodge is rarely necessary and, unless there is a strong impulse towards acts of violence, they are allowed to wander freely in this courtyard and carry on with all the innocent acts of eccentricity their natural exuberance suggests to them (1).

188. It is around this regular collection of long series of lodges and courtyards that a pathway planted with a row of lime trees runs to the south and east. The trees give it shade during the summer and tranquil patients whose insanity has degenerated into a kind of dementia walk about freely. In the eastern part of this pathway there is a dormitory for elderly women who have been reduced to a state of senile dementia. A servant girl attends to their needs and cleanliness. The other southern part of the footpath is adjacent to a kind of garden or promenade of about three acres, planted with young trees to give shade, with an ornamental pond in the middle. The hospice ends to the west with a sort of oblong forecourt onto which

the doors of a long row of lodges open; and on the parallel side is a long covered path where tranquil patients in the decline of their illness can walk about under shelter in rainy weather. Finally, those who are in full convalescence and whose reason is completely restored are taken to roomy dormitories which border the hospice to the north. Here they lay on very neat, tidy beds after having spent a large part of the day in the communal sewing room. At the very end of one of these dormitories, in a separate large room, there is an infirmary for patients who develop all sorts of incidental illnesses which can crop up depending on the season or other particular circumstances. And lastly, when the mental hospice was restored about thirty years ago, a double row of joined lodges, and other parallel lodges lower down than the hospice, were retained. These were for the isolation of people who had degenerated into idiocy and other patients who had reached a kind of degradation through the most awful debauchery and complete oblivion for all the rules of modesty and decency: this called for an isolated place to avoid contagion by example.

189. This distribution of patients according to the nature of the premises, the general conformities of taste and inclinations, and their state of calm or turmoil, shows the basis for the general order prevailing in the hospice and the ability to avoid all seeds of dissention and discord. The melancholic patients remain voluntarily in their lodges or wander about freely under archways of greenery which have the double advantage of providing visual relaxation and shelter from the heat of the sun. The fountain in the middle of their courtyard provides plenty of water, meeting their needs and brightening up their solitary quarters. The women suffering from dementia, and those whose maniacal insanity is in decline and for whom the least thing can exacerbate matters, enjoy complete liberty either in the courtyards and lanes designated for them or in the adjacent garden. This is grassed over and already shaded by young lime trees which grow higher every year. No unnecessary discomfort and no constraint is in general applied, and often patients who have recently arrived in a state of extreme agitation or fury regain their tranquillity a few days later because of the general arrangements in the hospice. In any collection of several hundred mentally deranged patients could one not always find rare examples of little intrigues, highly sophisticated deceitfulness or the diabolical plots which a spirit of discord can sow? And what an upheaval there would be if all these ferments of trouble and disorder could spread freely and not be concentrated in one or two isolated courtyards secured with fences! It is the same with more or less hot-tempered patients who could turn their blind fury against one another or anybody else nearby. The convalescent patients, although at the opposite extreme, must be no less the object of close surveillance to stop any communication with other patients, reaffirm a still vacillating reason by means of regular work, and to prepare them for their return to the outside world.

II. ON METHODS CURRENTLY USED TO CONTROL THE INSANE

190. The sustained use of chains is an admirable invention for perpetuating the fury of maniacal patients with their state of detention, for making up for the lack of enthusiasm of an unenlightened superintendent, for maintaining constant exasperation and a focused desire to get revenge in the patients' hearts, and for stirring up racket and commotion in hospices. These drawbacks had been an object of concern for me whilst carrying out my responsibilities as physician at Bicêtre during the first years of the Revolution, and it

was not without great regret that I could see no happy end to this barbaric and routine-minded custom. However, on the other hand I remained calm and relied on the skill of the superintendent of this hospice (M. Pussin), who was equally keen to end this neglect of true principles. Fortunately this happened two years later *(4th Prairial[1] Year VI)* and there was never any development better devised, nor followed by more outstanding success. Forty wretched patients who groaned under the weight of the irons for varying numbers of years were set free in spite of all the apprehensions registered by the Central Bureau, and they were allowed to wander about freely in the courtyards simply with the movements of their arms restricted by a strait-jacket. At night they were loose in their lodge. It was noticeable that this marked the end of unfortunate injuries suffered by the staff. They had often been struck or injured in an unforeseen manner by patients restrained in chains and constantly in a state of concentrated fury. One of these patients had been in this sorry state for thirty-six years and another forty-five years – however they could still move and walked about slowly inside the hospice. One still remembers one of these patients who had been in chains at the back of a dark lodge for eighteen years. As soon as he was able to see the bright sunlight he cried out in a sort of ecstatic rapture *'Ah! What a long time it is since I saw anything so beautiful!'*

191. The insane, far from being culprits who need punishment, are patients whose sad state deserves all the consideration due to suffering humanity and whose lapsed reason one must seek to restore by the simplest means. They may be reduced to a complete disruption of all their intellectual faculties and only obey blind impulses which drive them to disorder and all kinds of violence. In this case they are beyond any advice, and the personal safety of the patient and that of the others must solely be catered for by simply keeping him in his lodge. If he is very violent, a strait-jacket of strong cloth must be used to restrain the movements of his feet and hands, and keep him fixed on his bed by strong straps, which he cannot see, attached to the back of this garment. But this situation of extreme restraint must be temporary, to avoid the results of anger focussed against those around him which would in any case only aggravate his delirium. Certain serious and urgent circumstances may require firmer but more short-lived discipline: this can only be clarified by some examples. A young girl who had been thrown into a state of stupor and kind of idiocy by severe vexations and deep dismay had been cured, and had even become quite stout, but during her convalescence she stubbornly refused to do any work. The superintendent, to punish her, one day had her taken to the lower courtyard amongst the idiots. However she appeared to enjoy this kind of suppression and just cavorted and danced and ridiculed everything. So a corset with straps was applied, pulling her shoulders moderately backwards. The young girl seemed to stiffen and put up with this ordeal for a whole day, but the constraint she suffered made her ask for pardon and she no longer refused to do the sewing. If she became slack in her work she was laughingly reminded about the *velvet waistcoat* and she immediately became obedient. Another forty-year old woman was so furious and wild that she struck all the servant girls, and was on the point of battering one of them to death in her lodge at the very moment when she was feeding her. On another day she threw an earthenware pot at her head and seriously wounded her. A vest with straps was put on her tightly right away, forcibly pulling her shoulders back. She could not tolerate this constraint for longer than an hour. She asked for pardon and since then she has not struck anybody although she continued to be in a delirium for a long time. If she said abusive things, it was enough to mention the vest to

---

[1] *Prairial – Ninth month of Republican Calendar – Ed.*

her and she immediately returned to order and calmed down. It does not seem that this sort of restraint can be tolerated for more than a short time, for it leads first to a feeling of general discomfort and severe difficulty in breathing due to restriction of the chest muscles, followed by sickliness in the stomach and unbearable anxiety so that the patient is driven to ask for pardon and remembers it all for a long time. But neither such a restraint, nor any other, is entrusted to the staff – it is for the superintendent to carry out and make a special object of supervision.

192. Showers, considered as a means of restraint, are often[2] enough to lead a patient who is capable of it to obey the general rule of performing manual work, to overcome obstinate food refusal and to bring patients driven by a kind of turbulent but reasoned mood under control. The bath is made use of then. We can benefit from such occasions to refocus attention on the fault committed. Through the tap a stream of cold water is squirted onto the head, disconcerting the patient or dispelling a prevailing idea with a harsh and sudden sensation. If she persists in being obstinate this shower is repeated, carefully avoiding harshness of tone and shocking language likely to outrage. She is made to understand that, on the contrary, it is only for her own benefit, and with regret, that these harsh measures have been resorted to; and a few jokes are sometimes thrown in, taking care not to take this too far. Once the obstinacy comes to an end this restraint is immediately suspended and a tone of affectionate benevolence takes over. The success of this approach, in common use in the hospice, may be judged by the following observation. A patient with a strong constitution, subject for more than ten years to a periodic irregular recurrence of maniacal insanity, could not be restrained by the most energetic and violent means, which on the contrary had only exasperated her. She tore clothes, bed linen and blankets to pieces, and was reduced to lying on straw, striking the staff and scoffing so much at the methods of restraint that her parents withdrew her from another hospice, making up their minds to try the method followed at the Salpêtrière. This poor wretch was extremely gaunt on her arrival although very voracious, and there was nothing to equal her fits of anger. First, the attempt was made to correct the poor state of her health with some delicious food, but her previous habit of tearing everything up became much worse. She was given a moderately strong shower and a vest was put on her with straps at the back to fasten her to her bed until she asked for pardon. At the first sign of submission she was given freedom of movement, but a recurrence led to the same restraining measures being repeated, restoring more calmness and reserve. However then the superintendent became indisposed for twelve days and the patient, relieved of close surveillance, seemed to forget the lessons she had been given. She had resumed her habit of striking the servant girls, tearing everything up and endlessly throwing herself into frenetic fits of anger. The superintendent came back to work and threatened to punish her but she took no account of this. She was then taken to the bathing area, subjected to a forceful shower with cold water and kept immobile with a strait-jacket. This time she seemed to be humbled and dismayed, and the superintendent, to impart a feeling of terror, spoke to her in the firmest terms, but without any anger, telling her that in future she would be treated very severely. Her repentance declared itself with a torrent of tears which she shed for nearly two hours. The next morning and the following days were calm, the other symptoms progressively diminished and as a few months of complete convalescence left nothing dubious in her condition, she was returned to her family.

---

[2] I will consider baths and showers in connection with medical treatment in another section.

193. Another example which I once witnessed at Bicêtre will show the benefit of sometimes severely shocking a patient's imagination and instilling a sense of terror in him. A young man, at the time of the Revolution, was dismayed at the overturning of the Catholic religion in France. Overcome with religious feelings he became maniacal and was transferred to Bicêtre after the then customary treatment at the Hôtel-Dieu. There was nothing to equal his gloomy misanthropy: he spoke of nothing else but the torments of the next life and he thought that to escape it he had to imitate the abstinences and macerations of the old Anchorites. From then on he denied himself all food and towards the fourth day of this unshakable resolution his state of languor caused fears for his life. Friendly remonstrance, entreaties and everything else were in vain. He roughly pushed away some soup he was offered and actually removed the straw from his bed so as to lay on the planks. Could the compelling course of his sinister ideas be counterbalanced in any other way than by instilling a vivid and deep fear? Accordingly the superintendent (M. Pussin) presented himself in the evening at the lodge door with a spectacle calculated to frighten him. His eyes were ablaze, he spoke in a thundering tone of voice and there was a group of his staff pressed around him armed with heavy chains which they loudly rattled. A bowl of soup was placed close by the patient and he was very clearly instructed to consume it during the night if he did not wish to invite some very cruel treatment. They went away, leaving the patient in the very difficult state of vacillation between the idea of the punishment with which he was threatened and the frightening prospects of the torments of the next life. After many hours of inner turmoil the first idea got the better of him and he decided to take his food. He was then put on a diet suitable to restore him. Sleep and strength gradually returned, as well as the use of his reason, and in this way he escaped a certain death. During his convalescence he often confessed to me his cruel agitations and deep perplexities during that night of trial.

194. The patients who are the most difficult to manage in the hospices, the most remarkable for turbulent activity and the most subject to sudden explosions of maniacal fury, bear in general all the features of a nervous temperament about which I have already spoken in the article on maniacal insanity. It may be imagined how many patients with this temperament are dangerous, given that their strength and audacity is doubled at the time. The big secret for bringing them under control, without inflicting or receiving injuries in unforeseen circumstances, is to have multiple staff members advance in a show of force so as to give them something of a fright with the imposing sight and to frustrate any resistance with skilfully coordinated steps. If a patient of this kind is suddenly gripped by a frenetic delirium during one of his intervals of calm, and has an offensive weapon such as a knife, stick or stone, the superintendent, who is always faithful to his maxims of maintaining order whilst avoiding acts of violence, himself advances towards the patient, looking fearless. He moves slowly and gradually, and to avoid aggravating him he does not carry any weapon with him. As he advances he speaks to him in a firm and threatening voice, and with repeated summonses keeps holding all his attention so as to keep his eyes off what is going on at his sides. He gives the patient the precise and imperious command to obey and give himself up. The patient, somewhat disconcerted by the superintendent's proud attitude, loses sight of everything else. At a given signal, he suddenly finds himself besieged by members of the staff who had slowly and stealthily been moving forwards. Each of them seizes a part of the furious patient – one an arm, another a thigh or a leg. He is thus lifted up and carried into his lodge, all his efforts overcome, and what threatened to be a tragic scene ends up as a quite ordinary event. There are disorders cropping up amongst the patients like those which happen in

civil life, and to overcome them and restore calm measures are necessary which are soundly devised on experience and knowledge of men. Vigorous and prompt implementation of such measures is also called for. The strong tendency of mentally deranged patients, even in their periods of calm and convalescence, to fly into fits of anger for the slightest reasons is well known. A brawl breaking out between some of them, the plausible appearance of an injustice committed by an employee, the sight of the onset of an attack of maniacal insanity and any real or imaginary object of discontentment or grumbling can become an alarming focus of discord and disorder, and spread from one end of the hospice to the other like an electric shock. People gather, get restless, form into mobs as in public riots, and what dire consequences can these angry scenes have if they are not stopped right at the beginning? It is under such circumstances that I have often seen the superintendent boldly confront a tumultuous outburst, turn to the right and the left, seize the most rebellious, conduct them to their lodges and immediately restore tranquillity and calm.

III. NECESSITY OF MAINTAINING CONSISTENT ORDER IN HOSPICES FOR THE MENTALLY ILL, AND OF STUDYING THEIR CHARACTER TRAITS

195. The extreme importance which I attach to the maintenance of calm and order in a hospice for deranged patients, and to the physical and mental qualities which call for such surveillance, is hardly surprising. For there lies one of the fundamental bases of the treatment of maniacal insanity, and without it neither accurate observations nor a permanent cure can be achieved, however one insists on the most highly praised medications. What a calamity it is for unlucky maniacal patients to be directed with a blind routine, and abandoned to the happy-go-lucky attitude of an unprincipled superintendent with no morals, or, which comes to the same thing, be left to the rustic hardships and murderous treatments of other subordinate employees! The qualities necessary for treatment include wisdom, ardent zeal and constant and tireless attention to the moves of every patient, and to the strange twist of each patient's ideas and the particular character of their delirium. Indeed, what variations must age, constitution, acquired habits, the combination of maniacal insanity with other illnesses and the degree of the disturbance of mental faculties not produce! In certain very difficult cases several months of such study hardly suffice to make up one's mind and determine correctly what kind of approach to take (2). But in most cases, especially in reactive maniacal insanity stemming from profound vexation, experience every day bears out the success achieved from consoling talks and the happy device of reawakening the patient's hope and gaining his confidence. But using bad treatments or restraint methods which are too harsh aggravates the illness and often makes it incurable. After other unhappy events a young man lost his father, and then a few months later his tenderly loved mother. From then on then there was deep concentrated sadness, no sleep, no appetite and soon afterwards an outburst of a very violent maniacal state. He was subjected to the treatment in common use, such as copious and frequent blood-lettings, baths and showers and other extremely rigorous actions; but all these mixed curative measures failed. The same treatment was repeated twice and then three times always with equally little success and even with aggravation of the symptoms. The patient was finally transferred to the Bicêtre, labelled as being mainly very quick-tempered and dangerous. The superintendent, far from accepting this opinion blindly, set him free in his lodge from the first day, so as to study his character

and his outbursts. The gloomy taciturnity of this patient, his despondency, his pensive and concentrated air, and a few disjointed words escaping from him about his misfortunes, gave a glimpse of the root of his insanity. He was consoled, shown compassion with his lot, and little by little his angry defiance was dispelled and he was brought to look forward to his affairs coming together again. An encouraging incident followed close on this promise, as a little money each month was obtained from his guardian to make his life more comfortable. The first payments lifted him out of his despondency and gave him more to hope for. His confidence in the superintendent and his regard for him was boundless, and his strength was seen to gradually return, as well as all the external signs of good health at the same time as his reason righted itself. He who had been very ill-treated in another hospice and labelled as a most violent and fearsome deranged patient had become, through a gentle and conciliatory approach, a most docile and worthy man noted for his touching sensitivity.

196. Some character traits can render the patient liable to give in only after repeated alternating more or less fiery outbursts and the applications of wise and moderated restraint. 'In mental treatment', the editors of the Bibliothèque britannique say[3] 'the mad are not considered to be completely devoid of reason; that is, inaccessible to motives of fear, hope, or honourable sentiments . . . they must first be subjugated, and then encouraged'. These general propositions are doubtless very true and rich in useful applications, but to appreciate them fully some examples are needed, and it is on this point that the English remain silent. Here is another case history of this kind to be added to the preceding ones, which will give us grounds for satisfying ourselves that this secret is known about in France. The commendable father of a family lost his fortune and nearly all his reserves as a result of events in the Revolution, and deep sadness soon drove him into an insane state. He received the routine ordinary treatment of insanity with baths, water jets[4], repeated blood-lettings and the most inhuman disciplinary methods. Far from clearing away, the symptoms became worse, and he was transferred to Bicêtre as incurable. The superintendent, without dwelling on the advice he was given designating this patient as very dangerous, left him on his own for a while so as to study his character. Never has a patient given freer reins to his acts of eccentricity. He drew himself all puffed up with pride, thought he was the prophet Mohammed, and struck out right and left at everyone who got in his way ordering them to bow down and pay homage to him. The whole day was spent pronouncing alleged judgements of exile and death, and there was nothing but threats and offensive remarks against the staff. The superintendent's authority was scorned and unrecognised. One day, when his tearful wife came to see him, he even got angry with her and might have killed her if somebody had not rushed to her help. What good could gentle approaches and mild remonstrance do with a patient who looked upon other men as specks of dust? The order was intimated that he should calm himself, and when he refused to obey he was punished with the strait-jacket and an hour's seclusion to make him appreciate his dependency. The superintendent soon brought him back from his lodge, spoke to him in a friendly way reproaching him for his disobedience and expressed his regret for having been forced to take harsh measures with him. The insane lapses recurred the following day and the same disciplinary measures were used, followed by the same worthless promises to be calmer in the future. A further and a third relapse occurred, succeeded by punishment consisting of a whole day's detention,

---

[3] *Sur un nouvel Établissement pour la guérison des Aliénés,* by Dr D, Vol.VIII.
[4] *Pinel is referring to a harsh form of shower – Ed.*

leading to a noticeable calm in the ensuing days. A fourth outburst of his haughty and obstreperous temper caused the superintendent to feel the need to make a deep and lasting impression on this patient. He shouted out vehemently to him, sought to make him lose any hope of reconciliation, and promptly had him locked up, saying that in future he would be unyielding. Two days went by, and during his rounds the superintendent just responded with a mocking laugh to the repeated appeals made to him; but by a mutual agreement between the superintendent and his wife, the latter set the detainee free towards the end of the third day. She expressly recommended that he contain his fits of anger and not to expose her to criticism for having been too indulgent. The patient appeared calm for several days, and at moments when he could hardly contain his delirious lapses, just one look from Madame Pussin was enough to bring him back to order, and he immediately ran to dive into his lodge for fear of being found at fault again. These oft repeated inner struggles between the involuntary recurrence of insane lapses and the fear of indefinite detention increasingly accustomed him to master his will and control himself. He was filled with affection and esteem for those who controlled him with so much consideration and friendliness, and as a result all the former traces of his maniacal insanity were little by little dispelled. A trial period of six months was enough to render his cure complete and this respected family father then set himself with tireless energy to restore his ruined fortune.

197. The practice of living amongst the patients and studying their tastes and individual characters can, in certain instances, suggest a way of supporting forceful restraint and preparing for the return of reason which has lapsed. A soldier who was still in a state of derangement, and had undergone the Hôtel-Dieu treatment, was suddenly overcome with the single idea of leaving for the Army. After trying all the gentle approaches force was resorted to in order to make him go back into his lodge in the evening. He smashed everything to pieces during the night and was so furious that very strong restraining bonds were needed. He was left to give vent to his impetuous fieriness for the next few days, and there were fits of bitter anger all the time, and outbursts of fury. He only responded to the superintendent with streams of abuse and he appeared to ignore his authority. Eight days went by in this violent state and then at last he appeared to see that he was not his own master to do whatever he wished. In the morning, during the superintendent's rounds, he adopted a most submissive tone and kissing his hand said 'You promised to let me have freedom inside the hospice if I was calm: well, I call upon you to keep your word'. Smiling, the superintendent told him how pleased he was at this happy change of heart, spoke kindly to him and had all restraints taken away at once: they would from then on have been superfluous and harmful. Reason and calm became gradually restored, but since the illness had been deep-rooted and since it was important to avoid any relapse, convalescence was prolonged and after a hospice stay of seven months this soldier was returned to his family and subsequently to the defence of his country.

198. The skill of trying to redirect the single will of deranged patients, reasoning with them and making them aware of their dependency, assumes that their reason is not in a complete state of distraction. If one of them is dominated by a blind fieriness and driven by a tumultuous combination of ideas with no order or sequence, it is only possible to exert control by making use of the strait-jacket or strict seclusion. But if exercise of judgement still survives, another no less commendable secret for putting a stop to brawls between the patients, overcoming their resistance and maintaining order is to appear not to notice

their outbursts, not say anything which smacks of criticism, and even appear to share their views, and skilfully convey an impulse to them which they just think is their own. It is in this connection that the lady superintendent, Mme Pussin, seemed to me to combine these rare qualities. At Bicêtre I have watched, astonished, as she approached the most furious manic patients, calmed them down with comforting words and got them to accept food which they firmly refused from everybody else. One deranged patient who was in great danger because of stubborn abstinence became angry with her one day and, pushing away the food she served to him, showered her with the most outrageous language. This clever lady fell in for a moment with his delirious words: she jumped and danced in front of him, answered with a few quips, managed to make him smile and by taking advantage of this favourable moment to persuade him to eat she thus saved his life. And how many times have I not seen her stop brawls, which might have had disastrous consequences, using a happy trickery! Three deranged patients who thought they were the equal of sovereigns, and who each took the title of Louis XVI, fought one day over the rights to royalty and asserted them rather too vigorously. The lady superintendent approached one of them and drawing him aside asked in a serious voice 'Why are you getting into a dispute with those people, who are obviously mad? Is it not well known that you alone should be acknowledged as Louis XVI?'. Flattered by this tribute the latter immediately withdrew, looking at the others in disdainful haughtiness. The same clever device succeeded with a second of the three, and in this way at once there was no longer any trace of the dispute. One day a much stormier occasion made me appreciate the full extent of this happy richness of methods in the skill of controlling the deranged. A young man, who had been calm for several months and free inside the hospice, suddenly had an attack. He crept into the kitchen, seized a knife used for chopping herbs and only became more furious with the efforts of the cook and the staff to disarm him. He jumped up onto the table to defend himself and threatened to cut off the head of the first who dared to advance. The lady superintendent fearlessly took a skilful line. She strongly disapproved of the attack being made against the patient. 'Why', she said, 'stop this strong, robust man from working with me?' She spoke gently to him, urged him to go to her with the instrument he had seized, and even showed him the way in which he would need to use it to chop the herbs, feigning to congratulate herself on having such a helper. The patient, deceived by this innocent ruse, just busied himself with his work, and at a given signal he was surrounded by members of the staff who safely lifted him up and took him to his lodge whilst the instrument remained in the lady superintendent's hands. One could defy the cleverest man, most versed in knowledge of the insane, to grasp the safest course to take in alarming circumstances with any more subtlety and speed.

IV. THE IMPORTANCE AND EXTREME DIFFICULTY OF ESTABLISHING FIRM ORDER IN A SERVICE FOR THE MENTALLY ILL

199. The administration of a hospice for mentally ill patients is a miniature government and in it we also sometimes see petty vanities and the ambition to be in charge working in different ways, clashing, giving rise to stormy conflicts of authority and becoming continual centres of turmoil and discord. These drawbacks, associated with all public establishments, become rather more serious in a hospice for the mentally ill because any splitting of powers can paralyse urgent restraint procedures, excite natural exuberance and make the restoration

of reason more inaccessible and more dubious. This is especially so if all arbitrary seclusion and every terror device is forbidden and only the exact amount of restraint which personal safety demands is used.

200. A fundamental principle when preparing the way for the cure of maniacal patients is first to have recourse to forceful restraint, then use kindly methods to gain the patient's confidence and convince him that one is only seeking to do him good. The superintendent has to appear in both these different roles and command the staff to support his objectives. And what might happen in such a plan, so wisely conceived, if another authority clumsily steps in and has a conflicting influence? A widow who was taken to the Salpêtrière hospice appeared to have sound judgement and was solely deluded about alleged persecutions of which she thought she was the object, and which she said were carried out using electricity or certain magic spells. She often opened her windows at night and lent an ear to certain menacing sounds she thought she could hear in the distance and to treacherous plots hatched against her by invisible hands. She became violently agitated and could even become dangerous. Otherwise, during the day, she was calm when speaking of her fears and reasoned correctly about everything else. It was a crying injustice, she said, to keep her amongst the insane and she kept asking me for a favourable certificate to obtain her discharge. The superintendent tried to dissipate her imaginary illusions by means of friendly conversations aimed at acquiring some influence over her and gaining her confidence, but at this point another authority intervened with a reassurance agreeing to the patient's discharge. There were then little secrets and repeated conversations on lines opposite to the recommendations of the superintendent. The greatest hindrance was created to obstruct treatment, the exclusive delusion became deep-rooted and everything now suggests that the illness is incurable.

201. It would be superfluous and perhaps distressing to recall all the obstacles I have encountered in the past, at different stages of treatment, through these kinds of poisonous rivalries. On the one hand these came from justified, but somewhat, violent and angry resistance, and on the other from a caustic character, gloomy moroseness and the fierce intolerance of a sanctimonious soul under the specious pretext of protecting oppressed innocence. There were some young debased and most corrupt convalescents who, to escape deserved restraint, knew how to whimper to order so as to interest another authority on their behalf. On one side, there was a model of the most cantankerous and discordant personality, which succeeded in confusing everything, getting contradictory orders and paralysing all the resources of mental and physical treatment. Elsewhere there were grumbling and bitter complaints which a few convalescent patients deliberately let be heard on the pretext of having been persecuted for reading religious material. The harmful influence of these readings, the inner excitation and the consequent prolongation of the illness were underrated. This tiresome struggle, a drawback in a hospice for mentally ill patients which is part of a major hospice, can always be avoided by a judicious superintendent who is ready to sacrifice everything for the maintenance of order in such a public establishment. I no longer have to complain about those former unhappy conflicts of jurisdiction, the deplorable effects of which many of my old notes attest.

202. It is not easy to resolve the general question relating to the centring of authority for the maintenance of order in a hospice for the mentally ill, since one must above everything else take into account the zeal and respective capacities of the physician and the superintendent.

They may share the same principles and live in perfect harmony, and then the physician who has lofty views relies completely on the general superintendent for all matters of direction and regulation. Alternatively there may be an extreme difference between a very clever superintendent and a happy-go-lucky physician who is very restricted in his outlook, and in this case the former does not fail to take over all the authority: a very well-known hospice has long served as a remarkable example of this. How then should general rules be established which can suit such opposite situations? It is no less true that whatever the general administrative principles of a hospice may be, and whatever modifications they may receive from the times, the premises and the forms of government, the physician, owing to the nature of his studies, the extent of his wisdom and his powerful interest in the success of the treatment, must be informed and become the natural judge of everything that happens in a hospice for the mentally ill. And he undoubtedly must leave the execution of disciplinary measures to the superintendent, never giving him any sign of disapproval in the presence of the patients or the staff. Yet he must nevertheless fathom the causes of any turbulent events which may arise and privately make this the subject of a frank and kindly communication.

203. The purpose allocated to the mental illness division at the Salpêtrière in its long-standing role as a place of convalescence, after the treatment in common use at the Hôtel-Dieu, gave rise to countless abuses. All the authority had been left to the servant girls because of the weakness and incapacity of the lady superintendent. So a complete reform became necessary towards Year X when a new order of things was put in place. But this reform, to be sound, needed to be made with wise reserve. At first there were angry shouts and complaints were made against the innovations and the injustice, and it is easy to imagine the resistance and silent intrigues of more than forty servant girls who were deprived of their assumed rights to treat the patients with extreme harshness and now reduced to passive obedience. They bustled about in all directions, moaned and complained to me, but limited to the functions of my position and full of confidence in the uprightness and skill of the superintendent (M. Pussin) I left to him the free use of the powers at his disposal; and all the difficulties were overcome. Most of the servant girls asked to retire and were happily replaced, little by little, by convalescent patients known for their intelligence and zeal, and capable of adopting the gentle approach which was made an inviolable rule for them.

204. The servant girls, to preserve a sort of equality among themselves in the tyrannical suppression system they had formerly imposed on the patients, had evenly divided the most turbulent and the calmest amongst themselves to avoid any inequality. At the least sign of excitement or agitation the unlimited use of chains or close seclusion was dispensed with comfortless diligence, but this perpetuated shouts and tumult throughout the hospice and became a permanent obstacle to a sound cure. A much wiser distribution of patients was adopted by the isolation of the furious women, or those most agitated, in a fenced courtyard. Freedom was allowed for patients of all kinds who were tranquil and in the decline of their illness to wander about inside, with reciprocal communication between the convalescent patients in their workshop or in their big dormitories. A reduced number of servant girls have been able to meet all the requirements of the job, joining with other calm convalescent patients and young idiots who were capable of mechanical work in sweeping the courtyards and many other cleaning tasks. If there was some tumult through the unforeseen fury or

acts of violence of a patient, all the patients (3) assembled together at the first signal to work with the superintendent to restore order. But generally speaking all the difficulties and dangers seemed to pile up on the head of the servant girl in charge of the furious patients' courtyard. She was often exposed to receiving blows and wounds, and was closely watched on the matter of arbitrary seclusions, and reduced, with no other encouragement, to receive the same pecuniary remuneration as the other servant girls. Consequently this post was often vacant and it was very difficult to get the duties fulfilled. I must recall here that a country girl with a strong constitution and a gentle character devoted herself to fulfilling this difficult task during her convalescence. Having done so praiseworthily for six months she bought a new dress with the money she had saved. On the first day of the holiday this was torn up by a patient in fury. From then on she was completely disgusted with the job and she asked to leave the hospice.

V. PATERNALISTIC SUPERVISION TO BE EXERCISED IN THE PREPARATION AND DISTRIBUTION OF MEALS

205. The continual agitation of deranged patients, their uninterrupted muscle movements during their acts of eccentricity or fury, their raised body heat and the vigour they enjoy, naturally explains a kind of voracity which is peculiar to them and which is sometimes so extreme that some of them at intervals go so far as consuming two kilograms of bread every a day. One of the first objects, or rather one of the most hallowed duties, of my position as chief physician at Bicêtre (in Years II and III of the Republic) was indeed to inspect the patients' kitchen department carefully and go into all the financial details, comparing these with the rest of the hospice where I had found a lack of concern, clumsiness and neglect for the first principles in the preparation and distribution of food. By contrast I recognised that it would have been difficult to prepare the food in more discerning, economical and prudent a way than in the division for mentally ill patients. This is another worthy testimony to add to what I have already said (Second Section) about the superintendent of the deranged patients at Bicêtre. Care was always taken to have food in reserve for the following day so as to rectify vicissitudes or oversights in stocking and be able to provide for patients' urgent or unforeseen requirements. Care was also always taken in summer to set vegetables aside and have them cooked and kept in earthenware pots to supplement the diet in the winter. On days when there was plenty of meat, fat and bone marrow, some was kept back (4) for lean days to make the soup much more nourishing. A very intelligent method was used in cooking the meat for the soup, not like the usual routine in hospice kitchens which consist in subjecting the meat to fierce and prolonged boiling, making the flesh hard and tough and preventing the gelatine from separating. The broth was always prepared on the morning it was distributed and each share was carefully worked out depending on the hospice's needs. It was only boiled to remove what was called the scum from the pot or parts most solidified by the heat. The wood was then taken away and a kind of artificial oven was made with bricks round the pot to keep the meat at a steady sustained heat a little below boiling point for four and a half hours. This made the meat fibres pulpy and tender and the gradual solution of the gelatine into the liquid produced a restoring healthy soup. In this manner a way was adopted of combining the deference and consideration due to unfortunate people with the wisest and most attentive economy.

VI. DISASTROUS CONSEQUENCES OF THE SHORTAGES WHICH OCCURRED IN YEAR IV IN THE HOSPICES FOR THE MENTALLY ILL

206. I leave to politics, enlightened by memory of the past and the results of long experience, the task of deciding whether the real estate of the hospitals and hospices should be kept for them as inalienable property, under the regulation of a wise administration, or whether some other means should be resorted to of ensuring the funds necessary for the needs of sick or infirm indigents, linking them with all the vicissitudes of public finances. It suffices to recall here, to those fond of order, a few things I have witnessed with my own eyes, the memory of which will distress even the least sensitive of men. It was by carefully working out the nutritional needs of the patients, under the Constituent Assembly, that the daily bread ration for those at Bicêtre was raised to one kilogram; and for two years I saw the benefits of this healthy arrangement. I ceased to be the doctor at this hospice, but on one of the visits which I occasionally made as a kindness to the patients (4th Brumaire Year IV)[5], I learnt that the bread ration had been reduced to seven and a half hectograms, and I saw several of the former convalescent patients slip back into a state of insane fury, crying out that that they were being made to die of hunger. The harmful progress of the shortage subsequently even worsened, for the bread ration was successively reduced to around five, four, three and even two hectograms, adding a small supplement of biscuit which was often very bad. The consequence was as one would expect, and it has been recorded that just in two months (Pluviôse and Ventôse Year IV)[6] the total number of deaths in the psychiatric hospice was twenty-nine, whilst in the whole of Year II it had only been twenty-seven. It was a similar but even quicker and more deplorable result for the patients at the Salpêtrière, for in the course of Brumaire Year IV (5) the mortality was fifty-six because of the high frequency of diarrhoea and dysentery. Would we have had to bemoan these disastrous events if the hospice resources had been fixed and guaranteed? We know the answer to this point from the history of the period, given the fortunate change that took place in the hospices. We know the influence of carrying out a few wise measures taken by an enlightened administration and how many remarkable modifications it leads to. With the same amount of bread, a negligent and lazy individual will bring about unsatisfied needs, whilst another more clever and zealous one will have the skill of satisfying everyone, and even keep little extra sustenance back for unforeseen cases of severe hunger in some patients who need a double or even a triple portion. That is how in the mental illness division at the Salpêtrière M. Pussin, who always supervises the sharing out and distribution of food, has large, medium and small helpings put up so that the servant girls in their department can distribute them according to the patients' requirements. In this way nobody gets too much or too little and overall there is always a surplus which is kept for unexpected cases or put back in the breadbin. Furthermore I have never heard any complaints from any of the Salpêtrière patients over this fundamental matter. The adjoining table (Table 4.1) shows the general rules and the proportions followed in the distribution of victuals.

207. A public establishment for mentally ill patients which is part of a large hospice and does not have its own kitchen has the disadvantage of always being dependent upon the general

---

[5] *Brumaire – Second month of Republican Calendar – Ed.*
[6] *Pluviôse and Ventôse – Fifth and Sixth months of Republican Calendar – Ed.*

Table 4.1 Diet for female mentally ill patients at the Salpêtrière

Days		White bread	Wine for persons aged				Meat	Haricot beans or lentils	Prunes	Cheese (Compte or Marolles)	Grapes	Rice	Broth
			70 years	75 years	80 years	85 years							
		decagrams	cl	cl	cl	cl	decagrams	decilitre	decagrams	decagrams	decagrams	decagrams	cl
Sunday		72	12	24	36	50	25	"	6	"	5	"	96
Monday		72	12	24	36	50	25	1	"	4	"	"	96
Tuesday	Full diet	72	12	24	36	50	25	"	6	"	5	"	96
Wednesday		72	12	24	36	50	25	1	"	4	"	"	96
Thursday		72	12	24	36	50	25	"	6	"	5	"	96
Friday	Reduced diet	72	12	24	36	50	"	"	"	4	"	7	96
Saturday		72	12	24	36	50	"	3	"	"	5	"	96

Observations

Fat days In the morning the inmates receive bread, wine, meat and 48 cl of broth.
In the evening, dry vegetables, or 35 gm of rice and cheese, or grapes with 48 cl of broth

Lean days In the morning the inmates receive bread, wine, 15 cl of dry vegetable or 35 gm of rice with 48 cl of clear broth.
In the evening, 15 cl of dry vegetables, or 35 gm of rice and cheese, or grapes with 48 cl of broth

In season, they can have alternately dry vegetables, cabbage, choucrout, spinach, sorrel, pumpkin, potatoes. They can also have alternately salad, cherries, currants, apricots, prunes, pears, and grapes as a substitute for cheese.

institution, as much for the choice of food as for the times of distributing the meals. It must be agreed that this excessively close and frequent distribution throughout the day does not conform entirely with dietetic principles which always call for a predetermined period for the digestion to work – all the more since in the morning many patients are slaves to having something to drink. There was another rule formerly observed at Bicêtre when I was the physician to that hospice, where the kitchen of the mental illness division was completely separate from the communal kitchen of the hospice: the timing of meals was arranged in a more convenient way; with the first meal at seven o'clock in the morning, consisting just of bread; lunch between eleven o'clock and midday with soup and boiled meat on fat days; and for supper, bread and a few legumes, greens or root vegetables. Whatever the general arrangements may be, they need to be adjusted when carried out: one can imagine that a debilitated patient suffering from some kind of constant diarrhoea should not have the same food as a robust patient subject to constipation (6). Undiluted wine is far from suitable for a very agitated or furious deranged patient, but it is appropriate for strengthening an elderly woman who is reduced to a state of senile dementia.

VII. VARIED PHYSICAL EXERCISE, OR ROUTINES OF MECHANICAL WORK, A FUNDAMENTAL RULE OF EVERY HOSPICE FOR MENTALLY ILL PATIENTS

208. There is no longer a problem to be solved. It has now been shown by the most constant and unanimous experience that in all public asylums such as prisons and hospices the surest and perhaps only measure to guarantee the maintenance of good health, good behaviour and order is the rule of mechanical work, rigorously enforced. This truth is above all applicable to the facilities for mentally deranged patients, and I am strongly convinced that in order to prevail and be of sustained usefulness, an establishment of this kind must turn to this fundamental premise. Very few patients, even in their state of fury, need to be kept from any active work, as I have personally ascertained. And what a distressing spectacle it is to see mentally deranged patients of all kinds in our national establishments continually and idly moving about in pointless agitation, while others remain sadly submerged in inertia and stupor! What better way to maintain an agitated imagination, regular fiery outbursts of anger and all the lapses of delirious excitation in them! In contrast, regular work changes the vicious chain of ideas and steadies the faculties of understanding by applying them. This alone can maintain order in any gathering of deranged patients, and dispense with a crowd of pernickety rules which are often ineffective at keeping order. The return of convalescent patients to their previous interests, to carrying out their occupation and to their enthusiasm for and perseverance at a task has always for me been a good sign and the best founded hope of a sound cure. But we still have to envy, in a neighbouring country to ours, an example which should be more widely recognised. That example is not provided by England or Germany, but by Spain. In one of their towns (Saragossa) there is an asylum open to the sick, and above all to the mentally ill patients, from all countries all governments, and all religions, with this simple inscription: *Urbis et Orbis*. Mechanical work was not the only object of concern to the founders of this establishment. They wished to restore a form of counterweight to the distractions of the mind using the appeal and charm inspired by working the land, following the natural instinct which leads man to make the land fertile

and thereby provide for his needs with the fruits of his labour. From early morning patients are seen, some doing menial household tasks, some going to their respective workshops, and the majority separating into groups led by a few intelligent and enlightened supervisors. They cheerfully spread out into different parts of a large enclosure belonging to the hospice and share out between themselves, a little competitively, the tasks relating to the seasons, growing wheat, legumes, vegetables, and busying themselves in turn with the harvest, trellis work, grape picking and olive picking. In the evening they enjoy calm in their solitary asylum and a peaceful sleep. The most continuous experience has taught in this hospice that this is the surest and most efficacious way of restoring reason. Any noblemen who reject in contempt and haughtiness any idea of mechanical work also have the sad advantage of perpetuating their insane episodes and delirium.

209. 'Laziness, indolence and idleness; vices so natural to infants', said La Bruyère, 'disappear during games, where they are active, engaged, precise and display a love of rules and symmetry'. Are deranged patients not the same when they are convalescent and when they are offered scope for their natural urge for physical movement and exercise instead of a listless and idle existence? There is no principle on which ancient and modern medicine is more unanimously agreed. Recreational movement or a difficult task halts the insane wanderings of deranged patients, prevents blood from congesting in the head, steadies the circulation and sets the stage for sound sleep. One day I was deafened by the tumultuous shouts and eccentric actions of a deranged patient. Once a rural job that he liked was found for him, I was able to converse with him without seeing any agitation or confusion in his ideas. Nothing was more worth noting than the calm and tranquillity which once prevailed amongst the patients at Bicêtre when some Paris merchants gave most of them a manual job which fixed their attention and lured them permanently with a small salary. It was to perpetuate these benefits and improve the fate of the patients that around this time I repeatedly approached the Administration in order to obtain an adjoining plot of land for the convalescent patients to cultivate so as to accelerate their recovery. The storms of the Revolution (Years II and III) always frustrated this plan and I was restricted to subsidiary means employed by the superintendent, who was always ready to select staff from amongst the convalescent patients (paragraph 87). These principles are similar to those of the concierge at the mad house in Amsterdam (7). It would be a salutary step forward to attach a large enclosure to every hospice for mentally ill patients, or even better to turn it into a kind of farm where the rural work would be in the hands of the convalescent patients, and where the produce would serve for their catering and their expenses. It is Spain which gives us such a fine example to follow in one of its principal hospices. The patients who are suitable for work are divided at daybreak into various separate groups, each headed by a guide to assign tasks to them, and direct and supervise them. The day is spent in continuous activity which is only interrupted by rest breaks, and tiredness at night brings sleep and calm. There is nothing commoner than cures brought about by this active life, whereas the derangement of the nobility, who blush at working with their hands, is almost always incurable.

210. It is at the time of convalescence, and at the first hints of recovery, that the previous tastes as well as the love of fine arts, sciences or letters often begin to come back, if it was formerly a feature of their background. This first reawakening of talent must then be grasped

eagerly by the superintendent of the hospice in order to promote and accelerate the growth of mental abilities, as an example reported in Section II of this volume (paragraph 66) illustrates. Other facts serve to confirm this truism. I sometimes had difficulty in following the uncontrolled garrulity and stream of ill-assorted and incoherent words of a former man of letters who at other times lapsed into sombre and forbidding taciturnity. But if a piece of poetry which had once delighted him came back into his memory he became capable of steady attention. His judgement seemed to be regained and he composed verses in which there prevailed not only a sense of order and accuracy in his ideas but also a steady flight of imagination and very apt witticisms. I could only give a few fleeting hours to this kind of encouragement and mental exercise but surely continuation of care following my principles would have had a fortunate effect on this convalescent patient! Another, a musician, also driven to insanity by the events of the Revolution, held the most disjointed conversations and often only spoke in monosyllables which he intermingled with jumps, dances and the most insane and absurd gesticulations. A muddled recollection, when he was convalescent, reminded him of his favourite instrument, which was the violin, and thereupon I engaged his parents to provide this enjoyment for him which would help so much towards his full recovery. He seemed to regain his former dexterity within a few days and continued to practice for several hours every day for eight months, with a marked advance in tranquillity and restoration of reason as well. But at that time another deranged patient, full of fieriness and eccentricity, was admitted to the same place of seclusion. The company of the latter, who was allowed to wander freely in the garden, completely shattered the musician's composure. He broke the violin to pieces, abandoned his favourite pastime and his state of insanity was now considered incurable. This is a distressing and memorable example of the influence which the spectacle of acts of maniacal insanity has on convalescent patients and confirms the necessity of isolating them.

211. The stormy and quick-tempered character of deranged patients, even during their convalescence, is known. Most of them have extremely delicate feelings and they get annoyed at the least sign of an oversight, misunderstanding or lack of concern, and then abandon whatever they had previously taken up with the greatest enthusiasm and warmth. A sculptor, who was a pupil of the famous Lemoine, had failed in his plans and hard work to get to the Academy, and from then there was deep melancholy and continuous scuffles with his brother whose meanness, according to him, had stopped him in his career. His outbursts and acts of violence resulted in an arbitrary order for his seclusion as deranged. He embarked upon fits of fury in his lodge, broke everything to pieces and remained for several months in a most violent state of maniacal insanity. Calm eventually returned and he was granted freedom inside the hospice. His understanding was still feeble and he bore the weight of an inactive life with difficulty. Painting, which he had also taken up, seemed to appeal to his imagination and he wanted to try portrait painting. His plan was quickly supported and he made sketches for portraits of the superintendent and his wife. The resemblance was well captured, but still not well executed. He thought he could see a cloud before his eyes, and he was discouraged by a feeling of inadequacy, or just the remains of good taste, long ago learned from the study of the finest models. The talent which he had shown and especially the desire to sustain his budding activity and hold on to a clever artist for society's sake led the bursar at Bicêtre to commission a picture from him, leaving the choice of a subject to him in order to give him a freer range in his composition. The convalescent patient, as

yet only poorly restored, thought this free scope was beyond his ability and asked that the subject should be specified, and even that an exact outline, suitable to be taken as a model, should be drawn for him. His request was evaded and the only opportunity to restore his reason was lost. He embarked upon reactions of indignation, thought he could see evidence of scorn in this oversight, broke up his paintbrushes, palette and sketches, and haughtily declared that he was giving up culture of the fine arts for good. His feelings over this were so strong that an episode of fury followed lasting several months. Calm returned, but he then went into a state of languor and sort of daydreaming which was edging on dementia. I had him transferred to the infirmary to try the combined use of a few simple remedies and a tonic diet. Friendly talks, words of consolation and a little cautiously dictated advice were of no use. His initial inclination for work and for the fine arts seemed lost forever. Boredom, distaste for life and the most sombre and apathetic melancholy rapidly advanced. Absence of appetite, sleeplessness and diarrhoea put a final end to his unhappy existence.

212. The general rule of mechanical labour is no less mandatory for the idiots of one gender or the other who abound in the hospices, and the same outlook and principles have been taken up at the Salpêtrière as those whose happy effects I had seen at Bicêtre. It is sad to see several of these idiots, who could be usefully employed in some rough manual work, or the cultivation of vegetables supervised by a clever leader, constantly inactive or in a sort of stupidly drowsy state. Reduced to a kind of servile sheep-like imitation, it is enough to give them an example to follow and put some active and industrious man at their head, and they immediately absorb the same spirit and are capable of very sustained efforts. I have seen this myself during the planting of trees inside the Bicêtre hospice. The keenest man could not have set to work with more persistence and strength. The addition of a kind of garden or promenade of three acres, in the mental illness division of the Salpêtrière, gave a glimpse of all the benefits which could be gained from this approach, either from labour at a pump to provide the necessary water for a reservoir in the middle of the premises, or another kind of work appropriate for the ways and customs of country women who were accustomed to dig the ground and other rural work. But a splitting of influence and good will among the employees then held back the progress made in carrying on with these helpful measures, and just sticking to general work to keep the hospice continuously clean was all that could be done. Also, in the premises intended for patients who are getting better, and whose dwellings are mixed with the group of imbeciles who are far from being in the last stages of idiocy, a kind of rivalry has been observed between the two groups over sweeping up the courtyards, taking water in wooden buckets from various fountains in the hospice and, by sprinkling and washing the cobble stones, keeping them very clean. Above all, this keeps them constantly cool in hot weather, thus combining several benefits. This had greatly added advantages in relation to the calm and tranquillity widely prevailing in the courtyards. It also provided a useful diversion from the violent outbursts and hot-headed fits over the slightest provocations which these same people often displayed and could not curb on account of the deficiency of their character or the very weak influence of their intellectual faculties.

213. But the successful organisation of the hospice which an enlightened administration had carefully promoted afforded us an even more valuable resource to speed up the progress of convalescence. This is a large sewing room, which is adjoining to the convalescent patients'

dormitory. Here, they gather to pass nearly all the day in company, encouraged by a small wage which they collect each day and which ends up providing those who are most active with a small resource on leaving the hospice at the same time as they resume the working habit ready for going back home. One cannot overemphasise the fortunate influence of this regular foregathering of several people, freely discussing the interests of their family which they have abandoned for several months and hope after an unavoidable absence of variable duration to see again soon. In this way the days go by quickly in a mutual exchange of their fears and difficulties. The superintendent often visits them, either to see their industrious activity for himself, to clear up any persisting lapses in reason, or lastly to make a note of those who approach work carelessly and to decide about their future. This can lead to specific notes when it comes to the report I have to make when they go back amongst society. It is in this assembly that friendly conversations and kindly encouragement can dissipate sad and melancholic ideas. Here women who are not yet free of these ideas can be compared with those who are fortunately delivered of them and so can be taken as models to which to aspire. It is very rare to see patients who show themselves to be consistently industrious suffer a later relapse.

214. The natural tendency of demented patients to have fits of anger, and their way of making the most sinister interpretations of events and of bursting into babblings, shows the strong necessity of constant orderly management so as avoid embittering them. Hence the measures I have seen rigorously put into effect in the Bicêtre hospice. The time of opening the lodges is set depending on the season; that is, at five o'clock in the morning in summer, half past seven in winter, and always in the same proportion according to the length of the day in the intermediate seasons. Great attention is paid to removing night soils immediately and seeing to the cleanliness of the lodges as well as the courtyards. There is a general visit by the superintendent during the morning to satisfy himself that nothing has been omitted or neglected. Breakfast is distributed a little more than an hour after rising; and lunch at eleven o'clock precisely, with soup and a third of the daily ration of bread being served. Fresh attention is paid to see to the cleanliness of the lodges again after the meal. There is a third distribution of the rest of the bread and a few fat or lean dishes at four or five o'clock in the evening, depending on the time of year. The lodges are closed at dusk, on the ringing of a bell, and a first night watchman comes on duty until midnight with the instructions to make a round of the whole hospice every half-hour to help patients, avoid damage to the lodges from more furious ones, and prevent anything sinister happening. Another night watchman takes over from midnight until morning, carrying out the same duties and pointing out patients who have developed any incidental illness. In the morning the staff come back to see to cleanliness and carry out their other responsibilities. Their attentiveness and presence throughout the day is imperative to maintain order in case of trouble and intervene together if a brawl breaks out between the patients, or if there is a sudden and unexpected outburst of an attack of insanity. These same staff are expressly forbidden to have a heavy hand with the patients, even if they are provoked or struck. Tactics are taught; or rather certain skilful manoeuvres are shown to render the struggles and reckless audacity of some furious insane patients vain and powerless. In a word, the general control of the hospice resembles that of a large family composed of turbulent and angry individuals who must be curbed but not aggravated, held in check by a sense of respect and esteem rather than by servile fear when they are capable of this, and be supervised, most usually with gentleness, but always with inflexible firmness.

VIII. GENERAL PRECEPTS TO BE FOLLOWED IN MENTAL TREATMENT

215. One of the essential features in every well run hospice is having a general centre of authority who makes decisions with no appeal, aimed at keeping order amongst the staff, exercising correct restraint over turbulent or very agitated patients, and determining whether a patient is suitable for the interview requested by one of his friends or close relatives. This overall authority must lie with the superintendent, and there is general confusion if the doctor or any other employee is weak enough to give way to complaints made to them and set their wishes and instructions in opposition to those of the superintendent. A young girl, who had fallen into a deep melancholia and had been reduced for several days to a state of stupor and numbness, began to recover and take a little nourishment regularly. All that was needed was to await her full convalescence and, as the only thing to be worried about was the danger of somebody coming to visit her too soon, I had agreed with the superintendent to continue to keep her sequestered. I do not know by what trick someone, under some pretext, managed to obtain an entrance pass and permission to have an interview with her. Her reason became distracted again that same day and a state of sombre taciturnity developed with refusal of all food for two days. It required over a month of attentiveness and care to correct such a problem and for the practice of regular work to be restored. It is even more distressing sometimes to see coarse people permitting themselves to blame the superintendent's conduct groundlessly, speak disagreeably to him, and thereby seek to diminish the esteem and confidence which he deserves on so many grounds. This is what happened with the parent of another melancholic girl who haughtily protested that a disciplinary shower had been called a baptism, and as a result took the opportunity to make a vicious attack against the treatment method used in this hospice. Another even more serious offence was to allow this melancholic patient the freedom to walk about in the other courtyards of the hospice, and permit her to evade the communal rule of working which is so salutary for consolidating convalescence. The patient was thus removed from the jurisdiction of the superintendent, the suspension of the baths increasingly hindered the medical treatment, and the patient as a result remained incurable.

216. The well-founded hope of restoring people to society who seem to be lost to it demands the most assiduous and untiring supervision over this large group of deranged patients when they are convalescent or in their lucid intervals. This group must be carefully isolated in a special part of the hospice, to avoid all accidental causes of relapses, where they can undergo a rehabilitation[7] designed to develop and strengthen their grasp on reality. But what circumspection, enlightenment and wisdom is needed to manage persons who are generally very shrewd, touchy and of irascible character! How can they be kept under continuous steady control if an essential ascendancy over them is not exerted by dint of the rarest physical and mental qualities? Those are the fundamental maxims which I never cease to instil by means of examples, and I am more and more convinced of these principles on finding them in force in one of the best known hospices for deranged patients in Europe: the Bethlehem. 'It is a most important objective', said Haslam[8], 'to win the trust of these patients and instil feelings of respect and obedience; which can only be the outcome of

---

[7] *This rehabilitation refers to Pinel's concept of 'une institution morale' – Ed.*
[8] *Observations on insanity with practical remarcs on the disease etc*, by John Haslam, London, 1798.

superior judgement, an outstanding education and dignity in tone of voice and in manners. Stupidity, ignorance and lack of principles, backed by tyrannical harshness, can create fear, but it always inspires contempt. The superintendent of a hospice for deranged patients who has got them in hand controls and regulates their behaviour at will. He must be of a firm character and give an imposing appearance of authority when necessary; he must threaten little but do what he says; and if he is disobeyed punishment must follow immediately with close confinement. When the patient is robust and full of strength, the superintendent needs to be backed up by several men so as to inspire fear and achieve prompt obedience without difficulty or danger'. The same author nevertheless prohibits all acts of violence or corporal punishment, for if the patient is deprived of the function of understanding he is impervious to punishment and this is then absurd cruelty. And if he appreciates his error, he will deeply resent the blows he received and his delirium would be renewed or exacerbated by the desire for revenge.

217. A man in the full vigour of maturity, confined at the Bicêtre, believed he was the king and always spoke with an air of command and supreme authority. He had undergone the usual treatment at the Hôtel-Dieu, where blows and acts of violence at the hands of the staff had merely made him more angry and dangerous. How should he be handled? An imposing appearance of constraint could further embitter him, yet condescension might confirm him in his imaginary claims. So one had to await a favourable moment to get such a difficult character in hand, and this is how chance turned out. One day this patient wrote a letter full of anger to his wife, bitterly accusing her of prolonging his detention so as to enjoy being completely free. He also threatened her with the full weight of his vengeance. Before sending this letter he read it to another convalescent patient who disapproved of these fiery outbursts of rage and reproached him in a friendly way for trying to drive his wife to despair. This wise advice was listened to and accepted, the letter was not posted and was replaced by another full of moderation and consideration. The superintendent, informed about this obedience to friendly advice, saw that there were already signs of a favourable change developing. He hastened to take advantage of this, went to the patient's lodge to talk with him and gradually brought him back to the principle object of his delirium.

'If you are the sovereign', he said, 'why do you stay mixed up with all kinds of deranged patients?' He went back again the following days to talk like this with him, in a kindly friendly tone. He gradually got him to see the absurdity of his exaggerated claims, and showed him another patient who had also been convinced for a long time that he was invested in supreme power and had become an object of derision. The deranged patient felt shaken at first, but soon he put his title of sovereign in doubt, and finally he came to recognise his flights of imagination. This mental change took place over the course of two weeks and after a few months trial period this respectable father was returned to his family.

218. 'It is likely', said Montaigne, 'that the main belief in visions, spells and such extraordinary phenomena arises from the power of imagination acting more particularly upon the softer souls of the common herd'. It is especially to the fantastical illusions, touchy suspicions and fainthearted fears of melancholic patients that this wise remark can particularly be applied, and there is also nothing more difficult than correcting or abolishing them. For how to disabuse spirits, often limited, who take the imaginary objects of their ideas as reality?

One of them only sees traps and ambushes around him, and even takes offence at the kindnesses one would like to do him, whilst another, turned into a potentate, is offended at being given the least advice or anyone going against his supreme will. Some spend the night in contemplation, speak as if inspired, prepare acts of expiation in the name of the Almighty or devote themselves to an abstinence which exhausts them. Some of them think they have been condemned to death on various pretexts and try to bring this about by utterly refusing any nourishment unless some fortunate expedient ends their food refusal. One demented patient at the Bicêtre hospice, who had no delusion other than thinking he was a victim of the Revolution, repeated day and night in Year III that he was ready to meet his end, refused to lie down on his bed and stayed stretched out on damp cobblestones which could have paralysed all his limbs. The superintendent tried remonstrance and gentle approaches in vain, and had to resort to restraint. The patient was tied to his bed with bonds; but he sought revenge by refusing food with total obstinacy. Exhortations, promises and threats were all in vain: four days had already gone with no food whatever. A fierce thirst then developed and the patient drank copious cold water, hour by hour; but he firmly pushed aside even the broth he was offered or any other liquid or solid nourishment. He became extremely thin; he was nothing but a skeleton by the tenth day of this frightening fast, and a very foetid smell spread around him. His food refusal was no less unwavering and he limited himself to his usual fluid. His condition could only be despaired of by the twelfth day. At this point the superintendent told him that from then on he was going to stop his drink of cold water since he was so intractable, and for it he substituted a fatty broth. The patient then stayed floating between two contrary impulses; one was that of a devouring thirst, which drove him to swallow any liquid whatever, and the other was the firm and immutable resolution to accelerate the termination of his life. The first in the end overcame him: he hungrily took the broth and soon, as a compensation, he was given the free availability of cold water. His slightly restored stomach gave him a pleasant feeling and the same evening he agreed to take a further drink of broth. During the following days he gradually began to take rice, soup and other solid foods, and thus little by little he regained all the attributes of sound and robust good health.

219. A thorough knowledge of the nature of man, and of the general character of melancholic patients, has always made for an appreciation of the necessity of conveying sharp shocks to them, creating a powerful diversion to their grim ideas and working with vigorous and long-continued impressions on all their external senses. Some wise practices of this type were part of the glorious achievements of the ancient Egyptian priests. It may be that the industrious resources of the arts, the objects of pomp and magnificence, the various pleasures of the senses and the rising power and prestige of religion have never been deployed to a more worthy end (8). These ancient establishments, so worthy of admiration, but so much to be contrasted with our modern practices and the state of our hospices, no less show the objective which must be set in all public or private assemblies of melancholic patients. We need to show patience, firmness and sentiments of humanity in the way they are controlled, and constant attention in the department to avoid fits of anger and exasperation of spirits. We must also offer pleasant occupations varied with the difference in tastes, varied physical exercise, spacious accommodation planted with trees, all the joys and calm of rural ways, and, at intervals, gentle and harmonious music. This is all the more easy to obtain since there is almost always some distinguished artist of this type in these establishments whose talent is languishing for lack of exercise and cultivation.

220. Life events can be so wretched and so oft repeated, and can bear such a character of solemnity and despair, and can so directly attack honour, life or everything in the world that is dearest to one, that there follows an extreme sense of oppression and anxiety, an overwhelming disgust for life and the wish to see an early end to it. This progression is even quicker if one has an acute sensitivity and a vivid imagination, and if one is clever at exaggerating one's situation, or rather at only seeing it through a gloomy prism of melancholy. 'My blood flows in waves and torrents of despair', said one wretch whose case history Chrigton reports. 'This piece of bread, which I wash down with my tears, is all that is left for me and my family . . . and I am still alive . . . I have a wife and a child who resent their existence . . . The duty of every man is to model his conduct on his circumstances; reason demands this and religion can only approve.' This man, who was moreover endowed with good manners and an enlightened mind, took advantage one day of his wife's absence to end his life. A constant state of illness, a serious disorder of one or more of the viscera, or progressive wasting can further aggravate the tiresome feeling of existence and hasten a deliberate death. But from what can the irresistible wish for suicide stem when it is derived neither from true sadness of the mind nor physical pain. 'I am in a prosperous position,' one of these melancholic patients, whose case history I have formerly reported in a journal[9], told me one day; 'I have a wife and a child who make me perfectly happy; my health is not noticeably changed, and yet I feel drawn by a horrible longing to go and throw myself into the Seine.' Events bore out this disastrous predisposition only too well. I have been consulted over a young man of twenty-four years, full of strength and vigour, whose disgust for life tormented him in periodic attacks. He then threatened to go and drown himself or shoot himself with a firearm, but the sight of the danger threw him into terror without making him give up this disastrous plan for another time. He was always resolute, yet always postponed the plan. It is in such cases that psychological treatment must be applied with intelligence and zeal, adjusted to the individual character and ideas of the patient one has to persuade.

221. Keeping eccentric deranged people in permanent seclusion and restraint, leaving them defenceless to the brutality of the staff under the pretext of the dangers they pose – to manage them in a word with a rod of iron, as if to hasten the end of an existence felt to be deplorable, is no doubt a very convenient method of supervision. It is moreover the characteristic method of centuries of ignorance and barbarism. It is no less contrary to the results of experience which show that this state of insanity can be cured in many cases by allowing the patient a limited freedom within the hospice, leaving him free for any agitated activity which is not dangerous, or at least by limiting restraint to the strait-jacket, at the same time not omitting the other rules of mental treatment to which his condition is amenable. Nothing is more noticeable than the powerful influence exercised by the superintendent of a hospice for the mentally ill when he bears in his role the sense of his dignity and the principles of the purest and most enlightened philanthropy. Here I can quote for examples Willis, Fowler and Haslam in England; Dicquemare, Poution and Pussin in France; and in Holland, the concierge of the Maison des fous (9) of Amsterdam. The coarse man of limited understanding only sees cunning and well thought-out provocation in the shouts, outrageous language and insane acts of violence, and hence the extreme harshness, blows and barbaric treatment which the staff permit themselves unless they are well-chosen and constrained by a severe discipline. In these outbursts of maniacal insanity, on the other hand, the wise and

---

[9] Medicine enlightened by the Natural Sciences, 1792.

enlightened man just sees an automatic impulse, or rather the necessary effect of nervous excitation which one should be no more indignant about than the impact of a stone carried along by its specific gravity. He lets these patients have the fullest range of activity (10) which is consistent with their safety and that of others, skilfully conceals the means of restraint he uses, as if they only have to obey necessary rules, and gives way indulgently to them. But he also knows how to forcibly resist or skilfully evade their ill-considered ventures. The stormy times of attacks of maniacal insanity burn themselves out in this way, under studied supervision, while the intervals of calm are exploited to make these outbursts gradually less intense and less long-lasting.

IX. PRECAUTIONS CALLED FOR BY EXTREME EXALTATION OF RELIGIOUS OPINIONS

222. Religious opinions in a hospice for mentally ill patients must only be considered from a purely medical point of view: that is to say that one must dismiss every other consideration of public worship and politics, and that one must solely see whether it is important to oppose the exaltation of ideas and feelings which can arise from this source in order to work effectively towards the cure of individual patients. At the same time one must examine what precautions should be taken to arrest the progress of the malady and prevent its effects, which are so often harmful and sometimes very dangerous to a debilitated understanding or distracted reason. Examples may be taken as much (paragraphs 53, 54) from authentic English works as from the collection of my daily notes. The disorders that can stem from this source need to be widely known, all the more since they most often lead to despair and suicide.

223. A young girl developed the most furious maniacal insanity as a consequence of extreme religious scruples. At the slightest crossing of her will she called upon the fires of heaven to consume the guilty parties. On her arrival at the hospice she rushed about and threatened and struck out. She was taken to her lodge and a strait-jacket was put on her to control her. The superintendent came to see her a few hours later and joked with her about her powerlessness to bring down the fires of heaven since she did not even have the power to get rid of her jacket. She calmed down after three hours and was given the freedom to walk about in the courtyard for the rest of her treatment.

224. It is contempt and inflation with haughtiness and arrogance which must be curbed in maniacal insanity, especially if this is inspired by ill-intended devotion. A young deranged patient expressed herself on entering the hospice with extreme arrogance. She became violently angry with the superintendent because he presented himself before her with his hat on his head. The latter looked haughtily at her and took his usual commanding approach with her. He spoke, threatening her if she dared to show herself a rebel against his orders. This young girl, intimidated, immediately withdrew in silence to the back of her lodge, spent a quiet night and from the next morning became calm and remained so for the rest of her treatment. But it must be agreed that this way of mastering a patient who is deranged through devotion can only be applied in a few special cases, and that many others stand up with unyielding energy against all methods of restraint under the pretext that it is better to disobey man rather than the Supreme Being, whose direct inspiration they think they receive.

225. Sometimes pious melancholia is driven by endless scruples, deep despondency and the constantly present single idea of having committed unpardonable crimes that deserve eternal punishment. Is it possible to avoid a state of despair in any way other than by consoling talk and great skill in gaining the patient's confidence? An elderly nun who formerly taught young people was brought to the hospice in a state of deep melancholia. Different physical and mental measures had been tried for more than six months, but her ideas and feelings were always the same and she never stopped repeating to the superintendent that he was wrong for not treating her as the most criminal woman and not subjecting her to severe punishment. One day when she met him inside the hospice, and was resuming the same discussion, she received a sharp reply and the express declaration that he didn't want to listen to her any more because she always held onto the same ideas and showed no confidence in him. This melancholic patient withdrew in silence to her dormitory, thought very carefully about this humiliating scene, and paid justice to the superintendent's impeccable honesty and his sincere desire to work towards rehabilitating unfortunate deranged patients. Was not everything she had just heard from him not dictated by the most humane principles? That night she was deeply perplexed and experienced a kind of inner struggle between the idea of her so-called crimes and the friendly remonstrance of a man who was so far from being motivated by personal designs. This vacillation and tumultuous conflict of opposing ideas thus prolonged and calmly discussed brought about favourable changes in her, and she ended up by being completely convinced that her scruples were imaginary. She no longer asked for anything but to work diligently towards her recovery by making use of the available physical measures.

226. Should one accede to the repeated demands often made by pious melancholic patients to keep devotional books around them, to be able to read them assiduously at will or to seek for new consolations from their usual confessor? The question cannot be decided by simple reasoning and one can only answer from the results of experience. This shows that the surest way to perpetuate the derangement or even make it incurable is to give in, and the more one gives in, the less one succeeds in calming the worries and scruples. What a rich source of derangement for over-scrupulous consciences there is in the unhappy dissentions existing between the priests who have taken vows and those who have not! One of these prelates who accompanied the Pope on his last visit to France wanted to defer to the wishes of an elderly nun, and at my request went to the Salpêtrière hospice, but all that came out of this meeting was a new set of perplexities. Another deranged patient demanded loudly to be visited by her normal confessor; but on his arrival she refused to confess her sins to him and declared she was only willing to confess to Jesus Christ in person.

227. A deranged patient who had been calm for some time, and had been transferred to the sick bay to be treated for an incidental illness, saw a religious ceremony of last rites being carried out. Her imagination was immediately struck by the memory of her grandmother long since dead. She went up to the priest, shook him, grabbed his stole and called upon him in such loud shouts to return her grandmother that somebody had to forcibly intervene to stop this noisy scene. Nevertheless, she suffered a sort of relapse, with a recurrence of the delirium which led her to dig up the ground everywhere to look for her grandmother's tomb. After her recovery a pious book lent to her reminded her that everybody had their guardian angel; and from the following night she believed she was surrounded by a choir of angels and claimed she had heard celestial music and had seen revelations. Her book was

taken away from her and burnt; but all the same there was a second relapse, and treatment only became more prolonged and uncertain as a result. To avoid such setbacks, care is taken to remove certain pious melancholic patients from the sick bay whenever there is a need to carry out any religious ceremony.

228. They never cease in England to remark, in publications on deranged patients, upon the harsh intolerance of the Methodist sect and the often disastrous effects of their distressing doctrine, always full of threats of celestial vengeance and the torments of hell. Women with a lively imagination and frail understanding have no less to fear in France from sermons, confessions and pious writings from which emanate a dark tinge of melancholia and the sombre elation of fiery morality, calculated to reduce human frailty to despair. My daily notes taken at the time of the admission of deranged patients to the hospice can serve to show the quarters of Paris where this melancholy devotion predominates, whilst in others compassionate and enlightened piety sometimes delays the development of derangement ready to reveal itself only to flare up later as the result of other determining factors. A young servant girl endowed since a tender age with a lively and quick-tempered character was aware at thirty years of age of developing all the turmoil of a fiery temperament, even though she was at the same time very wise and pious. A kind of tiresome struggle then began between the inclinations of the heart and the severe principles of conduct to which she had become accustomed over a long time. These inner struggles and the alarms of an over-scrupulous conscience sometimes plunged her into despair and made her look for ways of destroying herself, such as poisoning herself or throwing herself out through a window. In these extreme perplexities she turned to a compassionate and enlightened confessor who tried to raise her courage and often gently repeated to her that she should become attached to God to regain peace in her heart. 'But I feel myself', this girl replied naively, 'more attracted to the creatures than to the Creator, and that is exactly what is torturing me'. The good priest persevered, talked to her consolingly and enjoined her to *await the triumph of Grace with resignation, following the example of many saints and even one of the great apostles.* Thus, far from raising fears about the future, he sought to restore calm in this agitated soul, countering it with the best remedy for great passions: patience, and time. But worries and prolonged wakefulness still ended up producing a derangement which was treated at the Salpêtrière following the same mental principles, and did not last long.

X. EXTREME RESTRICTION TO BE PLACED ON COMMUNICATION OF DERANGED PATIENTS WITH PEOPLE OUTSIDE

229. It is a great relief in nearly all human infirmities to receive compassionate care and the good offices of one's friends and family; and how many of these touching attentions are an even greater prize in the hospices where the patient finds himself separated from his family and often left to staff who only approach him with repulsive harshness! Why should a distressing exception be made for the mentally deranged patient, condemning him to a form of isolation until his reason is restored? An experiment has shown that deranged patients can hardly ever be cured in the bosom of their family (paragraph 58 *and following*). Willis, in the establishment he had set up in England, put severe restrictions on meetings of deranged patients with their former acquaintances – he only allowed these very rarely and solely in

certain cases for encouragement and as a reward. It is indeed noticeable that the patients whose isolation is most complete are cured the most easily. In the Bethlehem hospice an entrance pass is insisted upon for strangers, and at the time of admission of a deranged patient the family are given an authorisation to visit him just twice each week. In France the need to stop the unrestricted entrance of strangers and nosey parkers into hospices for the deranged has also been felt, and to be allowed into the one at the Salpêtrière express permission is required. Why were these prudent measures formerly always neglected in the hospice at Bicêtre where there was no limit upon visits to patients? How distressing it was to see these unfortunate folk serving as a spectacle and diversion for indiscrete people who often made a cruel game of embittering and harassing them! I once saw a deranged patient, who was getting better, fly into the greatest fury and violence against an evil joker who was provoking him through the window of his lodge. He dropped back to his original state and this relapse lasted for over a year. I can quote an even more deplorable example of these thoughtless visits. A foreign merchant who had become mentally deranged as a result of profound frustration and the loss of his fortune had been transferred to the Bicêtre after the usual treatment at the Hôtel-Dieu. The restoration of his reason with mental treatment was making rapid progress and I had coherent discussions with him without detecting any difficulty or inconsistency in his ideas. But in a few days everything changed. He learnt that his associates had seized a piece of personal property he still owned, and a woman was even so imprudent as to come to see him with some adjustments over matters he knew nothing about. He gave a great sigh and sank into a melancholia of dismay leading him to a complete dementia which has become incurable.

230. I am pleased to find the greatest conformity between the results of observations made in England and in France over the necessity of gathering demented patients together in public and private asylums to bring about, when possible, their sound and lasting cure. The deranged patient, Haslam says in the English work already mentioned, must be removed from the bosom of his family, where he always remains restless, and he must be held in a place of detention as soon as the illness is confirmed. The interruption of all communication with everybody close to him, avoidance of people used to obeying him and the idea of being dependent upon a stranger and not being free to indulge in whims, give continuous exercise for his mind if it is susceptible to this. Experience shows that deranged patients hardly ever recover under the immediate control of their friends and kin. Even visits from their friends whilst they are in their delirium always increase their agitation and untameable character. It is a well-known fact that they are then much less likely to be unwelcoming to strangers than they are to those who have been the object of an intimate relationship. Very often the patients who were furious and uncompromising whilst with their family become docile and calm when they are admitted to a hospice, and likewise some of them, who appeared recovered and to be behaving normally during their detention, resume their fiery agitation and delirium on returning prematurely to their family. However, during the progress of their convalescence, a few visits at intervals by their friends seem to have a very fortunate influence; they comfort them and open up a new prospect of hope and happiness for the future.

231. If the isolation of deranged patients is a general principle of treatment, what harmful effects must an encounter with the people one grumbles about, or whose presence can only reawaken unpleasant memories, not have on the subject in a public or private establishment,

even when the illness is declining or the convalescence is not yet fully consolidated! Are even the most focussed precautions on the part of the chiefs not sometimes at fault? A widow, after treatment, was already convalescent and had been given permission to receive visits from two of her daughters who were very hard-working and reserved in their behaviour. But on the other hand she had much to complain about over the disturbances and failings of another of her daughters who also wanted to pay her a visit. 'Ah! Miserable wretch!' cried the mother on seeing her, 'What a lot of difficulties and worries you cause your family! I am afraid you may drive me to despair'. She immediately withdrew into her lodge, spent the night in sorrow and tears; the next morning she was very agitated and dropped back into her previous maniacal state which persisted for about five months, and which was replaced by a kind of dementia which could almost be regarded as incurable.

232. It is difficult in some cases to fix the precise point during convalescence at which a visit from the relations can be permitted without danger, for this decision, or at least its consequences, are subject to several incidental circumstances, including the individual's greater or lesser sensitivity, the amount of attraction or aversion inspired by the visitor and various family interests. A young girl who was very haughty and full of arrogance during her state of maniacal insanity had returned for nearly two months to her normal character of modesty and reserve. She reasoned very soundly and asked insistently to be returned to the bosom of her family. It was felt that her sister could be allowed to have a meeting with her to plan the time of her discharge better, but the morning after her visit there was a kind of fiery agitation, incoherent muttering, repeated fits of anger and a frank relapse which lasted several months, calling for the usual treatment methods to be used once more.

233. I could give many examples of the sad consequences resulting from premature visits by family members or others who previously had particular relationships with the patient. I could again report a bigger number of examples of total refusal of such a meeting, when particular advice has been received, or invaluable information which should make it feared. However, I feel I should not omit one rare case even though it represents a kind of monstrosity in morality. A young girl of eighteen years, with the purest morals, and whom a father fit for public loathing had tried to prostitute for money in an evil place, had come to submit herself to this infamy, and had been overwhelmed by such enormous horror that a most violent insanity developed. She was transferred in the same state, after two months of treatment, to the hospice for mental illness, and the father had hardly heard of her convalescence than he had the shamelessness to appeal vigorously, even to the legal authorities, for permission to visit his daughter. This became the object of enormous concern for her, and the energy with which the mere idea of this interview was rejected may be imagined. One of her aunts fortunately became fond of her and removed her from the evil destination which the father was preparing for her.

234. It must not be forgotten that even during convalescence the influence of reason is still frail, and that in visits permitted to relations and friends there must be great caution so as not to excite strong emotions and bring on relapses. A young convalescent patient, who was to be collected by her mother from the hospice at a specified time, thought that her mother was very ill or even dead because she had not heard from her, and a kind of despair and mental disturbance ensued which lasted several days. Amongst other examples I can also quote another melancholic patient brought to the hospice who had a quite irresistible inclination

to suicide. Having been cured for over three months she fell, as a consequence of the same imprudence, into a kind of dementia which could now be looked upon as incurable. One day a priest came with a lady to visit the hospice out of curiosity, and his eyes became arrested on a convalescent patient to whom he drew attention in a peculiar way. The patient thought she was being pointed out as a criminal, especially as the object of her delusions had previously been being chased by priests. She thereupon felt deep indignation and from that day a true recurrence of her delusions developed despite all the care taken to disperse her fears and anxieties.

235. It is so usual for tender mothers still to retain these deep natural feelings throughout their periods of derangement that they must be spared, with the greatest care, the sight of infants who are unknown to them and whom someone has unwisely brought with them when visiting some convalescent patient. This is something that has sometimes triggered the stormiest scenes. A very agitated deranged patient, having seen an infant a stranger was holding by the hand and which she believed to be her own, immediately rushed to snatch her away. She struggled violently and cried out, and the frightened real mother went into a fainting fit that lasted over an hour. Another delirious patient whose illness was subsiding and was free to jump, gambol, babble, play a thousand innocent pranks and wander about at liberty in the courtyards, one day escaped through the entrance gate. She came by chance upon one of the porter's children who she seized, and violent steps were needed to get him back. She flew into fury, injured several servant girls and it was only with real difficulty that she was confined back in her lodge. The furious delirium which resulted lasted for several months.

XI. SUPERVISION MEASURES REQUIRED WITH CERTAIN PERVERSE OR UNCONTROLLABLE CHARACTERS

236. Maniacal insanity distinguished by furious delirium (paragraph 156) or a blind fury without delirium (paragraph 160) can persist for a variable length of time, or recur in periodic attacks with lucid intervals (paragraph 155), or the deranged patient may have his reason completely distracted, making him impervious to any advice or any kindly remonstrance. There is then no other option, if he is dangerous, except to keep him locked up or even hold him on his bed with the help of a strait-jacket and straps to prevent him from turning his blind rage back on himself. But a clever and experienced superintendent can sometimes spot effective ways to master him, even from the first days, using gentle means, and at the same time bringing an end to the fury and delirium, as in a striking example I have given (paragraph 154). Another example of this kind is no less remarkable. A young country girl, commendable for the purity of her morals, was coarsely insulted when she was menstruating by another woman and descended into a furious delirium. With difficulty nine servant girls, working together, managed to lock her up when she arrived. Three hours had hardly gone by when the superintendent carefully examined her, spoke gently to her and won her confidence. She became calm and tranquil the same day, and the next day she was already able to pass on to the convalescents' dormitory.

237. There are a few rare examples of unruly and cantankerous characters, otherwise show-ing no trace of any lapse of reason, whom one prefers to confine in hospices for the deranged

rather than mix with the guilty in detention centres, and which can be attributed to maniacal insanity without delirium. An elderly nun showed me a striking example of this at
the Salpêtrière. A servant girl approached her to be helpful and she heaped insults and the
most acrimonious epithets on her. Even the calmest patients were treated with no more
consideration, and there were endless threatening shouts, fits of anger and attempts to strike
out at everything. If she was given her food at meal times she threw it indignantly away or
craftily hid it so as to be able to complain that someone was trying to starve her. It was a
delight to her to tear her clothes to shreds and cry out that she was left with nothing and in
a state of nudity. She did not dare to stand up to the superintendent's authority when he was
there, but behind his back he became the continual object of her sarcastic remarks. Such
a focus of trouble and discord became dangerous for the other patients and she had to be
confined in a single lodge where the exasperation of this perverse and unsociable character
has hence remained concentrated.

238. I turn my eyes from the distressing memory of the historical details of the habitually
discordant and degenerate wickedness of a few other women who were worthy rivals of the
last one, and who appeared from time to time in the hospice. It is sufficient to make known
the way in which, in a best managed establishment for deranged patients, the most energetic
supervision becomes necessary when one carefully tries to avoid arbitrary repressive measures and seeks to prevent all sources of disorder and the progress of certain plots hatched
in silence. One of these women, unable to captivate an audience, disseminated the spirit of
faction and trouble which drives characters like this. She had concertedly planned a secret
escape from the hospice and had got everything ready with the greatest astuteness. She also
made use of the freedom she had been given inside, and the influence of a well-known name,
to gather information with others likely to share her views. There was an endless pompous
display of the great proceeds it would fall to her to divide up and the riches she would have
to dispose of in the future. She had promised some of them a guaranteed asylum in their
old age, others pecuniary reward and some of the servant girls had been won over with the
hope of embarking on all kinds of sensual delights in places of pleasure and enchantment.
The superintendent was singled out as the only obstacle to be overcome and the particular
object of her vengeance. It had been decided to get rid of him if he appeared by plunging
a knife into his chest at the time of the rising. This plot was so skilfully devised that they
had already got over the walls of the enclosure and the escape was partly executed when
the security guards who were called just in time stopped anything further. It can well be
imagined that internal security measures delivered the hospice of this dangerous woman
who had no impairment of reason other than dreams of profound immorality.

239. It is important to distinguish a kind of well-thought-out wickedness associated with
free use of reason, as in the preceding case, from that which stems from a state of illness
and must be submitted to a standard treatment even though the patient reasons soundly
and appreciates his condition and the irresistible urge which drives him to dissoluteness or
even to the most culpable actions. Before the use of chains as a means of discipline was
abolished at Bicêtre (paragraph 190) a deranged patient whose attacks of fury were in the
habit of recurring periodically for six months in the year was himself aware of the decline
in his symptoms towards the end of the attacks. He sensed the exact moment when he could
without danger be allowed free within the hospice. He asked for his discharge to be delayed
if he felt he could not yet overcome the blind impulse which drove him to very violent

acts. After the superintendent had come to gain his confidence through his compassionate character and gentleness, he confessed in his calm interludes that during his attacks it was impossible to curb his fury. If anyone appeared before him he thought he could see the blood flowing in their veins and felt an irresistible desire to suck his blood and tear his limbs with his fine teeth to make this sucking easier.

240. I have shown elsewhere (paragraph 190 and following) the restraint methods which enlightened progress and a sense of humanity seem now to call for and which are established in the Salpêtrière hospice, and in Dr Esquirol's nursing home, which is directed according to the same principles. The difficulty of getting these measures adopted elsewhere stems from that of combining two objectives which seem incompatible: the energetic discipline of a patient aimed at resisting his insane will; and the happy gift of winning his confidence by convincing him that one has only acted with severity in his own interests, in order to work towards his cure in a more certain way. This presupposes great zeal and special skill. A young person of seventeen years, caringly brought up in her paternal home, but with extreme indulgence, descended into a cheerful and frolicsome delirium for no reason that could be established. Taken to the hospice for deranged patients in a singularly agitated state, she jumped about, danced and carried out a thousand irregular movements. A start was made with a few laxative drinks and a few baths, and the superintendent with his wife also treated her with the greatest gentleness and all the consideration designed to win them her confidence. However, she maintained her haughty character all the time and only spoke of her parents with bitterness, reproaching them for having had her confined in a hospice. To subdue this inflexible character, the superintendent took the opportunity of the bath to speak forcibly against certain unnatural people who dared to rise against their parents' orders and ignore their authority. He warned her that from then on she would be treated with all the severity she deserved, since she herself was opposing her own cure and was concealing the basic cause of her illness with insurmountable obstinacy. The young person remained deeply moved, and the following nights felt a kind of inner conflict between the feelings of arrogance which dominated her, and the memory of the signs of kindness shown to her aimed at curing her and returning her promptly to her family. She ended by admitting to her faults and made an ingenuous confession of how her reason had become distracted as the result of a thwarted inclination of the heart, and she named the man who had been its object. From then on there was a most favourable change; she recalled all the perplexities she had felt in the midst of her feelings of adversity and admitted that she was now relieved. She could not adequately express her gratitude to the superintendent who put an end to her continuous agitation and brought back tranquillity and calm to her heart. Convalescence then began and continued to make rapid progress.

241. The memory of firm methods of repression used by the superintendent can provoke in some deranged patients a deep resentment or even concentrated hatred, and it is not until their reason is completely restored that they end in doing him a ringing justice and giving him not just recognition, but sentiments of real affection. One young woman, the continuous object of her parents' kindness since her tender years, came to suffer at home a delirium which was so furious that six very strong men had difficulty in controlling her. Sent to the hospice for deranged patients in this violent state, the use of acidulated drinks and some laxative made her pass darkish material for several days, and the symptoms had already diminished, but the forceful methods of restraint which were still used – baths,

showers, and the strait-jacket (paragraph 192 and following) – became unbearable for her. They provoked a sort of concentrated hatred in her against the hospice superintendent who, on the other hand, was asked in frequent letters from the parents to persevere and not to relax his efforts to subdue this violent and inflexible character since the cure could not be achieved in any other way. The resulting exasperation for the young patient was nevertheless harmful to the treatment and convalescence advanced in slow steps. On an agreed day the parents went to the hospice and admitted that they themselves were the original cause of the severity of the restraint methods used, confessing that they had continually requested it. From then on the patient thought she saw a veil fall which had hidden the truth from her. She appreciated all the assiduous care lavished on her, became calm again, began to laugh and her convalescence made rapid progress.

242. The diversity of temperaments, tastes, ages, sex etc, necessarily introduce great variety in ways of managing the mentally deranged, and in the choice of methods for gaining their confidence and maintaining constant order in the hospice. It is the fruit of skill and experience which suggests clever ways, in particular cases, for handling a deranged patient and arresting the course of his exuberance. But to succeed the superintendent needs a combination of two rare qualities (paragraph 216): a constant commitment to fulfil his responsibilities; and an air of openness and candour which is natural and not artificial, and leads the patient to ask for his advice in the perplexities he faces. Sometimes it is necessary to know when it is the right time to move beyond the tone of authority and command to stop a bout of exuberance or exaggerated pretensions. The former cook of a titled lady had been transferred to the hospice for the deranged with all the signs of maniacal insanity without delirium. Some time afterwards, she became agitated, irritated, alternately shed tears and prided herself that she was soon going to regain her job. She further thought she was privileged, became very unruly, and took little notice of instructions she was given: she even went as far as striking a servant girl who had woken her up too suddenly that morning. She also replied haughtily to the superintendent who reproached her for her lapses: so it was necessary to have recourse to force to restore order, and a few hours of seclusion were enough to make her realise her dependence and make her calm and docile from then on.

243. A woman who had reached the point where her maniacal state had begun to decline still had fiery fits of anger at intervals which she could not overcome. One day she came to grab a knife and threatened to slit the throat of everybody who went against her wishes. The superintendent was informed, and he fortunately got the servant girls to intervene and overcome the patient without any accident, and had her taken to the bath. As she had already regained her reason, he pointed out to her how dangerous her outbursts were and had her given a strong water jet on the head, which was repeated the next day. At the same time he showed her other people who were taking baths around her but to whom water jets were not given because they were peaceful and had never sought to wound anybody with a dangerous weapon. After the third day of this active and well thought-out discipline, the fear of the water jet constantly before her imagination had a calming effect through its mental influence, and after three months of observation and treatment this woman was restored to her family. Another patient deranged through piety had become less deluded but was still unsociable. She became angry all the time over the most frivolous matters: it was a crime to dare to sing, or speak to somebody nearby, and upon the least movement anyone dared to make there were bitter complaints and grounds for quarrelling. The superintendent similarly had

her taken to the bath and pointed out how much her presence caused trouble and disorder everywhere. He explained very precisely to her the reasons which had made him decide to give her a strong water jet to curb her fits of anger whereas he abstained from this for the other people who were also having a bath. Three similar episodes during the course of a week were sufficient to inspire serious reflections in this convalescent patient about the extreme exasperation caused by her character. She became calm and restrained, and from then on took up regular work in the sewing room (paragraph 213). In general, the doctor and the superintendent must support each other on the need for severe and impartial justice in disciplinary measures taken against deranged patients, and the importance of acquainting them with the purpose of these actions when they can appreciate this. This is all in order to increasingly gain their esteem and confidence, and bring back to their mind the calm so essential for obtaining a sound and lasting cure.

244. But are not pure morals needed to achieve this kind of return and its beneficial effects? Can such morals be expected from some unruly or perfidious women who become deranged through shameful vices, debauchery, drunkenness or the vilest intrigues? A young very dissolute person had no concerns over heaping the most outrageous abuse on her parents for having taken her to the hospice. All gentle approaches and consideration were superfluous and she constantly remained inflexible and persistent in her demands for a prompt discharge. This became an insurmountable obstacle to the success of her treatment; and even made her condition worse by bringing on a true delirium over several objects. Another very dissolute young person only gave out murmurs during her stay in the hospice and appeared to have vowed an implacable hatred against everybody who annoyed her. Every method tried in her treatment was useless and serious deeds of which she had previously been guilty resulted in her being taken to the prison at Saint-Denis. It has been the same with several women taken to the Salpêtrière at different times for excesses of debauchery or drunkenness.

245. Constant care and supervision is needed to watch over the general distribution of the deranged patients into different departments (paragraph 189), moving them around from one to the other depending on their favourable or retrogressive changes. The care and supervision must always be encouraging, sometimes reprimanding, checking in detail all the internal regulations and routines, and avoiding contagion with bad morals (11). Calm must be maintained everywhere and all objects of trouble and discord must be removed! It would certainly be all too easy to abandon some deranged patient in the back of his lodge as an uncontrollable being, or even to weigh him down in chains and treat him with extreme harshness, as if one was merely charged with removing him from society for ever and waiting for the natural end of such a cruel existence. But does not the most repeated experience lead to the rejection of this approach which is all too common, and to its ranking it amongst the most harmful prejudices? Must it not be an inviolable rule, in the management of every public or private establishment for deranged patients, to grant the insane patient all the freedom which his personal safety, and that of others, can allow, and to make any discipline proportionate to the greater or lesser gravity and danger of his outbursts? Another inviolable rule is to rigorously prevent coarse harshness and violence from the staff. Finally one should gather together all the facts which could help enlighten the doctor in the treatment, study carefully the individual varieties of morals and temperaments, and ultimately employ either gentleness or firmness, with a conciliatory approach or an imposing tone of authority and inflexible severity.

XII. PRECEPTS TO FOLLOW IN THE MANAGEMENT OF MELANCHOLIC PATIENTS

246. It is from a quite different angle, and almost in a form opposite to maniacal delirium, that melancholic delirium (paragraph 168) reveals itself. Where there is overexcitement and exuberance in the former, there prevails in the latter a deep despondency or even a state of stupor and a continuous succession of suspicions or endlessly recurring fears over the most frivolous grounds. The management of the patients in this latter case calls for no less skill and zeal than in the former, aimed at abolishing exclusive prejudices and restoring courage. A very rich man with the normal manly strength who remained sedentary for several months became morose and subject to the most fainthearted fears. A great voraciousness followed the loss of appetite and made him take unlimited food at all hours of the day and night. This melancholic patient could hardly have any sleep. He went to bed at four or five o'clock in the morning, spent the night in constant fear, thought he could hear words in a low voice, carefully closed his door, worried a few moments later that he had not shut it properly and kept returning to check his mistake. Another idea might come into his mind then, so that he would get up from his bed to examine his papers, separate them in turn and put them together again, thinking he had forgotten something, and worried about the dust on the furniture. He felt there was a great instability in his ideas and wishes, he was both wanting and not wanting, and always tormented by suspicions and slights. He also often complained of spasms and what he called nervous shooting pains in the stomach, and because of a fear of breathing outside air he always stayed indoors. He knew he was wrong not to keep himself clean and agreed in good faith with this, but confessed he could not change the way he was. Firmness, regular use of light laxatives and horseback riding cleared up this melancholia.

247. A young person sank, for no known cause, into a sombre moroseness and suspected everyone around her of wanting to poison her. The same fear pursued her after she left the paternal home and took refuge with one of her aunts. Her suspicions went so far that she refused all form of food, and then she was transferred to a boarding house where no more success was achieved, whatever could be tried. She was then taken to the hospice at Salpêtrière and as she was tranquil she was put in the convalescents' dormitory. The noise and tumult she created during the night forced her to be moved and she was confined in a lodge where she again carried on with her touchy and pettifogging mood. An inconsiderate visit made to her by a stranger only aggravated her melancholia and from that same day she absolutely refused any form of food. The strait-jacket was ineffectively applied to constrain her to eat and it was necessary to resort to a disciplinary water jet. She promised everything at the time, but on leaving the bathtub she repeated the same refusals. The next day some food was brought at the time she was in the bath with the injunction to take it if she wanted to avoid having her head submerged in cold water, and she obeyed this time without showing any repugnance. Signs of compassion shown to her, together with comforting and gentle talk, finished in winning her confidence. She took to working diligently, and little by little her imaginary fears vanished.

248. The grounds which lead melancholic patients to refuse all food are very varied, as numerous observations made on deranged patients in hospices bear out. In one case the patient thought there were toads in her stomach and in order to starve them to death she thought she had to refuse any kind of nourishment. Another melancholic patient was persuaded that

somebody wanted her life and that some harmful substance was always mixed with her food to kill her, giving rise to something of an invincible repugnance to eat it. A mother, known for her extreme attachment to her family, and who had been thrown into a very deep melancholy by domestic setbacks, looked upon food offered to her as a portion intended for her children and indignantly pushed it away. The expedient of the water jet had to be resorted to several times to prevent her from dying from cachexia. A young person who had been publicly harshly reproached for having had a baby from an illegitimate love affair was so upset that it was only by the most pressing exhortations that one managed to get her to eat and thus sustain her unhappy existence (12). In some cases everything fails and the melancholic patient succumbs.

249. The collection of my daily notes on the many causes, varieties and appealing glamour of the devotional melancholia which can flood the wards of the hospices, and even become contagious there without the closest vigilance, would provide an inexhaustible fund of strange facts and spicy anecdotes for a hoaxer. Here there is a young person who is terrified through abandoning herself too indulgently to reading novels. There, someone with longings of the heart against which a priest has fiercely inveighed and adjudged to be seen as deserving eternal flames. Then there are the extreme perplexities of a frail and over-scrupulous soul who has committed a dreadful crime, that of making her confessions to a non-juring priest. In some cases a legal marriage sanctioned by civil laws and not by ministers of religion has been threatened with eternal disapproval, and in others the stormy times of the Revolution have been harkened back to, and a sensitive woman has been gravely reproached for having omitted attending public worship for several years. Then there are mysterious societies of privileged brotherhoods who have skilfully fired up piety and raised it to the level of rapture and ecstasy. Sometimes also there are gullible and not very industrious mothers who would rather head for sermons and churches than commendably undertake housework. So I will be discrete and restrained, and limit myself to bringing up to date particular examples of this sort which false piety alone can marvel at like so many models to follow. But it is sad and distressing to see so many victims crammed every day into the hospice who have now become incurable as the result of having obstinately rejected the wise advice given to them, on the pretext that it is better to obey God than man. Those one has been able to cure were endowed with sound judgement which allowed them first to weigh up opinions, next to face up to doubts and uncertainties, then to provoke fresh enlightenment with judicious questions. They have then come upon the true elementary knowledge of universal timeless and ubiquitous morality, and adjourned religious practices at the time of their cure. In this way a few have been drawn back from the abyss into which they were running. But pride, ignorance and prejudice, and perhaps also a too deep-seated state of the illness, have made a certain number of them impervious to all the remonstrance and indications of compassion lavished upon them. Their confidence could not be won, and they sank little by little into a kind of daydreaming or habitual dementia which permanently excluded them from society and reduced them to complete nonentities.

250. The most thorough supervision is barely adequate to prevent any communication between the devotional convalescent patients and the most melancholic ones, and also to carefully remove all the exterior signs of piety such as devotional books, images, crosses and relics. The most repeated experience demonstrates that relapse often results from these sources, and they can also often be a serious obstacle to the success of treatment. An

attempt was made elsewhere to cure a melancholic patient whilst allowing her to continue to retain a wooden Crucifix on her chest, but the illness only intensified, increasing her perplexities and despair to the extent that one day she seized a pair of scissors to kill herself. Transferred to the hospice, one of the first steps taken was to remove what she called the sign of salvation from her. Little by little her former feelings were dispersed, whereupon treatment met no further obstacles. One of these melancholic patients who had become more tranquil had been transferred to the infirmary for some minor indisposition and a few days later certain religious ceremonies were performed for a dying patient in the next bed. She immediately stood up, recalled the memory of the death of her grandmother who died some time ago, shook the priest, took him by the stole and surplice, shouting loudly for her grandmother, with the result that there was a very noisy scene and a real relapse (13). Formerly, on Holy Thursday, certain religious ceremonies were celebrated in the dormitory for very elderly women who had slipped into dementia. However, drawbacks associated with this practice caused it to be done away with and it no longer takes place except in the infirmary. Again, care is taken to remove the devotional melancholic patients whose condition could be aggravated by this spectacle.

251. Another matter is even more to be feared in the hospice for deranged patients and calls for stricter supervision. This is the irresistible tendency to suicide which often accompanies melancholia and is warned about at the time of admission. Very varied methods can be employed to carry out this deadly plan. A few melancholic patients have tried to throw themselves from one of the convalescents' dormitory windows, so they have had to be fitted with bars; others have tried to put a lace round their neck to strangle themselves; some have swallowed the most disgusting objects to poison themselves and some have gone as far as swallowing pins. A woman who was of very gentle character and tenderly cherished by her husband developed this black humour following her confinement and sent her family into despair with her repeated attempts to kill herself. In the first days of her admission she could not adequately express her extreme disgust for life, nor conceal her repeated efforts to free herself from it. Sometimes it was verdigris she was looking for to poison herself; sometimes she found a quicker way and seized a stone, using it with redoubled strength to strike her chest although with no effect other than to cause a large bruise. On another occasion she went off alone and tried to strangle herself with a lace. But all her efforts were in vain. From time to time there was some other attempt whose dire consequences were foreseen, and of which she was finally disabused by gentle approaches, the use of temperate baths, diluted drinks and assiduous work. Another young melancholic patient had so tightly gripped her neck with a lace to strangle herself that her face was livid and she had already lost consciousness. It was only by prompt action that she was saved, but hardly had she come to than she fixed in indignation upon the servant girl who was looking after her and even tried to strike her, bitterly reproaching her for restoring her to an existence which had become unbearable for her. (This was a girl who had been seduced and then abandoned by her lover at the time of her confinement.)

252. It is no mean task to undertake to choose the method and the tones to adopt in countering the strange ideas of so many melancholic patients, with their individual varieties of character and of the prejudices which dominate them. Some are enlightened, benevolent, sometimes very sensitive, timid and endowed with very modest manners, while others are deceitful, close, full of pride and prejudice, and become completely incurable if one shows them any

misplaced indulgence. A well-born lady, who had sunk into unhappiness and devotional melancholia, was so sensitive that for having been simply told that she would receive visits as soon as there was no longer any danger for her or other people, she answered with intense indignation: 'But does somebody think I've got rabies?' and it took several days to calm her down and put right this unseemly behaviour. Another, on the contrary, who was very imperious and used to being blindly obeyed by an over docile husband, stayed in bed for part of the morning and then demanded that he should bring her drinks on bended knee. In the ecstasies of her arrogance she ended up believing that she was the Virgin Mary. Would one succeed in curing her and taming this haughty character by appearing to approve of these pompous daydreams? Should it not be the same in respect of an obliging old man's servant who regarded him as the guardian of her own fortune, and who as soon as she heard of the death of somebody who was very rich, approached the authorities to acquire their estate as an unquestionable right? If one shows condescension towards gloomy melancholic patients, they only become more stubborn and more imperious, and one ends up by making them incurable. Thus the superintendent of mentally ill patients who lives all the time in their midst carefully studies, at all hours, the particular object of their individual delusions. He prepares and puts into practice a mental reorientation designed to support the fortunate results of physical treatment.

253. In the system generally adopted in the hospice for the mentally ill, featuring much indulgence and reasoned severity, what results could be achieved if the staff were not kept in complete subordination and were just allowed, as in so many public and private establishments, to speak to the unfortunate melancholic and other patients with savage harshness and rule them with a rod of iron? Furthermore, the closest supervision is exercised over the servant girls as over the other patients, and scrupulous care is taken to exclude those who are known to have a harsh and coarse character, only accepting docile and industrious convalescent patients (paragraph 203). One must always to be on guard against their little animosities and antipathies. The utmost premium is put on ensuring that they not allowed, in any case and under any pretext, to strike or be violent in any way, but they are obliged to lend reciprocal help in perilous moments and set their combined efforts against the fiery resentment and outbursts of blind anger of some patients. A convalescent patient, who became a servant girl during the course of her treatment, was suddenly grabbed by a patient who caught her by the hair and knocked her to the ground in an effort to strangle her. To get free and make her lose her grip this girl gripped the patient's thigh in her finger nails and gave her a wound like a bite (paragraph 204). After this there were great rumblings, lively discussions and grave criticism over a wound caused by a servant girl, and complaints by the girl over the impossibility of avoiding such an act of violence in the situation to which she had been reduced. The two opposite sides were listened to, statements from witnesses were taken and after thorough deliberation it was decided that the accusation was unfounded. The servant girl remained in her job, deemed to have limited herself to legitimate self-defence to save her life. Is this constant attention always to exercise rigorous justice and prevent anger within an establishment for the mentally ill not the surest guarantee of interior calm and good order? And is the trust accorded to the superintendent not derived from the authority that necessarily results from an invariable combination of ability and righteousness?

254. But what becomes of an establishment devoted to the mentally ill if the superintendent's authority comes to be ignored or shared with someone else, and if appeals can be made

against any strict judgements he reaches? The most difficult and upset melancholic patients are always looking for a protector on the pretext that they are being oppressed. They flatter him for being a support and indulge as a consequence with increased relentlessness in their pipedreams. Thus I am careful to refrain from any measures connected with the domain of the internal management or discipline, and listen neither to complaints nor objections. I am always on guard against deceitful ways which can be used to evade the internal rules and, what is even worse, to perpetuate the distraction of reason or aggravate it.

255. I have no wish to revive bitter memories, but I can only deplore again the sad series of constant power struggles formerly waged between a former general surveillance agent and a particular superintendent of the mentally ill. These struggles in some cases caused medical treatment to fail, as several of my daily records bear out. The melancholic patients, always absorbed in their singular ideas, were then perturbed and spent time dreaming up new ways to defend their cause. Precious time was lost in sterile discussions and their illness ended in becoming chronic and incurable. The drawback would have been nil if the above official, who wanted to exercise all his rights, had sacrificed his animosities for the public good and had been willing to come down from his lofty sphere in order to get accurate information and practice conciliatory ways. There were often scenes full of anger and bitterness which went on even in the presence of patients, as if to turn them against the superintendent and cause him to lose the confidence which is so necessary to him in working towards their recovery. I only consider these matters in their simple relation to medical treatment and leave to the administrative authorities the task of increasing the powers to maintain the order and consistency of the department. But what successful results could I obtain myself if the chief of surveillance was not looked upon internally as invested with total authority for the prompt and final execution of all disciplinary measures?

NOTES TO FOURTH SECTION

1. The architect was asked to modify his plan and, instead of courtyards six metres wide ending at the side with ground floor lodges, that he should make them ten or twelve metres wide and put ground floor lodges on either side with a first floor above. He was also asked to allow for a parallel double row of lime trees to provide shade for places the strong sun sometimes makes unbearable – some unfortunate deranged patients are only too inclined to do anything which is bad for them and overexpose themselves unwisely to the sun. Furthermore, during summer and spring, heat becomes excessive between this double row of lodges, which is bad for the treatment of patients who are very agitated and in a state of fury. This would have the additional benefit of providing space for the erection of the lodges.
2. A man who was formerly attached to a prince's house through his appointments, and driven to maniacal insanity as much by the overturning of his old ideas as by that of his fortune, only revealed his delusion about his imaginary greatness when somebody mentioned the Revolution to him or else in certain moments of agitation. Otherwise in the hospice he maintained the outward appearance of courtesy and decorum which had been his custom in the past. If anyone contradicted his opinions he immediately withdrew without any abruptness or mutterings, just confining himself to a respectful salute. The exclusive idea which generally occupied him however was that of his

almighty power, and if he had an outburst he uttered threats with all the weight of his wrath and announced that he could easily bring down the heavenly fires and shatter the world. One single consideration held him back; and this was fear of destroying the army of Condé, whom he admired, and who according to him was destined to fulfil the Eternal's designs. It is extremely difficult to influence the imagination of such a patient, either with gentle means or with active restraint methods. An outburst was needed on his part which put him in the wrong and justified treating him vigorously; and this happened after about six months of his stay in the hospice. One day when the superintendent was complaining to him about the dirt and rubbish he had left in his lodge, the patient became violently cross with him and threatened to kill him. This was a suitable time to punish him and convince him that his power was imaginary; but since the relations intended to withdraw him from the hospice within a few days, it was decided not to attempt anything.

3. In the private establishment, so well known and deservedly so, of Dr Esquirol, each patient has a domestic servant exclusively attached in his service who always sleeps next to him and even within his room if it is judged necessary. All these domestic servants are ready to come together as a frightening crowd to intimidate a patient if he should have some momentary excitation which made him to violent. The patients never stay in their rooms, they walk around in a spacious shady garden or rest in what is called common room. The furious patients are free to walk about in strait-jackets in the courtyard which is partly shaded by a pleasant grove. Several convalescent patients go for walks outside the house, each accompanied by his dedicated domestic servant.

4. To give a fair idea of the parental cares undertaken by the superintendent and his wife, I will mention that fatty and lean food was served alternately each day of the week, and that on the lean days the food provided in the hospice was arranged in a manner to allow one pound of butter to sixteen pounds of rice, which makes about three and a half pounds of butter for the lean soup for about two hundred patients. As unpleasant speculation about the provisioning was still being made over this subject, most often more than a pound of salt was added to this quantity of salted butter. So what could the soup be other than a kind of hot salty water, since there were only two pounds of butter to four hundred pounds of soup? At the tastings I made I was struck with astonishment to still find a soup of good quality. I soon found out how the superintendent managed to get by, either by keeping back a little meat or vegetables from the previous day, or by making use of bones which had been discarded elsewhere, or were used for lucre by being crushed and the copious gelatine extracted. The way of making rice soup was no less sound. Instead of flooding it with water just a little was added and left until it was all absorbed whereupon some more was added, kept hot in a separate bowl. The cooking was completed by successive additions of water.

5. At that time I was charged by the Administration to investigate the causes of this mortality through a precise observation of the prevailing illnesses, and this is the conclusion of my report.

'I think one must principally attribute this mortality to the shortages prevailing in the psychiatric department during last spring and summer. In fact, before the 1st of Germinal[10], each patient had one and a half pounds of bread each day, and one hundred

---

[10] *Germinal – Seventh month of Republican calendar – Ed.*

pounds of it was allowed for the soup for the whole hospice. On the 1st of Germinal the hundred pounds were stopped, and the ration of bread for each patient was reduced to one pound until the 15th of that month. From the 15th till the 30th the ration was only twelve ounces. The reduction was taken still further for the first eight days of Floreal[11], as the bread ration was only eight ounces. At that time ship's biscuits were issued for the soup; but two hundred pounds of bread were withheld from the whole hospice, reducing the normal ration to six ounces. When the biscuit was stopped, on the 1st of Thermidor[12], the ration went back to twelve ounces of bread. The voraciousness of patients of either sex was known. So the shortages impacted mainly on the mental illness hospice, and the consequences were diarrhoea and disastrous dysentery'. (*Bicêtre, 27 Brumaire Year IV.*)

6. In Dr Esquirol's establishment meals are generally ample, fortifying and based on the healthiest food prepared, I may add, without spices. The first meal is served at nine o'clock, and varied depending on the condition and state of mind of the patient, and sometimes several of them need to be given a second lunch. Dinner is at four o'clock. The convalescent or calm patients and those who are only agitated intermittently are admitted to Dr Esquirol's table, and the others, as long as they are not dangerous, dine in a common room, each at their own table and waited on by their domestic servant. The small remaining number eats in their room. Everything which is served comes from the common table, where the portions are put up showing where they are to go. Each patient drinks water with a few drops of wine in it as they wish. Supper consists of legumes and fruit.

7. It is remarkable, M. Thouin said, that a house containing so many people should have so few servants in its employment. I only saw four or five permanent staff, all the others being taken from amongst the convalescent patients, who, excited by the concierge's example and chatter, eagerly participate in looking after those who need help. They fulfil this task with all the more enthusiasm because they received similar help themselves from their predecessors. There is no fear of the service flagging, because there are nearly as many nurses as patients, and they are controlled by a man belonging to the staff who is allocated to each room. This economical and, above all, very moral practice is utilised in all the hospices in Holland. The result of this is that the poor are better treated and the costs of the staff, officers and senior managers, who are so numerous and highly paid with us, are practically nil.

8. At the two remote ends of ancient Egypt, which was then thickly populated and strongly flourishing, there were temples dedicated to Saturn, where the melancholic people crowded and where priests, taking advantage of their trusting credulity, supported their so-called miraculous cures with all the natural means that nature could suggest. There were games, recreational exercises of all kinds set up in the temples, voluptuous paintings, seductive images everywhere exposed to the patients' eyes and pleasing songs and the most melodious sounds often delighted their ears. They walked in gardens full of flowers or in groves adorned with refined art. Sometimes they were made to breathe fresh healthy air, on the Nile in decorated boats, or in the middle of rural concerts. Sometimes they were taken to smiling islands where, under the symbol of some divine protector, they were shown new and ingeniously staged spectacles, and choice societies.

---

[11] *Floreal – Eighth month of Republican calendar – Ed.*
[12] *Thermidor – Eleventh month of Republican calendar – Ed.*

Every moment was in short dedicated to comical scenes, grotesque dances and a system of diversified amusements born by religious ideas. Could a matched and scrupulously observed routine, the travel needed to get to certain sacred places, the continuous feasts set up deliberately along the route, hope fortified by superstition and the skill of the priests to create a favourable diversion and drive away sad and melancholic ideas all fail to suspend the feeling of distress? And would they fail to calm the worries and often bring about salutary changes which care had been taken to promote in order to inspire confidence and build up the reputation of the tutelary divinities? *Nosograph. phil.* Tom.III, page 94, 3rd edn.

9. A madman, at the height of his vigour and very strong, who had been brought tied up and gagged on a wagon by his family, scared all those who had brought him and nobody dared to untie him to take him to his lodge. The concierge sent everybody away, chatted for a little while with the patient, gained his confidence and after untying him persuaded him to be led into the new dwelling place which had been prepared for him. Each day he made progress with his spirits, mastered his confidence and brought back his reason. This man went back to the bosom of his family, to which he brought happiness. *(Description of the House of the Mad of Amsterdam,* Décad. Phil. Year IV.)

10. t has been easy in the past for me to judge the benefit of avoiding too close a seclusion for the insane. When the most wild and most furious in the hospice of Bicêtre were held in chains in their lodges, they were continuously agitated, day and night. There was nothing but shouts, din and tumult, but after the use of the strait-jacket had been established, and these patients had received the freedom of wandering in the courtyards, their wildness evaporated in continuous exertion all the day. They bustled about and tormented one another harmlessly, which at night left them in a calmer and more tranquil state.

11. Experience every day shows how necessary it is to have seven or eight lodges in a separate part of the hospice where one can keep certain deranged patients who are not furious, but very unruly and uncontrollable, in a longer or shorter state of isolation and seclusion. Amongst this number one may include: 1° those who cannot be submitted to the general rule of work, and, always acting badly, take pleasure in harassing the other patients and provoking and endlessly stirring up matters of discord, without the usual disciplinary methods being capable of inducing the least reform in them. 2° Religious devotees who think they are inspired, continually seek to create new proselytes and take a perfidious pleasure in inciting deranged patients to disobedience under the pretext that it is better to obey God than men. Gentleness, threats and disciplinary measures are all equally unsuccessful with these characters who are always ready to behave in the opposite way to the impression which needs to be communicated to deranged patients in order to cure them. 3° Women who during their bout of insanity have had an irresistible propensity to steal everything they can get hands on, who go into the lodges of other patients seizing everything they find and give rise to disputes and endless brawls.

12. It is difficult to imagine the many measures and the perseverance needed in a well organised and zealously controlled establishment to overcome this utter refusal of food. First gentle means are tried, with pressing invitations to open the mouth which is kept stubbornly shut. If resistance continues and the patient is unwilling to chew the solid food he is offered an attempt is made to get him to take nourishing drinks, soup with rice, noodles or milk, tipped into the mouth with an iron spoon to part the teeth which the patient keeps firmly clenched. If this method is not enough and the

drink itself is rejected, a baby's feeding bottle is used following M. Pussin's technique. The nostrils are pinched, and as the patient is forced to open his mouth to breath, the opportunity is take to get an amount of liquid swallowed, and this procedure is repeated several times on the same and following days. In the event of all the methods I have just mentioned failing, I have an elastic feeding tube purchased which is introduced down one nostril; and through it a little liquid is passed into the stomach, maintaining the patient's strength whilst waiting for him to make up his mind to take nourishment voluntarily. Finally, there have been cases where ill-understood religious principles have led to an insuperable resistance being mounted, leading to a belated death.

13. During the convalescence of this same melancholic patient, another woman furtively obtained a devotional book for her which she read surreptitiously and very carefully. The same M. Pussin found her bathed in tears, sighing away and continually repeating that she well knew that her children were dead and had been cut in pieces, and that life was unbearable. It was natural to attribute this impression to a dream but some pious reading was also suspected, because she was caught in the act in an out-of-the-way place with a devotional book about the Guardian Angel, revelations and ecstatic visions. It was taken away from her and torn up in front of her. This initially threw her into a sort of consternation but a few days later her mistaken impression became obliterated, and convalescence then made rapid progress.

5

RESULTS OF ANCIENT AND MODERN EXPERIENCE IN THE MEDICAL TREATMENT OF THE MENTALLY ILL

256. I do not know whether any area of the physical sciences presents at first sight more impenetrable obscurities, and inspires in an author a more warranted mistrust in his strengths, than the historical exposition of the rules to be followed in the treatment of the mentally ill. The most scrupulous anatomical studies have uncovered practically nothing about the true seat, or character, of mental derangement. How can one know, master and learn to rectify the different defects or lapses of understanding when its functions in health are so difficult to appreciate and distinguish properly from one another (paragraphs 2, 3 and following)? A few popular ideas, purely empirical processes or odd isolated facts have up till recent times formed the basis of the treatment of mentally ill patients but how can such limited and shaky experience be relied upon?

257. A spell of several years in hospices for the deranged of either sex has opened up a rich source of education for me which is perhaps the most solid and the least subject to error. Before adopting any principles on methods to be used I restricted myself to the most simple ones, and on many occasions I left the illness to run its natural course to see what beneficial resources nature could produce when not thwarted by extraneous interference. To achieve my objective it was necessary to establish and maintain regular order and smooth running in these hospices, and it was in this respect that I was fully supported (Fourth Section) at the Salpêtrière by an exceptional man, M. Pussin, who was the superintendent of the mentally ill patients. So I was able to study very carefully not only the characteristics of the different species of mental alienation and their principle varieties, but also their individual course at different stages. In this way nothing was left to chance and I was able to distinguish superfluous or harmful treatments from those which are of direct and indisputable usefulness.

Medico-Philosophical Treatise on Mental Alienation.
Philippe Pinel. Translated by G. Hickish, D. Healy and L.C. Charland.
© 2008 John Wiley & Sons, Ltd.

I. ON THE PRACTICE OF STRIKING DERANGED PATIENTS AS A MEANS OF CURING THEM

258. The lot of the human species is deplorable when one comes to think of the frequency and numerous different causes of insanity, and of the countless circumstances which can be adverse for those who suffer from it even in the most happily run institutions. If one wished to keep every mentally ill patient closely secluded within his family, repeated experience shows that this would be imposing an insurmountable obstruction to the restoration of his reason. On the other hand, if we dedicate public asylums to large collections of mentally deranged patients and add together all the benefits of such a site and the extent and layout of the premises, yet still more is needed. This includes rare qualities of enthusiasm and discernment, and a happy mixture of imposing firmness with heartfelt compassion and sensitivity which is essential for looking after these forsaken souls. They are subject to so many failings, bizarre whims and sometimes such outbursts of blind fury, that all one has any right to do is to pity them. Would it be possible in any other way than from enlightened experience and constant attention to be able to sense the approach of these bouts so as to prevent accidents from their onset, or to severely restrain the brutality of the staff and punish their negligence? The same experience and attention are needed for removing the incidental causes of episodes and, while these last, eliminating everything which could aggravate the delirium. When the episode is over the resulting debilitated and lifeless state which itself can become disastrous has to be attended to. Then all the opportunities the calm intervals provide must be exploited to accelerate the cure using the means found most dependable from enlightened experience. But what would become of a hospice even with the best choice of superintendent if the doctor himself, full of prejudices, restricted in his outlook, and endowed with utter confidence in his own ideas, shows himself to be less interested in the public good than in asserting himself and haughtily exercising sole supremacy?

259. I have set out (Fourth Section) the nature and fortunate results of gentle methods and of the use, in a few cases, of an approach involving fear or firm and steady opposition to the dominant ideas and inflexible obstinacy of some deranged patients. On other occasions a courageous, imposing and determined manner free of any insult or any sense of bitterness or anger, and consistent with sacred human rights, is employed. This is enough to show how much this course differs from the crude harshness, blows, wounds and I dare to say the horrifying and sometimes murderous treatment which can occur in mental hospices where the staff are not held under the most watchful and severe supervision. Why do the writings of the ancients, particularly those of Celsus, bring a kind of intermediate method (1) to mind: a system of curative measures based on severe punishments, hunger, blows and chains to contain the patient when advice and gentle ways become useless? Why have public and private establishments been organised along similar principles? A farmer from the north of Scotland of Herculean stature rose to fame for the treatment of maniacal insanity, according to Dr Gregory. His method entailed setting the patients to the hardest agricultural work, varying their tasks, some as beasts of burden and others as domestic servants, and in the end reducing them to obedience with a shower of blows at the least sign of revolt. A very famous kind of monastic establishment, in one of the southern parts of France, was managed on similar principles. Every day one of the employees went round the lodges and when a patient behaved eccentrically, became noisy, wouldn't go to bed at night or rejected food

etc, he gave him the clear order to change and warned him that his insistence on these lapses would be punished the next morning with ten blows with a cosh. The verdict was always executed punctually and if necessary it was even repeated several times. Reward was no less precise than punishment and if the patient showed himself to be submissive and docile he was made to eat his meals in the refectory next to the teacher as if to test him out. If he forgot at the table and made the least mistake he was immediately warned about it with a hard blow on his fingers with a stick, and then he was told with calm solemnity that he had been bad (2) and must watch his behaviour more carefully. But in all the cases I have just quoted, have the legitimate limits not been exceeded; and should they be allowed if surer and more generally favourable results can be achieved by simpler and more humane methods? Is this not like the education of children, where blows and repulsive pedantry were once hallowed as established principles but are now banned in a more enlightened century? Do the Turks find nothing more admirable than the absurd despotism they inflict on the modern Greeks, and could any lesser tribute be paid to the liberal ideas and magnanimous character of the ancient peoples of these countries?

260. It would perhaps be descending into vagueness to set down standard and uniform rules for the use of blows and corporal punishment in the management of deranged patients that would apply to all populations. How could one make sure that the black people living in servitude in Jamaica, or the slaves in the Indies, shaped by an oppressive system all their lives, would not be subjected, in the case of mental derangement, to the same harsh and despotic jungle laws? But should the favourable effects generally to be expected from fear in the curing of insanity, and the acute sensitivity of the Frenchman and his violent reaction against any offensive abuse of power whilst any flicker of reason remains, not call for the gentlest disciplinary measures? And do not all observed facts arise from application of these principles? What hot-headed reactions or indeed what bursts of rage and indignation have I not seen in the past arising amongst certain patients when hoaxers coming to visit the hospice at Bicêtre made a barbaric game of harassing or provoking them! Even in the patients' infirmary, which was isolated from the hospice and beyond the supervision of the staff, how many times has it happened that because of the stupid gibes of the nurses or their brutal harshness, calm patients on the road to recovery slipped back into outbursts of fury after uncalled-for vexations or acts of violence! On the other hand, deranged patients transferred from elsewhere and designated on their arrival as very angry and very dangerous because they had been exasperated by blows and bad treatment, suddenly seemed to change their natures when someone spoke gently to them, sympathised with their troubles and gave them the consoling hope of a happier lot. Convalescence thereafter made rapid and straightforward progress. And finally does the most constant experience not show that to make the effects of fear lasting and sound, this sensation must be associated with that of respect as reason is regained? This implies that any discipline should not have been undertaken out of anger or arbitrary harshness, that only force proportionate to the degree of resistance was used to overcome the patient's exuberance, and that one was solely driven by the desire to restore him to his old self, as shown by a frank and friendly explanation immediately upon his repentance. These are the principles I have adopted and confirmed with numerous examples (Fourth Section) and which are the results of the most reiterated experience. One was undoubtedly a long way from having the advantages of the setting, the position of the premises, the expanse and the internal layout as Dr Fowler had in

his establishment in Scotland, but I can testify, after observation over several consecutive years, that the same maxims of the purest philanthropy preside over the management of the mental patients at this hospice. The servant girls are not allowed to lay a rough hand on the patients under any pretext whatsoever, even in retaliation. Furthermore, strait-jackets and limited lengths of seclusion are the only punishments inflicted and, failing success with gentle methods, an imposing display of disciplinary measures as part of a shrewd strategy sometimes achieves unhoped-for cures.

261. In maniacal insanity of recent onset, as in other acute illnesses, very often it is rather less the violence of the symptoms than a deceptive appearance of calm which should give rise to concerns about grave consequences. Has experience not shown that attacks marked by the most angry and most tumultuous mental breakdowns generally gradually subside and end by fading away provided they are not very long-standing and are treated judiciously. And that a dose of variable strength of an antispasmodic can sometimes calm down and even arrest the violence of the symptoms of a maniacal patient who is overcome with blind fury, embarks without respite on a string of piercing shouts and threats, never stops rushing about, causing a fracas and taking not a moment's rest even for several months on end, and who tears everything up, even pulling the straw of his bed to pieces. However, observation also teaches us that in many cases a sound and lasting cure can be achieved with gentle and moderate methods, abandoning the patient to his tumultuous agitation and only using the amount of discipline necessary for his personal safety and that of others. This can usually be accomplished by using the strait-jacket or camisole. He can also be helped by avoiding exasperating him with uncalled-for harshness or offensive language and sparing him from any source of annoyance or anger, either while being attended to or while being fed. Any sharply expressed refusal or curt reply when he asks at an inopportune moment to be set free needs to be guarded against, and if his request is declined this should be on understandable grounds. Finally, strict discipline within the hospice has to be maintained, particularly making the most of intervals of calm to set the patients to serious occupations or hard labour. These simple experience-based principles are borne out by the fact that some mental patients who had sunk into a kind of imbecility or idiocy through the excessive use of blood-lettings became cured after fifteen to twenty days of delirium or acute and critical maniacal insanity. A young soldier was taken from the Vendée army in Paris in a state of fury and subjected to the then usual treatment at the Hôtel-Dieu with repeated blood-lettings from the feet. After the last one there was an excessive haemorrhage when the tourniquet slipped off, followed by a prolonged state of syncope. He was transferred to the Bicêtre in the last stage of debility and languor, with diarrhoea, a pale face, speechless and with total obliteration of the functions of understanding. His father who visited him was dismayed at his state and left some money to relieve his lot. Steadily increased healthy nourishment gradually revived his strength and vigour. Then warning signs of an attack became apparent, with redness of the face, gleaming eyes, febrile shaking, extreme agitation and finally marked delirium. This patient ran about in the hospice with a precipitate gait, provoking, insulting and upsetting everybody he met with his derision, but as he abstained from any acts of violence he was left to wander about freely amongst the convalescent patients. Twenty days went by in this delirious state, then calm returned, and his reason, which was first feeble, was subsequently completely restored by means of regular work and exercise. His stay in the hospice was prolonged for a further six months to make his cure sounder and he was returned to his family towards the end of autumn. This delay was a necessary precaution against any relapse.

II. IS THE PRACTICE OF FREQUENT BLOOD-LETTING IN MENTAL ILLNESS BASED ON ENLIGHTENED EXPERIENCE?

262. A young girl of fifteen years, away from her family, fell into a state of deep frustration and soon afterwards her reason became distracted. A country surgeon who was called in fixed his eyes on the patient and declared that *all the trouble came from corrupted blood, that it was supposedly a type of blood characteristic of maniacal insanity, that it all had to be taken off and a cure would result.* So he carried out the blood-letting but the most violent fury developed immediately afterwards and the patient was taken to the Salpêtrière. Is this surgeon's old refrain of blood-lettings not repeated every day from one end of the Empire to the other, at the onset or during the course of every mental breakdown? And do even very well educated men not allow themselves to be dragged along in the stream, without looking at the true results of repeated experience?

263. I have always been on guard against any practice which was merely based upon superficial appearances, and does the practice of blood-letting in maniacal insanity not turn solely on redness of the face, sparkling eyes, an animated look and other dubious signs of too much blood and its violent rush to the head? Sound judgement should reject futile conjecture and vague reasoning which in the effort to appear truthful is all the more subject to error. When there is uncertainty about not acting, or acting in a reckless way, sound judgement embraces the first, while also endeavouring to benefit from all the facts that can enlighten it. When deranged patients are admitted to the hospice, care is always taken to question their relatives on the matter of blood-letting, and if this has been carried out they are asked about the result. The answers most regularly given testify that the condition of the patient has always deteriorated immediately afterwards. I think I should not omit something strange which happened in Year XIII. Two young people of the same age and similar temperament arrived on the same day. One of them had not had a blood-letting and she became cured in two months. When a copious blood-letting had been performed on the other she became reduced to a kind of idiocy and did not regain her speech until towards the fifth month, and her full complete recovery was not achieved until the end of the ninth month. Some time afterwards the singular example was seen of a melancholic patient who had had five blood-lettings from the foot and three from the jugular vein, and who then sank into such a state of debility and stupor that for several days he was unable to take any nourishment.

264. It is not just to contradict myself but to enlighten myself that I have sought facts from all sources that have turned out in favour of the direct effectiveness of blood-letting for maniacal insanity, but all I find gives fresh grounds for doubt. Amongst the patients admitted to the Salpêtrière, those who had had no previous treatment are precisely those who were easiest to cure. I have eagerly gone through a collection of selected observations published in England on maniacal insanity, and although there is restraint on the matter of blood-letting, the very cases where it was carried out on the most obvious grounds led me to regard it as having been harmful, or at the least superfluous. I see that in one of these cases a young person of eighteen years with a florid complexion and signs of congestion around the head was able to be bled with impunity, but it is noticeable even in this case that after only four ounces of blood had been withdrawn her arterial pulse rate dropped from eighty to sixty and syncope occurred and the vein had to be closed. Several other active remedies

were subsequently used. In this case, to which cause can a cure be attributed which comes about several months later? In another case of distracted reason occurring at the change of life a dry cough, restless nights, disturbing dreams, reddened eyes and headache led to recourse to a few small blood-lettings, and it was acknowledged that the extreme weakness and debility which followed put a stop to its further use. Lastly, in a third case of maniacal delirium which was made worse through the patient being left for a long time exposed to indiscrete questions and stupid jokes from ignorant people, why not restrict oneself to simple isolation and gentle treatment, without recourse to blood-letting *ad deliquium* which is one of the most hazardous and foolhardy methods one could allow oneself?

265. Since I have been directing treatment in the hospice for mental patients blood-letting has become a very rare and epoch-making event. But one must also avoid becoming extreme in one's ideas, and a cause has perhaps never been more compelling than in the following case of a thirty-six-year-old girl who had developed a maniacal delirium following a severe fright and was continually crying out. Her monthly periods had stopped, her face was very red and alert, her eyes were bright and her conjunctival blood vessels looked injected. A moderate blood-letting from the foot was made. However, soon afterwards the patient went into a state of complete idiocy to the extent that she was constantly walking about swinging her arms and continually plaintively calling out the words *the stone without water*. After remaining for over two years in this state, she at last came to herself again as if from a long dream. She resumed the habit of dressmaking and left the hospice the following month fully cured. I would like to think that the blood-letting did not produce this prolonged state of idiocy, but could it have prevented it? I am far from wanting to pronounce a general exclusion of blood-letting but I believe that cases for its judicious use are exceedingly rare.

III. ON TREATMENT BY BRISK IMMERSION OF DERANGED PATIENTS IN COLD WATER

266. Van Helmont, whose disorganised imagination seems to have stretched to all the dreams one could have had in the seventeenth century, wanted to transfer a popular and barbarous procedure already used for hydrophobia to the treatment of maniacal insanity. I refer to total submersion which he had looked upon as a very simple remedy. One must groan to see such a hazardous and dangerous method confidently put forward by the famous commentator on the work of Boerhaave, and thereafter passed on as a point of doctrine in the schools of the last century. Subsequent and often repeated animal experiments have destroyed this fragile edifice and it is now known that submersion can be fatal within a few minutes. A little more self-restraint is applied in certain establishments for mental patients and the procedure is restricted to suddenly immersing the patient in cold water, lifting him out immediately and immersing him again in the same water several times. The old method is no longer used, but that being the case is the new one not also completely superfluous? For Van Helmont's bizarre idea was to destroy the patient's wild ideas by going right back to their earliest traces, which could only happen, according to him, by obliterating these ideas, so to speak, by a state neighbouring upon death *(idcirco inveniendum erat remedium quod posset occidere, necare, tollere aut obliterare præfatam illam amentiæ imaginem)*[1]. But one should blush to

---

[1] *'Therefore, a remedy should be found which could destroy, kill, remove or obliterate that previously mentioned thought of madness. – Ed.*

insist on this medical delusion, perhaps even more insane than the ideas of the patient whose distracted reason one wishes to restore, and I will restrict myself to a few considerations regarding brisk and repeated immersion of the patient in cold water.

267. The use of immersion in a cold water bath has not been omitted from amongst the treatment precepts given by Dr Cullen, and he recommends plunging the patient into cold water by surprise, keeping him there for some time and frequently tipping water onto his head whilst the rest of his body is submerged in the bath with the direct intention all the time of rousing a slight shiver and producing a refreshing effect. But can one turn a blind eye to the countless drawbacks associated with this practice? Have the combined effects which a cold sensation over the whole body, the violent means used to carry out this immersion, the forced swallowing of a certain amount of water, the fear of imminent suffocation from which the patient cannot save himself, his angry and tumultuous efforts to escape an imminent danger, and his concentrated wrath against the staff who carry out such oppressive measures all been taken into account in terms of the impact these could have on an irascible character? What a lot of other abuses are inevitable in the process, likely to raise the patient's exasperation to a peak. These include the derision and coarse harshness of the staff, for instance, who make a sort of recreational game out of his unhappy situation, and the contempt and insulting language with which they greet his cries and bitter complaints. In short, a remedy which should only be administered regretfully often changes into a kind of coarse and barbaric amusement. I have sometimes questioned patients treated elsewhere by this method and then transferred to the Salpêtrière, and they could not adequately express to me the indignation which memory of these odious vexations excited in them. One of them, who had been treated for eighteen months in a well-known hospice, and who had often been submitted to this terrible ordeal, only spoke of it with loathing and assured me that after this bath she was always more angry and more furious.

268. A young man of twenty-two years, of robust constitution, had suffered setbacks as a result of the events of the Revolution. He exaggerated the ills of the future, became deeply saddened, could not sleep and then was suddenly seized with a most violent maniacal fury. He was subjected to treatment for acute maniacal insanity in a town in his Department, and they were especially lavish with cold baths there during which it was customary to submerge him briskly with his limbs tied. His delusion was to believe he was an Austrian General. This led him to adopt a commanding tone all the time, and his fury was redoubled at the time of the bath because he only saw there a blameworthy neglect of the respect due to his rank and distinctions. Such treatment merely made his condition worse and his parents made up their minds to send him to Paris, to a boarding house, in order to entrust him to my care. He seemed very angry and very violent on my first visit and I sensed the necessity of going along with his illusion so as to win his confidence. I always showed deference and respect, and always gave the appearance of being disposed to receive orders from him rather than to give them to him. I said no more about baths; he was treated gently, just had diluted drinks, and was free to walk about at any time in a pleasant garden. These diversions, physical exercise and a few friendly conversations I had with him now and then gradually restored calm, and towards the end of the month he no longer showed me any haughtiness or defiance. The re-establishment of his reason took place slowly, but at the end of three months I could no longer detect any trace of his former delusion. But towards autumn and the following spring, at the first approach of a kind of nervous excitement indicated

by a more lively expression, a little more talkativeness and exuberance, I got him to take whey as a purgative at intervals for a fortnight, and then a few tepid baths for the sake of cleanliness so as not to reawaken his previous repugnance. Any outbreak of an attack was thus prevented and the stay in the same boarding house was extended for a year as a safety measure. On leaving, he went into the countryside where for ten years he has divided his time between consultancy work and farming without having shown the least sign of his previous delusion.

269. The use of the cold bath, says the English author already quoted, has nearly always been combined with other remedies and it is difficult to decide to what extent, taken on its own, it could be useful in maniacal insanity. Its use separately from any other treatment has been too seldom repeated to be able to reach any firm conclusions. 'I can however give an assurance', adds the same author, 'that in many cases the cold bath has produced, within a few hours, paralytic conditions, especially when the patient was in a state of fury and of plethoric constitution'. Feriar, another English author, seems less indecisive: he has made up his mind in favour of cold baths for melancholia, and in favour of hot baths for maniacal insanity. This is without quoting any example other than that of a maniacal patient who was reduced to a very parlous state by the use of these latter baths, then treated all at once with tonics, moderate doses of opium, camphor, purgatives and finally promptly cured by the use of electricity. Does such complexity of treatment not prolong the uncertainty and doubt rather than dissipate it? To settle the question I am going to report here the fruits of my own experience of baths in general.

270. One must always be careful of arguments, even the most sophisticated, for the direct action of any remedy whatsoever. However, fresh weight is added if the authority of the men most famous in medicine and most given to thinking for themselves can be quoted in support although it always takes constant and fully discussed experience to clear up any uncertainty. I leave all that can be put forward in favour of lukewarm baths to be taken at its proper value: the benefit of relaxing the skin, promoting perspiration, stabilising circulation, preventing a rush of blood to the head, securing a peaceful sleep etc, to prove their efficacy against melancholia and maniacal insanity. But it cannot be denied that outstanding observers such as Cælius Aurelianus, Alexander of Tralle, Aretæus, Prosper Alpin etc have not recommended them in any special way. The turmoil of the Revolution in Years II and III deprived me at Bicêtre of several things needed to use them, but everything came together again in Year X at the Salpêtrière hospice, enabling the trials at different stages of these illnesses to be resumed. For nearly eight years these baths have become the fundamental basis of treatment for both maniacally insane and melancholic patients as their effectiveness has become increasingly evident. Their use has been varied and they have been supported with other ancillary methods. Twelve bathrooms are in active use for a large part of the day. Patients are generally admitted at all stages of their illness and the baths are variously continued or suspended depending on the greater or lesser intensity of the symptoms. There is in general no reluctance, no fear and everything goes off calmly and with the greatest propriety since the bathrooms are screened. The patients are supervised and encouraged, the most unruly ones are brought to order, and any circumstances which might call for special modifications are examined without anything being allowed to upset the general progress and unity of this simple method of treatment.

271. A happy combination of the shower with the bath adds greatly to its effectiveness and reduces any drawbacks that could arise from it to the minimum. In each bathroom and directly above the patient's head is a pipe which by means of a tap can deliver a stream of warm water from a height of three feet (3) depending on the intended objective. It can be regulated depending on the symptoms but is generally very gentle and limited to a single shower. It is only towards the end of the bath and just for a few minutes that the shower is administered, when the blood circulation has been drawn to the surface of the body and one wishes to reduce its pressure in the head by cooling. The showers are often omitted as the maniacal insanity declines or during convalescence, when baths are still used intermittently, but they are resumed on the approach of a bout of maniacal insanity, or indeed when it has already developed. In all cases those violent water jets are forbidden which are inconsiderately administered elsewhere, letting a column of water several lines[2] wide fall on the patient's head from a height of seven or eight feet, for longer or shorter periods at the will of the staff who can bring their small-minded prejudices and hard and useless coarseness to bear on this as on many other matters. The shower is only ever administered at the Salpêtrière by the superintendent personally and he controls it with intelligence and with all the attention the circumstances call for. If there are only signs of a moderate agitation in the head, the shower is confined to letting cold water drip on the patient's head, to provide gentle cooling, as much by the contact of this liquid as by the resultant constant evaporation, something which perhaps gives better results than putting snow on the top of the head as is done in England.

272. What confusion there is in expressions, unless the way they should be understood is not precisely determined! It is not enough to prescribe the shower vaguely if one does not carefully determine the circumstances for its application. All the preliminaries to its use and the precautions to be taken need to be specified. Care must be taken to indicate the areas on which the stream of water is to be successively or intermittently directed, as well as the exceptions which preclude its use or restrict its duration and force. Omitting the latter can lead to a double impression of bitter cold and a violent impact on the head, and extraordinary pain there. Other sympathetic effects also result in the region of the stomach, the liver and the lungs, as direct experiments have proved (4). What exasperation and what tones of despair must this tumultuous collection of most heartbreaking sensations not provoke! At the Salpêtrière, however, the word shower must awaken completely opposite ideas. It is never entrusted to servant girls who could make a cruel game of it or a means of taking secret revenge. Care has been taken to eliminate any source of terror from it, and even to familiarise the patients with the procedure, laughingly recalling the threat of a little sprinkling of water on the head to those whose reason is not completely distracted and who are just having some setback. The superintendent himself, going through the sewing room where the convalescent patients are gathered, sometimes makes a joke about it. Moreover he only ever gives a shower towards the end of a bath at the temperature of 22 to 24 degrees on the Réaumur thermometer, and it is never prolonged more than one or two minutes, reducing it to a very fine spray directed successively on different parts of the head. In winter the patient is immediately afterwards put in one of the beds in a small room next to that of the baths, and in summer she is taken back to her own bed. If she complains she is consoled,

---

[2] *1 line = 3.175 mm – Ed.*

encouraged and reminded that if she has been made to suffer a little this was only to restore her more quickly to good health. It is in general a false system to sustain an atmosphere of terror, seeking to annoy deranged patients for no reason, and provoking their natural irascibility. On the contrary, one should try hard to create calm as a fundamental point of treatment. At the Salpêtrière, rigour and firmness are only used to subdue the patient, return her to order and make her docile. As soon as she is subdued and resigned, and her reason begins to come back and make her accept her faults, then everything changes for her and she has nothing but gentle and kindly manners awaiting her.

IV. TREATMENT TO BE FOLLOWED DURING THE FIRST PHASE OF MANIACAL INSANITY

273. An establishment devoted to deranged patients can combine the benefits of its situation with those of a large enclosure and spacious and convenient premises. Something fundamental is missing if because of the internal layout it is not possible to isolate the patients depending on whether they are in the phase of extreme intensity of symptoms, or the phase of marked improvement, or of convalescence. The layout must also make it possible to prevent them from communicating with one another. This is as much to prevent relapses and facilitate observation of all the in-house regulations as to avoid unexpected changes which are in no way part of the even course of the illness but can hamper its progress and can sometimes even set up insurmountable obstacles. The methodical separation of the patients depending on the three stages already mentioned greatly facilitates efforts to take the respective steps for their feeding, hygiene, psychological care and their successive advance towards recovery or maintenance in their current state. This lays the basis for a kind of permanent school for learning about the different disturbances of understanding and their various slight distinctions depending on recognisable features. Can the observant doctor anywhere else learn and correctly apply the fundamental rules of treatment and familiarise himself with the different degrees of impairment of reason? And is there anywhere else where he can learn to recognise those degrees of impairment which respond more or less quickly just to time and diet, those which constitute the greatest obstacle to their cure because of being deep-rooted, and finally those which demand the use of certain medications even for the judicious and enlightened individual who wishes neither to overrate their effects nor to overlook their benefits?

274. Recent maniacal insanity resulting from accidental causes can initially take different forms (paragraph 152) but constant observation shows that, when nothing obstructs its course and it is successfully supported by careful management (paragraph 150), the symptoms only retain their full intensity for a certain time. It also shows that the method of driving the disability to an advanced degree with blood-lettings and strict starvation only disrupts its course, makes this longer and sometimes recurrent, and may even lead to a state of stupor and a kind of idiocy. If the patient is very violent, one should just set oneself to breaking up his impetuous fieriness and contain his struggles by restricting the movements of his arms and legs with a camisole attached to the wood of the bed with straps (5). This should usually only go on for a few hours, and then a strait-jacket can be used which just restricts the arms and does not interfere with walking about during the course of the treatment. If there is just

a frisky maniacal state without any danger, freedom of movement is similarly allowed all day to let over-agitated mobility evaporate, so to speak, and especially to calm the extreme irascibility which stems from the derangement and which is likely to be merely aggravated by seclusion and restraint.

275. An observant doctor cannot confuse maniacal insanity with what is called malignant or ataxic fever, which is very dangerous as is shown by examples sometimes seen in the mental patients' sick room. So one should not go by the febrile appearances which deranged patients often exhibit in the early stages, such as pallor or redness of the face, a rapid pulse and very fetid smell, since this state soon responds to diluted and acidulated drinks. Moreover, this state is very often the effect of rigorous starvation first imposed on the deranged patients, which they are forced to continue for a long time even though regular observation shows that they are generally very voracious. Because of this they also often develop a scrawny delirium which complicates the original disturbance and adds to its violence. One of the first objectives to be fulfilled on their arrival in the hospice is to provide them with plenty of food. Then just with careful management, a most favourable change is often seen to take place within a fortnight. One of the most striking examples of this abuse is that of a lady who had been bled several times and condemned at home for over a month under the doctor's orders to a diet which was so rigorous that she was not even allowed to have any lean broth in the torments of her ravenous hunger. She had gone to the extreme of chewing and swallowing several handkerchiefs and was in a state of extreme languor when she was transferred to the hospice. A start was made by letting her have the kinds of food she longed for most, and she was given moderate sized but frequent meals. Her delirium, which had been so furious at home with her family that four very strong men could hardly keep her in her bed, subsided significantly. Towards the eighth day she was allowed to wander freely in the infirmary with just a strait-jacket. She continued to be provided with the most substantial food – dairy produce and chocolate for lunch, fatty soups, meat and fish for diner with a few plates of vegetables, and in the evening cooked fruit or jam. Towards the fifteenth day she was given freedom of movement and she was at the stage of walking about in the courtyards in just a frock coat like the convalescent patients.

276. The treatment and support of deranged patients in the first stage of the illness is an amalgamation of several physical and mental measures. Their isolation from the family environment, and the manner of controlling them, is adapted according to their particular state. Attention is paid to feeding them and clearing the stomach if it appears to be over-loaded. Care is taken to end their seclusion as soon as this is possible and getting them to breath fresh outside air all day. Complete or limited freedom of movement is granted to them as long as they are not dangerous. Acidulated drinks with which their thirst and inner ardour are counteracted are supplied for them. The art of grasping their first lucid moments to encourage and calm them, special study of their individual character and their abnormal ideas, and finally the closest surveillance to eliminate everything which could exasperate them whilst at the same time opposing their lapses with inflexible firmness are all important. Their agitation, however violent, does not generally thwart matters for it stems from the nature of the illness, and all the means of holding it in check are provided for. One tries to produce general relaxation with gentle medicaments of slow-acting effect, reduce vital energy with mucilaginous emulsified or acidulated drinks, intermixed at inter-vals with laxatives to prevent the effects of constipation which is habitual for them, and to

correct insomnia with some light sedative To these internal remedies the use of temperate baths is added, taken on alternate days (paragraph 203), sometimes with a gentle shower at the end of the bath. Nothing is hurried or rushed. From time to time all medicaments are suspended for a few days to allow nature to develop her protective powers, and then those measures which can support her are resumed in turn. The pressure of fluids towards the head is thus gradually reduced, slowly advancing towards the intended end whilst leaving nothing to chance. The bouts of agitation and rambling gradually calm down, the lucid moments become more frequent and the patient, on becoming fit to pass from the first to the second division, is ready for further improvements.

277. Just setting out the general rules of treatment leaves out the modifications which may have to be made and the considerations needed in particular cases over a host of accessory circumstances. Would a plethoric young person who was subject to haemorrhages be managed indiscriminately in the same way as a weak patient who was exhausted and subject to spasmodic infections? And could a venesection which would be useful for one not be out of place and harmful for the other? Most deranged patients of either sex obtain great relief from temperate baths, but a few can only bear cold baths. Would one use exactly the same methods for a breakdown caused by fright in a young person as for that which can be brought on by what is known as the change of life? Would one not give consideration, in selecting treatment, to maniacal insanity coming from the revulsion at a patch of dry skin, erysipelas or any other rash? Quite opposite excesses can equally trigger a maniacal delirium such as a very hard-working life on the one hand or an apathetic state on the other, an enforced chastity or the unbounded pursuit of pleasures, sobriety carried to the last stage of abstinence or the continually increasing abuse of alcoholic liqueurs. Through all these modifications to which the general method is subject, and which can in turn call for the use of antispasmodics (6), laxatives, tonics or relaxants, a fundamental principle which everything rallies around can always be seen. This is, that in this illness as in many others, nature tends to cure and to restore the functions of understanding to normal (paragraph 200), apart from incurable cases about which I will speak afterwards. It is just a matter of keeping faithful to the general laws of good health, encouraging supportive measures and allowing them time to take effect. Thus, for example, in maniacal insanity produced as a consequence of confinements, with milk secretion disturbed or diverted to the nerve roots, the necessity has been suspected of applying a vesicant to the nape of the neck, and repeated experience confirms the efficacy of this practice every day.

278. 'Medical books,' Montesquieu exclaims, 'those monuments to nature's fragility and the power of science which make us tremble when they treat even the slightest indisposition by indicating these can bring death in their train, but which accord us complete security when they speak of the virtue of the remedies as if we were immortal!' Should this discriminating critic's jibe, so applicable to a great mass of medical writings adorning or overloading our libraries, not come back to mind when in works on maniacal insanity one constantly hears the futile terms *brain disturbance, preparation of the humours prior to their evacuation, a focal source of bad matter, so-called revulsion or repulsion* etc? Are these same philosophical reflections proposed for a large inventory of powders, extracts, juleps, syrups, potions, topicals etc designed to overcome mental alienation? And what should we think of the law so religiously observed right up to our days of repeated blood-lettings with no distinction between the underlying causes, sex and individual constitution, species of insanity and

the stage of the illness? And is it right to mix up the true results of observation with the discrepancies of a doctrine which stems from prejudices, the spirit of hypothesis, the rule of pedantry and ignorance, and sometimes the authority of famous names?

279. A deluge of tedious writings and useless compilations, the ridiculous language of the schools and the passion to explain everything are aberrations common to almost all the sciences – but what do Aristotle's ancient doctrine and Descartes' vortex matter to modern physics? Has medicine itself, in the judgement of men of the severest taste, not set the example since its cradle of the wisest and most circumspect progress and of healthy and rigorous logic? And who can deny these qualities to Hippocrates? Does what some ancient authors like Aretæus, Celsus and Cælius Aurelianus write on maniacal insanity not bear the most refined spirit of observation? In contrast, carefully study certain authors such as Forestus, Horstiius, Plater, Valeriola etc on their scientific explanations and the extreme excess of their polypharmacy, and what precious facts have they passed on to us about this illness! Even more precise ones are found in collections in the Academies, periodical publications and personal compendia of observations. Feriar, and Dr Perfect in England, and Laughter in Germany, have carried out trials on a few simple remedies and they also show that research is truly under way. The progress I follow further extends the realm of science and shows within what boundaries the prescription of medicaments should be restricted. Often judicious waiting, supported by mental or physical management, can be enough. In other cases the illness is beyond all resources. The following then is a list of the tasks I have set myself to fulfil in the present state of our knowledge: To give the greatest importance to the history of mental alienation and to make a strict distinction between the different species of alienation, so as to avoid administering treatment uselessly or hazardously. To bring the management and internal regulation of nursing homes and hospices for mental patients under clear rules, since it is impossible to treat them successfully in the bosom of their families. To make a case for the need for premises that enable the methodical separation of these patients according to the stages of the illness clearly appreciated. To put diligent supervision, enlightened care and strict maintenance of order in the department at the forefront. To indicate the simple remedies which experiment seems to authenticate, and the precautions, stage of the illness and the species of alienation which can ensure their success. And, finally, to learn to reserve the use of some powerful remedies, which other circumstances could render superfluous, harmful or reckless, for extreme cases and for those hitherto regarded as incurable.

280. A collection of the personal observations reported by doctors on the disturbances of imagination of melancholic patients, the illusions which dominate them and the expedients (7) of varying degrees of ingenuity tried out to cure them, would make an inexhaustible fund of quite surprising anecdotes. They might look like fairy tales if the hospices were not swarming with similar examples – all the more striking for being the stumbling block of all the resources which medicine has to offer. Melancholia consists, in the extreme intensity, of an idea which is exclusive and liable to absorb all the faculties of understanding, and this intensity is the reason why it is so difficult to eliminate. If one pretends to think in the same way as the patient he revels in his idea, whilst if one argues with him he gets angry. If his state stems from some physical trouble it may sometimes respond to laxatives, but often the resultant debility only augments and exacerbates it. It is only by combining the use of cinchona with opium that one can put right melancholia marked by atony and extreme

despondency, of which I could quote many examples. If suppression of a skin eruption or discharge is the cause, drainage or cautery becomes necessary. Feriar, when consulted by the friends of a young man who had sunk into the most profound melancholia, asked several questions regarding its causes. He learnt that, for several years the patient was subject each spring to a herpetic eruption on his back which extended up to his shoulder, and that the clearing up of this eruption had been the occasion of the onset of the illness: he prescribed drainage to the neck. From the third to the fourth day a discharge of foetid material developed. The mental state thereupon changed and successively improved. Complete recovery then followed as the result of sustained physical exercise, sea bathing and a tonic diet.

281. Melancholic delusions present yet more obstacles to a cure for nothing can be expected from the spontaneous efforts of nature, and mental treatment is needed to give strong support to physical measures. A certain set of ideas prevails which delights the imagination and binds itself to a dominant passion. There is a kind of enchantment which listens neither to pieces of advice nor to reprimands, and is often combined with extreme irascibility. One patient may dream of nothing but honours and dignities, another gets lost in mysterious religious notions; and some of them utterly refuse to eat. Something much gloomier occupies others – an irresistible urge for suicide. Whatever the exclusive ideas may be which seize the melancholic patient's mind, be they bizarre or reasonable, he often hangs onto them with an obstinacy which nothing can dispel, and which makes him indignantly reject any other idea which is suggested to him, whereas in every other respect his judgement is sound. It is even worse still when utterly bombastic pride and most exaggerated claims come to aggravate this sombre and atrabilious mood. A young man under my care in particular demonstrated a frigid and disdainful haughtiness, at times scarcely speaking a word. From the start I foresaw that he was completely incurable, which experience and the passage of time only confirmed. Just the opposite state, a humility which is more than Christian, poses no less difficulty for a cure unless one manages to get the upper hand of the melancholic patient's mind and completely win his confidence. An elderly nun with a weak and over-scrupulous character developed the habit of reproaching herself for the slightest omissions, thinking she was the most criminal woman. Why, she said, not take everything away from me, or punish me severely? Such was the constant subject of her objections and complaints in the hospice, and this one day attracted an abrupt response from the superintendent aimed at getting her to pull herself together (8). Thereupon she began to have misgivings and doubts about her situation, since a man full of uprightness was not concerned about it. She mistrusted herself, began to ask for enlightened advice and after that her recovery advanced rapidly.

282. Sometimes it is much less by medication than by mental means, and especially by active work, that the melancholic patient's sad ideas can be satisfactorily diverted, or indeed their incorrect associations changed; but how difficult it is to prevent relapses!

283. One day in one of the most turbulent periods of the Revolution, a workman expressed some thoughts in public about the judgement and sentencing of Louis XVI. His patriotism thereupon became suspect in his quarter and because of a few vague signs and a few threatening words whose anger he exaggerated, he went home one day trembling all over and in deep dismay. He could no longer sleep, his appetite was gone, he could not face work and was constantly full of fear. He ended up believing he was a victim destined to die. He was regarded as having become deranged and was transferred to the Bicêtre after

the usual treatment then given at the Hôtel-Dieu. The idea of being condemned to perish by the guillotine absorbed him night and day. He endlessly repeated that he was ready to meet his fate since nothing could save him. Regular work and doing his job (he was a coat tailor) seemed the most likely means of changing the vicious direction of his ideas, and the Administration was encouraged to grant him a small salary for repairing the clothes of other patients in the hospice. There was nothing to compare with his enthusiasm and ardour to make himself useful. He wasted no moment of the day and after working hard for about two months he appeared to be completely changed. There were no more grumbles, no reference to his so-called death sentence; he even spoke fondly about a six-year old child he had appeared to have forgotten, and he showed a strong desire to have his company. This reawakening of his sensitivity seemed to me to be a most promising sign and this source of happiness was restored to him. There was then nothing more he wanted; he always set to work with renewed pleasure and never ceased repeating that his child, who was always with him, was the joy of his life.

284. Experience has shown the effect of a few simple remedies for avoiding the return of melancholic bouts which lead to suicide, but it has often also shown their ineffectiveness, and at the same time the benefit of strong and vivid emotion in providing a solid and lasting change.

285. A workman with a sedentary job came to consult me towards the end of October 1783 because of loss of appetite, excessive and inexplicable sadness, and an overwhelming urge to go and throw himself into the Seine. Definite signs of a gastric disturbance led to some laxative drinks being prescribed and for a few days also some whey. His bowels became looser, and the melancholic patient, who was very little tormented by his destructive ideas during the winter, was altogether free of them in the summer, and his cure looked as if it was complete. But as autumn set in there was a further return of the problem. A sombre and darkened veil spread over the whole of nature, and there was an irresistible draw to the Seine to end his life. He said he was only held back by the thought of abandoning a child and a wife he cherished tenderly. This inner struggle between natural feelings and the frenzied delusion which armed him against his own existence was short-lived this time. There was soon firm evidence that he had carried out his disastrous intention, acting on his blind despair.

286. A man of letters who was prone to over-eating, and had recently been cured of tertiary malaria, began towards the autumn to sense all the horrors of an urge to suicide. With alarming calmness he weighed up the choice of different ways of killing himself. A journey he made to London seemed to build up the strength of his profound melancholia to a fresh level and the unshakeable resolve to cut short his life. He picked a time late at night and went onto one of the bridges in the capital to throw himself into the Thames. However, the moment he got there, thieves attacked him to rob him of what he had with him, which was actually virtually nothing. He became indignant and struggled to get free, but this was not without experiencing deep fear and great turmoil. The fight came to an end and at that moment a kind of revolution in the melancholic patient's mind took place. He forgot his original objective, returned home in the same state of distress as before, but completely rid of his sinister suicide plans. His cure was so complete that, living in Paris for ten years, and often reduced to precarious ways of living, he has never felt the least distaste for life (9).

This was a melancholic mental illness which yielded to the feeling of terror produced by an unexpected attack.

287. Blind credence in demonomania or the devil's influence should be hardly surprising in the writings of Wier[3], which were published around the middle of the seventeenth century and which are as relevant to theology as much as to medicine. These were errors of the times which should be pardoned in an author who was so careful in describing the formulas for exorcisms, the gift of predicting the future attributed to the Devil, the treacherous and cunning tricks he plays when taking human form, and the features of famous people he has borrowed in various places to show himself on earth. 'When a man', said the wise Richard Mead, 'tears up his clothes and walks about naked, strikes everybody he meets with terror, gives himself deep wounds, is so furious that he breaks the strongest chains, hides himself in the most lonely places and wanders about among tombs, and finally shouts out that he is possessed by the Devil; these are merely acts of madness, and that', he adds, 'is all what we are told is possession by the Devil boils down to'. And one only has to go into the hospices for the insane to reduce all these supposed possessions, or rather these imaginary ideas of melancholic or maniacally insane patients, to their true value. A convalescent patient employed as a servant girl was frightened by the threats of one of the other patients and on one of the following nights she was struck with the idea that the Devil had given her four slaps on the face. She even thought she saw him in the corner of her lodge under the bed sheet and blanket, which had rolled onto the ground as a result of her restless movements and great agitation. She was frozen with fear and at times uttered loud cries, finding herself in complete darkness and subject to all the illusions of her distracted imagination. The superintendent had the door opened, ordered a lighted candle to be brought and himself unrolled the piled-up linen to show her that the Devil was certainly not hidden underneath. He spoke firmly to this visionary, reminded her of the evidence of confidence she had always given him and exhorted her to keep calm. It was prudent not to leave her in a place where everything could bring back an unhappy memory to her and so she was transferred to another lodge. She was made to examine all parts of this so as to reassure herself thoroughly against the presence of the supposed Devil. A few baths and dilute drinks gradually calmed her melancholic delirium and this young person went back to her normal work.

288. It is known that once, at Besançon, the feast of Saint-Suaire was celebrated in the presence of a great assembly of deranged patients considered as possessed, who were brought from far away to be cured in the belief that the Devil could not fail to be driven from the bodies of the possessed by this religious ceremony. With an immense crowd of spectators seated in an amphitheatre round an elevated area, and some supposedly possessed people controlled by soldiers and agitated with movements of fury and frightening contortions, priests in ceremonial regalia proceeded gravely to the exorcisms. Inside the church, and out of the common view, there were the melodious sounds of warlike music. At a given signal, a kind of standard or blood-soaked flag in the name of Saint-Suaire was raised in the air and displayed at three different times to the sound of the cannon in the citadel. The profound commotion communicated itself to the assembled crowd, who cried out in great enthusiasm *miracle! miracle!* The pretentious and solemn spectacle was such that each year the cure of the possessed was ascribed to the effects of supernatural power. It is reasonable to rule out

---

[3] Joannis Weiri, *Opera omnia, in-4°*, Amsterdam, 1660.

anything supernatural from this ancient custom, even if there have been some cures, and just see in this the combined result of many strong impressions calculated to bring about a profound change in some deranged patients, dissipating the illusions of a distracted imagination.

V. ON THE USE OF REMEDIES OF VARYING ACTIVITY, DESIGNED TO SUPPORT GENERAL MEASURES OF TREATMENT

289. The use of hellebore for madness, the choice, preparation and administration of this plant, the preliminary remedies, due precautions to support its action and avoid harmful effects, were all a very important matter of doctrine for the ancients. Experience had shown that this drastic substance could sometimes produce violent over-purgation, intractable vomiting, convulsions, intestinal inflammation and even death. I go back, for knowledge about these details, to the articles *Hellebore, Helleborism,* which I have inserted in the Methodical Encyclopaedia. The disuse that this remedy has fallen into will no doubt give rise to few regrets, either because its administration is considered to have been reduced to blind empiricism or because it lacked any sound basis – that is to say, any historical knowledge of the symptoms and different species of mental alienation. Medicine, which is now enlightened by advances in chemistry and botany, is much more successful in the choice of laxatives and emetics, as it now has very simple ones, and their action can be precisely determined and not attended by any danger. But these medicaments must always be viewed as accessory means of treatment, which are now used with more discretion given our wider outlook and more reliable resources amongst the collection of other mental and physical measures. I have noted in speaking of bouts of periodic maniacal insanity that they are mostly preceded by a kind of constipation and extreme sensitivity of the intestinal tract, so that if a copious drink of a chicory decoction is given in time, with some purgative salt, freedom of the intestine is restored and all the forerunners of a further outburst of the attack are eliminated. This is a truth so well-known in the hospices and based on such a large number of cases, that a patient afflicted with these intestinal conditions has hardly been moved to the infirmary when he is given some of this laxative drink, and most often the next attack is averted, especially when the maniacal insanity is subject to irregular periods corresponding to seasonal variations. I have also very often noticed that spontaneous diarrhoea developing during the course of an attack of maniacal insanity, or when it is subsiding, has all the features of a crucial bowel movement and can be an omen of an imminent cure provided the patient is managed prudently; and on this point my observations are in agreement with those made in England.

290. The general spirit now prevailing in all the physical sciences must make the explanation of phenomena in medicine increasingly plain, but in eliminating all arbitrary reasoning the constant relationship which seems to exist between certain affections thought to be separate but which are in a kind of mutual linkage, needs no less to be recognised. Among these are disorders of the stomach and the abdomen, which correspond to lapses in understanding and angry fits of the will. The brain no doubt appears to be the seat of false feelings and illusions of judgement, but the stomach and the intestines sometimes exert a very strong influence over these derangements, and gradual changes brought about to the functions of

the latter visibly have very clear effects on the former. On this point one cannot be unaware of a general consistency between the ancient physicians and the best observers amongst the modern ones, be they French, English or German. Dr Perfect, who has published a wise collection of observations on mentally ill patients in England, generally combines the use of emetics, and often of purgatives, with other methods of treatment and recognises often that it is necessary to correct a stubborn constipation which is an effect of the illness and which in turn foments it. So he prescribes alternatively, with a warm bath, sodium tartrate and potassium tartrate, either alone in a barley concoction or combined with a sweet sugary substance such as manna. He has these drinks taken for two or three days and then suspends them for one or two weeks and repeats them again in the same way. Sometimes he has them taken in an almond emulsion, depending on the circumstances of age, sex or individual sensitivity. Elsewhere he speaks of these subsidiary means in moderate terms and has looked upon them as a sort of appendix to the other general methods of treatment. The customary drinks he prescribes in these cases are guided by similar views. These are sometimes simple or wine flavoured whey, barley concoction with Arabic gum and sugar, and a light lemonade or orangeade, and sometimes other similar mucilaginous, sweetened or acidulated drinks.

291. Observation in France has led to the same results, which therefore should not be dismissed. In this hospice for mentally ill patients, as in Dr Esquirol's establishment, each set up nearly ten years ago, the habitual use of the same sweet drinks and baths, interspersed from time to time with a laxative or cathartic of greater or lesser strength depending on the circumstances, is also adopted. There is solely this difference in the second of these establishments, that the people undergoing treatment generally come from rich families, and pleasant drinks, sweetened water, lemonade, orangeade, barley decoctions with different syrups, almond emulsions and whey either nitrated or mixed with some saline or purgative substance can all be provided there in abundance. This is something which cannot happen in a national establishment, where order and strict economy must prevail. In other respects there are in France the same matters of regret as in England, since in both countries the deranged patients are often not given regular and combined treatment until after they have gone through the harsh ordeals of confused polypharmacy managed in an empirical manner. Thus, for example, the English doctor says that a patient, before coming under his care, had been bled four times in three months, and that vesicatories had been applied to the occiput, back and arms, drainage had been performed to the nape of the neck, light laxatives had been followed by violent cathartics, and foetid gums and other sedatives had had no effect, nor had emetics, scarified cupping or cold baths. Instead of diminishing wayward flights of reason, all these different methods that were hazardedly tried merely augmented it. It would be easy to quote several more examples taken from the same author, and to liken them to what happens in France before admission to the hospice creating such an obstacle to proper treatment. I go by them all in silence, for there is no difficulty in imagining them, and they all spring from the same cause – a general ignorance of the true principles of the treatment of mental alienation. But it is important to draw attention to a very grievous symptomatic complication, a feeling of burning heat, which sometimes develops during attacks of maniacal insanity or as they fade in autumn. I have often had occasion to see this condition amongst the patients at Bicêtre (10), and sometimes it became so violent that I have seen some of them roll on the ground with signs of the most extreme distress, and die a few days later without sedatives or mucilaginous preparations having any effect in arresting the disastrous progress of this grave intestinal disorder. At the same time considerable

dryness of the skin was noted. As the hospice at Bicêtre lacked the benefit of providing baths for them, at that earlier stage I only had drinks, which were inadequate to prevent or cure this condition. A lucky chance, or rather an odd circumstance, led me to turn to ordinary bramble leaves (*rubus dumetorum*, L.) taken as a decoction, and the first trials gave such successful results that the staff were sent into the countryside to gather a reliable store of these leaves so as never to be without them when they were needed, and to be able to remedy the problem as soon as it appeared with one or even two pints of this concoction taken daily. I must undoubtedly attribute the rarity of these symptomatic diarrhoeas, or the capacity to counteract them just as they appear, to the frequent use made by patients of baths at all stages of their illness. However, in some intractable cases, particularly when patients who have recently arrived at the hospice are attacked with this intestinal disturbance following a rigorous diet or stubborn food refusal, this simple medicament has been used most successfully. A lady who had lapsed into maniacal insanity following childbirth had been submitted at home to a rigorous diet for more than a month. As a consequence, by the time she reached the hospice she had contracted a diarrhoeal complication which filled her with worry and had already reduced her to the last stage of exhaustion and debility. A few days later she was started on the bramble leaf decoction, of which she took nearly a pint daily, and eight days later a diminution in the diarrhoea was noted, so marked that this only occurred during the night and soon came to an end.

292. The course which Dr Locher, physician of a hospice for deranged patients in Vienna, Austria, has followed deserves to be known about because of the trials he has made of certain remedies, even though the results were uncertain. He seems to dismiss any internal regulations, the historical study of the symptoms of alienation, its division into distinct species, the isolation of patients into separate departments and pathological anatomy research as all counting for nothing. He only accepts the general distinction of insane delirium and melancholia, with no differentiation in the treatment. Casting a quick glance at the general ways used to treat this illness, he very succinctly reviews the use of emetics, diluted and acidulated drinks, blood-lettings, vesicatories and, finally, of narcotics or opium preparations which he gives at night to avoid insomnia. If the illness persists, he adds, one must promptly pass on to more effective treatment for fear of it becoming chronic, and with this in mind he has tried using antispasmodics. Musk was first tested out on six maniacal patients (he says nothing about the character of the maniacal insanity) and was given from 15 grains (13 decigrams) down to one scruple (7 decigrams) as a bolus with syrup of kermes. Sweating was then promoted by subsidiary means. This remedy was continued for three months, without however achieving any result other than to impregnate the whole hospice with a very strong and disagreeable odour. The use of this antispasmodic was then replaced with camphor, whose efficacy according to Locher derived from its combination with vinegar acid in a mixture. From then he was led to trying distilled vinegar which he had taken after dinner at a dose of one and a half ounces daily, in dessert spoonfuls every quarter of an hour. Nine patients were cured in the space of one, two or, at the very most, three months. But it is clear these trials were incomplete and they have contributed little to medical progress, owing to the failure to identify the specific character of the illness.

293. The apparent contradiction in the results of experiments on the value of camphor indicates the necessity of not limiting oneself to the generic characteristics of the illnesses, but of always going back to those of the species. Kenneir reports, in the Philosophical

Transactions[4], four examples of maniacal insanity cured by the administration of camphor. Feriar, another English doctor, in contrast says he has used it in all kinds of doses for this illness without obtaining any success. Locher, the Vienna doctor, is of the same opinion following his own experience. What does such a divergence of opinions show except that some have used camphor for certain species of insanity and others for very different species or varieties. Amongst the English doctors the one who has used camphor under different forms most consistently and most repeatedly is Dr Perfect *(Annals of Insanity)*. He most commonly prescribes it combined with sugar and vinegar as follows:

Pr. Camphor	50 grains
Sugar	6–8 ounces
Warm Vinegar	12 ounces

Make a mixture: to be taken by the dessert spoonful at intervals, especially in the evening and at night.

294. But as taking this remedy has often been combined with purgative drinks, how can its efficacy be accurately assessed? Thus, for example, in one of these cases the doctor had inserted a drainage between the shoulders, in the direction of the spine, which yielded a heavy discharge. At the same time he had the patient take, every three days for six successive weeks, an emulsion of almond in which manna and potassium tartrate were dissolved, and a drink made up of a barley decoction and manna solution was also added. In the morning on intermediate days, at different times, a glass of the preceding mixture was taken, to which a few drops of a mixture of volatile alkali and compound tincture of lavender were added. It is astonishing that in a century when chemistry has spread so much light on pharmacology, and where the study of natural history should have communicated a true observational talent to doctors, anybody could allow himself to use such a complicated remedy to which it is so difficult to assign any direct effects. The same doctor has commented that in the space of ten days this patient had become calmer and sensible, and that she had obtained a rest appropriate for her recovery at night. That may be true, but how to establish a relationship between the effect and such an impenetrable cause? By distancing ourselves from all this monstrous polypharmacy and keeping to clear principles it is recognised that camphor possesses a sedative quality, and that the acids have this more or less pronounced property, and finally that sugar just acts as an intermediary to facilitate the solution of the camphor in the vinegar. So I use the aforementioned mixture in cases of severe maniacal excitation. I have a few spoonfuls given in the evening to calm the symptoms, and this gives favourable results. But as one must be prepared for all circumstances, and sometimes cannot overcome the revulsion some patients bear for this remedy which is disagreeable, I substitute a sugared or honeyed almond emulsion in which a half or a whole grain of aqueous extract of opium is dissolved for some patients. This gives results which are more certain and less variable. It is only by employing single remedies, or at the most remedies combined in twos when their properties have been noted separately, that one can reach definite results when treating the particular species or individual variety of insanity one seeks to cure. It is in this connection that I approve of the association of cinchona with opium proposed by Dr Feriar for melancholia in which there is atony and extreme despondency, as well as for secondary idiocy following the over-energetic treatment of maniacal insanity. This doctor mentions a young man of

---

[4] Abridged from *Transact. Philosoph. Méd. et Chirurg*, Paris, 1791.

sixteen years who had a kind of taciturn delirium with distorted features, yellow skin and a weak and faltering pulse. He prescribed two gros's[5] of an electuary of cinchona with two grains of opium for him, to be taken morning and night. Little change was noted for a few days, but in the following fortnight progress towards recovery was very pronounced and the cure became complete. The remainder of the illness, indicated by swelling of the legs, responded to massage with mustard powder.

295. The criticism rightly made of doctors for their blind faith in a sumptuous array of medicaments and the weakness of their often illusionary powers will not distract the man who is, on the contrary, very restrained in their use and aspires to the true principles of science. Such a doctor draws his main resources from the accumulation of all the physical and mental factors likely to lead to a favourable change, after having in addition thoroughly delved into the case histories of the progress and different stages of the illnesses. I hope that reading this work will show that these fruitful ideas are no strangers to me. Medication comes into the general plan as a secondary means and it is only then that they are opportune, which is something quite rare. It will be easy to see the truth of this remark when subsequently considering the treatment of mental alienation in its various aspects, be it according to age, sex, the successive stages of this illness, its recent or long-standing duration and, finally, its frequent association with hypochondria or other illnesses.

VI. CONSIDERATIONS RELATING TO MEDICAL TREATMENT IN THE SECOND AND THIRD STAGES OF MANIACAL DELIRIUM

296. A particular example reported in full detail (paragraph 150) has enabled the general course of maniacal insanity, and its different stages, to be appreciated. I then (paragraph 187) showed the internal arrangements in the hospice for deranged patients and how they had been divided into three different departments depending on the extreme of maniacal insanity (11), its decline or on convalescence. Throughout the Fourth Section the internal regulations relating to the different stages of maniacal insanity, or different forms of mental alienation, were set out. In a word, I have just submitted the different methods used to remedy maniacal insanity considered in its first stage, and the results of enlightened experience, to an impartial scrutiny. Now I pass on to the same medical treatment in relation to the second and third stages of the same illness.

297. The premises allocated to the second section of deranged women (paragraph 189) – that is to say, those whose delirium is declining – provide the general benefits to be expected. It is not enough, in order for them to be transferred there, that just a few lucid moments and some return of tranquillity should have been noticed. A still more promising change is needed, the sense of a return to their own existence, an end to the earlier agitation, a resumption of previous habits and the replacement of the preceding state of agitation or fury with only a few momentary lapses. There is also sometimes a vague restlessness which rises up in irregular movements, running about with no particular object and with disordered and disjointed perambulations. During this intermediary stage, or rather during this progressive advance towards the complete restoration of reason, these patients with diminished understanding

---

[5] 'gros' is an old French measure of weight equal to one-eighth of an 'once' (the French ounce) – Ed.

stay in their lodges, in turn standing and sitting, but unconstrained and with complete freedom of movement barring some transient agitation from an incidental cause. They walk about under the trees or in an adjacent spacious enclosure and some, getting closer to the convalescent stage, share in the work of the servant girls, busying themselves in drawing water, removing dirt from the lodges, washing the cobblestones and carrying out other more or less energetic heavy tasks. If any return of symptoms of agitation, or appearances of a relapse likely to spread tumult and disorder around them is detected among these women, this is immediately remedied with baths or diluted drinks. If this state persists, they are returned to the treatment courtyard, whereas if the improvement is maintained and restoration of reason becomes more evident, the trial period is shortened and early progress to the convalescents' dormitory is anticipated. Continuous experience has shown how in this state of weakness of understanding, one single mistake, one premature visit by a relative or friend or indeed any distressing piece of news, can sometimes stir up strong emotions and bring back the former disturbance of reason. A woman who was calm and reasoning for over a month received a very upsetting letter, which was hidden in a bag of laundry, from her family. From then on she could not sleep, her agitation gradually increased and a severe delirium developed. She spent nearly six months in the treatment courtyard before any improvement could be seen. Calm and reason then slowly came back and this woman returned to her family after a long convalescence.

298. One of the most valuable changes brought about in the hospice is the addition of large isolated dormitories to accommodate the convalescent patients and ensure complete restoration of their reason before their return to the outside world: these are the premises intended for the third division of the deranged patients. These dormitories, where complete propriety prevails and which are, furthermore, well aired, contain about eighty beds. They are subdivided into four sections which allows free communication between them, and which has the advantage of providing a staged transition to confirmed convalescence. There is the greatest calm everywhere in this part of the asylum and, to make this more certain, the convalescent patients are engaged in working in a large knitting and sewing room (paragraph 188), and are encouraged to compete for a little pay. One of the fundamental principles is to keep away any matter for discontent or acrimony and any grounds for chagrin or worry. The gentlest and most industrious servant girls are carefully selected, mealtimes are very punctual, meals are carefully prepared, there is the closest surveillance to avoid any subject of dissention or turmoil and constant attention so that women with an untameable or cantankerous character, or those who are on the point of relapsing, are sent back to the second division. One must also be continuously on guard against premature discharges. Constant experience shows how much these different things must be carefully supervised. A young convalescent patient suddenly became agitated during the night. She left her bed, was talking volubly, now and then giving high-pitched shrieks, and conveying something of a fright to her neighbours. From that night three other convalescent patients slipped back into a temporary state of disturbance and this made it necessary to send them back to the second division; and the young girl back to the first, to receive treatment once more. No doubt it is very agreeable, at this convalescent stage, to be visited by neighbours, renew old relationships, take an interest in some family affairs and so to prepare for an early return to society, but it is also useful to point out the drawbacks sometimes associated with these meetings. One young victim of an unfortunate love affair had just regained full possession of her reason. Her neighbours thought she was completely cured, strongly pleaded for her

discharge, and far from accepting the advice they were given to defer this for a few days, they returned in strength to smuggle her out. However she was recognised at the gate and taken back into the hospice, which annoyed her considerably and caused her to relapse.

299. I return again to the private establishment that I mentioned, which is managed following similar principles. It is during these family visits or walks that Dr Esquirol skilfully applies mental treatment as the mental alienation subsides, and during convalescence. He consoles one, encourages another, and converses with a melancholic patient seeking to dispel his imaginary illusions. He studies the coherence of their ideas and tries to disentangle the unwitting disorders which maintain their distracted reason. Sometimes he counters their false prejudices whilst sometimes he appears to go along with their exaggerated opinions, or even to participate in their frivolous whims in order to win their good will and thereby open up the way for a successful outcome with sound advice. As soon as the patient shows unequivocal signs of convalescence, he is admitted to the communal table with the doctor, and after a few days of this test he goes on to the part of the establishment intended for convalescent patients, where he stays for a shorter or longer period to confirm his complete recovery. There, with no frills, the accommodation combines strict propriety and everything which could be pleasant for the patients, together with the facility to walk about in an adjacent garden. There is then complete liberty, the domestic servants' influence ends and the doctor lives informally with his convalescent patients. They have lunch, play billiards and have games together. Some of the evening is spent in a large room to enjoy music, and when no problems are anticipated the patient is freed to go to walk with his servant in the Botanical Gardens, or go by carriage into the country.

300. The sudden switch from a state of delirium to sound reason is a bad sign, for this is the usual character of periodic maniacal insanity, which is most often incurable. An intermediate state, and an improvement which come about in stages, indicates a sound reestablishment of mental faculties so long as nothing disturbs this natural tendency. This is the purpose of the innumerable precautions taken in the convalescent patients' division, and the strict surveillance exercised to catch the least features of a relapse the minute they appear and take steps to stop any further developments. Care is also taken, as soon as these signs are recognised (Second Section), to use temperate baths or some gentle shower, prescribe mucilaginous or acidulated drinks, and resort to gentle laxatives, either an emetic water or a purgative salt solution etc to correct the constipation which is then common. Particular circumstances can also call for the application of leeches or a vesicatory and sometimes a light sedative if nervous excitation is too evident. It is mainly by gentle and consoling talk that hope should be sustained, courage raised, early discharge from the hospice anticipated and every true subject of dissatisfaction and dissention dismissed. Everything is in order if, despite minor agitation, the facial features retain their tranquillity and the taste for work remains. But if the patient remains idle and reticent, or if his features become animated and nothing settles his fickle restlessness, and, above all, if for the slightest thing he gives way to the fieriest fits of anger and becomes completely exasperated, then there is everything to be feared for the future. In this case the treatment, with any appropriate modifications, has to begin all over again.

301. One of the commonest prejudices against the treatment of maniacal insanity, or rather an idea which has become popular, is that this illness is always subject to relapses and

that any cure is only apparent. Consequently this is one of the points on which it has been important to stick to the result of a long series of carefully assessed and recorded facts, and this is to be found in the following section. In the meantime it suffices to observe that these relapses are a consequence either of premature discharges from the hospice pressed for by the family, from a subsequent state of distress and from bad treatment received within the family or, finally, because the illness had already become periodic for many years and must be looked upon as incurable. An example will show to what harsh extremes convalescent patients may be reduced on their discharge, and whether there is then any doubt that the illness has been precipitated a second time by a physical or mental cause. A young girl treated in the hospice, after a state of complete delirium of several months, was so well recovered that she remained employed looking after other patients for more than three months without showing the least sign of distraction. So she left the hospice and went to the house where she had previously been in service, but being rejected by her previous masters under the pretext that the maniacal insanity could come back again, she unsuccessfully sought other means of support and became deeply distressed. As she was of Jewish origin she hoped to find other means of subsistence in Strasbourg amongst the Jews, and she undertook this journey exposed to all the vicissitudes and in a state of complete destitution. She encountered nothing but refusals, abandonment and scorn everywhere, and ended by being taken back to the hospice reduced to extreme despondency and having fallen into a melancholic stupor. Dismay showed on her face. She thought she was doomed to perish on the scaffold, causing her to sigh deeply and beg for mercy. During the first two months she ate very little, stayed crouching at the back of her lodge and obstinately refused to go out. Gradually she seemed to come out of this state of stupor and at intervals showed transient glimmers of reason which became increasingly prolonged. Efforts were made to dissipate her fears and she was given to understand that she would not be obliged to leave the hospice. She regained her courage on reminding herself of the good care already lavished on her and soon afterwards she regained her cheerfulness and enjoyment of work and became fully convalescent. One cannot but be moved by the fate of many mental patients, so often victims, even after they have been cured, of peoples' prejudices and ignorance.

VII. CRITICAL ENDING OF ALIENATION SOMETIMES PRODUCED BY SPONTANEOUS ERUPTIONS

302. There is wide agreement on how medicine should be envisaged amongst wise minds and this conformity, one imagines, does not consist in multiplying the formulae of medications. It rather lies in skilfully combining the resources of mental and physical management to produce a slow and lasting change, especially in chronic illnesses. In some this combination is used to promote the appropriate preservative effects of nature to end with an unexpected cure. Ancient and modern physicians have recognised that mental alienation sometimes comes to an end with varicose veins, rectal bleeding, dysentery, spontaneous haemorrhage or an intermittent fever. But these successful endings, either slow and gradual, or by a sudden and unexpected outburst, are certainly not the outcome of a sedentary and apathetic life and a doleful and silent despondency. They result from an approach wisely adapted to the character and constitution of the patient, the particular species of the derangement and its stage of development, and after that the powerful influence of physical exercise, music,

reading, change of place and travels (12). Almost all the facts reported in this Treatise attest that the derangement resulting from a mental cause responds most often to the salutary effects of nature when this is not obstructed. Two examples will show what these resources are, even when the cause of the derangement is material or physical.

303. A young man involved in hunting under the former government was given the task of rubbing mercurial ointment onto the skin of some mangy dogs. He contracted a kind of scabies from this with small pimples, rubbed himself with citrus or sulfur ointment and seemed to be cured of this skin infection. But soon afterwards he became completely disturbed, behaved in an eccentric way and embarked upon exuberant and disjointed chatter with no coherence in ideas, whilst at other times being lost in sombre taciturnity. The usual Hôtel-Dieu treatment although continued for two months failed, bringing about no change. He was taken to a boarding house in the Saint-Antoine suburb for the winter of 1788, where I had the opportunity of seeing him. At first ordinary methods were tried, with relaxing and purgative drinks and a few sedatives in the evening, and he was more tranquil. In the spring he had a prolonged course of purified vegetable juice and lukewarm baths, and it was after this that an erratic inflammatory affection spread to different parts of his skin. Sometimes a red swelling was noticed over the central part of his tibia. Topical emollients were applied but, instead of forming an abscess with pus, this swelling disappeared after four or five days. Large pustules appeared successively on the arms, thighs and legs, and then dried up after a little oozing. The chest was also successively affected with a feeling of suffocation, difficulty in breathing and the appearances of a kind of asthma, and this seemed to clear the head, for periods of calm were noted. Eight months went by with these incidents without any lasting noticeable change in the power of his intellectual functions. The patient was one day taking a lukewarm bath when a swelling in his right parotid region was noticed. The next day the swelling was hard and red, and emollients were applied. There were signs of fluctuation on the seventh day and, following incision with a lancet, pus was drained. There was copious suppuration for the next twenty days, with formation of a scar. The workings of nature here were in no way equivocal, for the ending of the abscess was the moment of the full return of reason. The patient left his boarding house with completely sound reason and I have seen him four years later leaving no doubt about his cure.

304. I have also witnessed another example of the ending of melancholia with jaundice. A jeweller suffered a bout of maniacal insanity for no known cause and was taken to a boarding house in the Saint-Antoine suburb where I was often called (this was in 1786). He was in a kind of gentle and tranquil delirium and was walking almost all the time in the garden or in his room, speaking in a low voice, with a faint smile. He responded accurately to the questions that were put to him, ate normally and was very peaceful during the night. Bouts of deep melancholia developed during the spring and in the autumn. Then, for one and a half to two months there would be a sombre taciturnity, a refusal to answer when questioned, an altered facial expression and a kind of lurid colour. At each of these seasons he had purgative drinks, cold baths and showers, and then purified plant juice. These remedies only led to a transient improvement. They were continued for five years without detectable and lasting progress in his mental state. Jaundice suddenly appeared towards the middle of October in the year 1791, for no apparent cause and as if through a salutary act of nature. Just diluted or acidulated drinks with lemon juice were taken and the jaundice gradually cleared up after two months, since when his reason has been restored without any relapse.

VIII. DIFFICULTY AND IMPORTANCE OF DECIDING, IN PARTICULAR CASES, WHETHER DERANGEMENT IS CURABLE: A REMARKABLE EXAMPLE

305. The possibility of curing mental alienation in a given case is one of those questions to which the answer may have grave implications as well as being difficult and complicated. Experience has no doubt shown, be it in England or in France, that it is quite common to see religious melancholy, maniacal insanity complicated by epilepsy, idiotism, dementia, and regular periodic maniacal insanity go on for a whole lifetime. But would prudence allow anyone to pronounce on their absolute incurability? Even in cases of irregular periodic maniacal insanity, which offer so many favourable chances of a cure (paragraph 39), what a lot of circumstances there are which can get in the way! Nevertheless, it is the judgement of the doctors that is called for first and from this can follow a legal ban, a divorce or the passing of an inheritance or large fortune (13) over to different hands – and sometimes a crown. What extensive knowledge and discernment is needed to grasp the true character of the mental derangement and to pronounce upon the future in these cases! What moral standards, despite every temptation, are needed to avoid obeying any extraneous impulse! I am going to give a few examples where the decision was simpler and easier.

306. A gardener who had been married for a few years began to be tormented by jealousy, suspecting his wife of having an affair with a priest. He took to drowning his sorrows in drink, sank into a violent state of maniacal insanity and was taken to the Bicêtre after the former usual treatment at the Hôtel-Dieu. He had more bouts over several months, but during his calm intervals he enjoyed complete reason and he got to sharing in the duties of the staff. It was then easier for him to overindulge in drink and during his excesses he felt the return of all the fury and storms of his earlier jealousy. His wife demanded a divorce and I had to give a verdict on whether there still remained any hope of a cure. The likelihood that the patient would have fresh attacks in his own home, his tendency to drunkenness and the acts of fury and violence of which he was capable left me with no hesitation, and I was of the opinion that his seclusion should continue so as not to compromise the safety of his family.

307. An elderly merchant who had fallen on hard times as a result of shady deals ended in becoming deranged, but he was deluded on only one point: that of *getting rich from the business of billiards*. The least opposition to this idea made him furious. The free use of his reason which he showed over every other subject, but which was not enough to obtain a favourable certification from me, gave rise to endless complaints, petitions to the administrative bodies and pleas to ministers on the grounds that he was the victim of his wife against whom he shed curses and threats. Frequently repeated conversations had made me aware of his single delusion, and of his hateful and violent disposition. The story of this was passed on to the official authorities, with the grounds for my fears. This put an end to the series of hospice intrigues. A kind of senile dementia began to accompany his earlier distraction as this patient was over seventy years of age and I made known the need for indefinite seclusion in my report.

308. It is always an important matter to establish whether the head of a family, or the possessor of a large fortune, should be declared to be deranged and whether his condition is incurable. A similar brief handled legally is yet another matter if it concerns a sovereign,

since the answer to this question can lead to a change of government and can have an influence on the misfortune or prosperity of a whole nation. This was the position in England in 1789. On the one hand there were fears on the part of the ministry and those who were attached to the government of the day; on the other hand, there were the intrigues and ambitions of those who wanted a regency council, which seemed to spread unrest everywhere, and gave place to very serious discussions in the British parliament. A small number of enlightened doctors were chosen to direct the King's treatment, or rather to act in a subordinate way with Dr Willis who was specially charged with all aspects of mental and physical management as well as the prescription of remedies. This prescribing led to much jealousy and intrigue on the part of the establishment doctors against what was commonly disdainfully known as an 'empirical'. A legal report had already been made fifteen days before and parliament sought a new one to judge whether the symptoms were diminishing. A committee formed from its numbers was charged with collecting the opinions of the doctors separately and drawing a conclusion from these in order to enlighten public opinion. This report (14), which at once radiated deceitful reserve, a wilful intention to be inconsistent and skilfully advanced prejudices, is a very strange passage worthy of being featured in the philosophical history of medicine. The first doctor questioned, Mr Pepys, at first declared that His Majesty's condition permitted him neither to appear before Parliament nor to attend to affairs, that no likely conjecture could be made over the duration of his illness, and simply that more calmness was noted in his mind than before and one could now speak with more assurance of his early recovery. Willis took a more positive stance and stated that if all his other patients were in the same frame of mind he would have no doubt over their early cure, but added that nevertheless he could not specify when this would be. His Majesty, according to him, could not read a single line of any book fifteen days before, whereas he was now in a position of reading several pages and even making pertinent remarks about what he had read. He said that if he had refused once or twice to sign the daily bulletin this was because he noticed some concerted reluctance, giving the impression of *the influence of somebody special*. Dr Warren came next, and clearly stated that he saw no sign of convalescence nor any remission of the symptoms, that all he had seen for a few days was one lucid interval of a few hours, but that this hope had been far from sustained, and in a word that nothing seemed to justify the reassurances which had been given to the Prince of Wales. Dr Warren also complained about Willis's letters and reports, as being little related to the truth. There were then various quibbles over the form and wording of the bulletins: one was put together as follows: *His Majesty passed yesterday quietly, has had a very good night, and is calm this morning*. Willis objected to this report as being inadequate in not showing any lessening of the symptoms or any hope of a forthcoming cure. Another grave subject for dissent: a particular bulletin ended with the sentence: *Is this morning as he was yesterday*. One of the doctors objected and wanted to substitute *continues to mend* as being more expressive. A third went for another variation: *Is this morning in a comfortable way*. However both sides protested at not being given any kind of guidance. Dr Baker was in turn questioned, and he stated that he saw no sign of convalescence; he felt that at such an age this illness would not be curable. His Majesty always seemed to him to be in the same condition and he exclaimed that what was called a good night was one with three or four hours sleep. Dr Reynolds wanted to bring everyone together; he said that His Majesty was calmer and more docile, that he was in a better general state of health, that he found him to be under favourable circumstances likely to lead to an *improvement*, but that he still saw no change in the principle illness. It was natural that faced with these wavering opinions the Government settled for the one which was most favourable, and which Dr Willis's success came to justify. Superficial and conjectural science, Montaigne exclaimed, is what gives rise to such opposite opinions. I would say weakness, and everyone's capricious condescension means that the spirit of openness and strength of character which combines so well with talents and enlightenment is lost, and dragged down in a whirlwind of intrigue.

IX. PRUDENT MEASURES TO BE TAKEN IN DISCHARGING CONVALESCENT MENTAL PATIENTS

309. Great sensitivity, and consequently a disposition that is proximate to relapse, tends to characterise deranged patients when they are in convalescence unless the latter is firmly established. A fright, a bout of anger, deep chagrin, hot weather, some intemperance or even suddenly going from detention and restraint to freedom can disturb them in a way which would not affect them under other circumstances, and bring back bouts of maniacal insanity when they have not long subsided. This is how patients taken back too soon into their family slip back again and are returned to the hospices many times. A grenadier in the French Guard who was one of the first to launch an attack at the time of the fall of the Bastille became elated with a limitless ambition, and being frustrated in his dazzling expectations he sank into a violent maniacal delirium. He remained in this state of fury and distraction for four more months after arriving at the Bicêtre, then calm returned and his mother hastened to take him back before his reason had become firmly re-established. There was a further relapse at home with his family and he had to be taken back to the hospice. The same mistake was made twice more with the same result. Then the mother, now wiser from experience, no longer pushed for the convalescent patient's inopportune freedom. He spent two years calmly with no attacks, left the hospice at the beginning of winter and had no further relapses.

310. Hot weather, and sometimes the return of cold weather, although much less commonly, can bring on bouts of irregular maniacal insanity. So it is prudent around these times to make use of some preventatives for convalescent patients who have been discharged from hospices, and get them to use some relaxant, either internal or external. A hard-working farmer, who had fallen into maniacal insanity as a result of the effect of the burning sun during the heat of the harvest, was cured after a stay of about a year at Bicêtre. He was returned to his family with the express recommendation to take diluted and laxative drinks, with a few baths, each year as spring approached. These precautions saved him from any attacks for the next two years, but the third year he neglected them and relapsed. He was then taken back for the second time to Bicêtre after the former usual treatment at the Hôtel-Dieu. His maniacal insanity was again very violent for five months, and after a slow recovery he was once again returned to his family. The past example had taught him a firm lesson and it became hardly necessary to recommend him to make use of ways to save himself from a recurrence.

311. One of the invaluable potential capacities of well-organised hospices is that it permits one to impress actively the conviction on susceptible patients that they are subject to a higher power destined to control them and shape their will and whims (15). This idea, which must be continuously put to them, stimulates the functions of understanding, arrests their insane

rambling and gets them gradually used to restraining themselves, which is one of the first steps to recovery. If their discharge is premature and they are sent home to their family too soon, their feeling of independence and freedom to follow their whims sometimes carries them beyond the limit. This gives rise to departures from discipline or to vivid experiences likely to bring back their earlier disturbance. I was once pressed to authorise the discharge of a convalescent patient towards spring, and the following were my grounds for refusing in my report. 'I have carefully examined the above named... detained in the hospice, and although at the present moment he appears to have free use of his reason, I think that it would be imprudent to allow his discharge; for he was during the first three months of his seclusion in a furious delirium and did not appear calm until the onset of last winter. It still remains for him to undergo the trial of the hot weather season to judge his recovery properly. There are grounds for thinking that if he goes home now, the joy of regaining his freedom and seeing his relations and friends again would be too striking, especially for a poorly restored reason, and could cause a relapse. I think therefore that his discharge from the hospice should be delayed until the decline of autumn...' (*Bicêtre, 15th Germinal*[6] *Year II*).

312. So as not to compromise public safety it is essential to exercise the greatest reserve in certifying the cure of maniacal insanity, and this is what leads me to add two examples here, which I picked from my records. 'I certify that JR, aged twenty-two years, and detained as a mentally alienated patient at Bicêtre, may be regarded as cured of maniacal insanity since for about one year he has shown no sign of impairment in reason, even during the hot weather...' (*Bicêtre, 20th Fructidor*[7] *Year II*).

313. 'I certify that TD, aged twenty-one years, and detained at Bicêtre as a mentally alienated patient, has shown all the signs of the restoration of his reason for about four months. There are all the more grounds for considering him to be cured in that his disturbance had followed an acute illness, that he had arrived in the hospice in a wasted state and that his reason returned very gradually at the same time as his health' (*Bicêtre, 20th Fructidor Year II*).

314. The exact timing of the discharge of a patient after standard treatment is something which is very difficult to decide and, without going into subsequent details here, the notes I have collected at the Salpêtrière hospice reveal the following comments:

315. 1°. Repeated observation shows that when the patient's relatives fuss to take him out before convalescence is confirmed in spite of the good advice given to them, a relapse usually occurs which, far from being attributable to us, on the contrary confirms the practice we follow in relation to each period of the illness. Having been made more prudent by these unfortunate incidents when the relatives have to send the individual back after a relapse, they leave him there for a longer space of time until the convalescent state is no longer in doubt and there is then no fear of the same thing happening again.

316. 2°. Some maniacal insanities become periodical and recur with intervals of calmness and set or indeterminate relapses over many years. All one can then expect from standard

---

[6] *Germinal – Seventh month of Republican calendar – Ed.*
[7] *Fructidor – Twelfth month of Republican calendar – Ed.*

treatment is to diminish the violence and duration of the attack; but when once the pattern of relapses has become deep-rooted one can no longer hope to break it, and the disturbance generally lasts a lifetime, with intermissions of varying length and regularity. So there are patients who come back in turn, after a fixed period and a shorter or longer stay in the bosom of their family. In such cases carefully directed and discerning treatment can have a good influence on the relapses which must be expected, and can alter them in a remarkable manner.

317. 3°. During the ordinary treatment and during the second and third periods of the maniacal insanity there still remains a transient agitation which can take on the full character of a relapse, either because of the weather or because of other physical or mental causes. Then, at the approach of an apparent relapse, use is made alternately of relaxing drinks and of temperate baths: this leads to lasting calm and prevents further disruptions in reason. Sometimes, too, these temporary troubles are brought about by imprudence on the part of the family, either from letters reaching the patients or from premature visits. A delay in the success of the treatment results from this, and a stay in the hospice not just for several months but even for a few years in some cases, is needed to achieve a consolidated cure. This state may also sometimes become incurable. One patient was already convalescent and she was allowed to meet regularly with two of her daughters who came to see her. This also seemed to be very agreeable to her and to contribute to accelerating her convalescence. This woman was then visited by another of her daughters whose depraved habits and reprehensible conduct had given great distress to all the family. 'Ah! You are here, poor wretch!', her mother told her with deep emotion; and from that day she dropped into a state of stupor and numbness which lasted for over six months no matter what I tried, and I presume this state is incurable.

318. 4°. In order to bring about the successful reforms in the hospice, and to introduce a regular system of moderation and gentleness in the service, convalescent patients have been admitted who through their character, strong constitution and love of work can also make themselves useful to the patients. It is remarkable to see them carrying out their tasks, sometimes with shaky reason, gradually gaining self-confidence after their initial efforts and then advancing in big strides towards an established convalescence. People of all ages have been working in this way for several years with impunity and these established facts are the answer to the contrary prejudice that relapses are inevitable.

319. 5°. Certain women of the common classes only become deranged after excessive drinking which has become a habit, and staying for some time in the hospice easily restores their calm and the full use of their reason, but on being given their freedom they go back to their favourite weakness and a relapse closely follows. So the certificate I issue on their discharge anticipates this; and what is there to be done about it?

320. 6°. Experience constantly shows that nothing affects the restoration of reason so much as the confidence one is able to inspire in the patient, provided that he is susceptible to this. He then becomes docile and submissive; he correctly appreciates all the effort being put into his recovery and his mental faculties thus exercised then expand with ever-growing benefit. Furthermore, the doctor and the superintendent of the mental patients' hospice will have constantly worked with common accord towards fulfilling this fundamental objective,

and I leave it to the reader to guess whether this is by a haughty approach and harshness of manners[8]. But with only a few testimonies of kindness to show to patients after they are under control, how is one to get the upper hand of certain inflexible characters who are dominated by unshakeable and sombre pride, and see nothing beyond their exclusive daydreams? It is rare to see such a striking example as that reported by an English author already quoted. A middle aged man had first been remarkable for his talkativeness and his sombre and touchy mood: he was always anxious, quarrelsome and ready to lose his temper. His character became more bitter after a few reversals of fortune, and he became jealous, misanthropic to the highest degree, and insufferable to his own family. It was then that his delirium burst forth. He drew exchange notes for enormous sums, even on bankers with which he had no connection. At last consigned to a mental nursing home, he behaved with all the arrogance of an oriental despot. He thought he was the Chancellor, the Duke of Batavia, and he demanded the homage only paid to sovereigns. This bloated pride, against which all the methods tried were in vain, gradually degenerated into a state of stupor and incurable idiocy.

321. 7°. In a general treatise on alienation one cannot expect a mass of details concerning the cause, age, sex, complexion and other accessory variations which can only be recorded in individual collections of observations. Here it suffices to set up the true principles and show the extreme difference that must exist between the results of sound knowledge of mental alienation and certain popular practices or purely empirical trials.

322. 8°. The path I have followed in the case histories of the symptoms of alienation, and in the manner of directing its treatment, has always been subordinate to rigorous observation of the facts considered with wise reserve, and I believe I have been on guard against the seduction of novelties whose benefits one can sometimes involuntarily overestimate. I have no doubt that one day there will be a reaction in favour of the ancient method of copious blood-lettings, acts of violence, unexpected baths and well-cemented iron chains. It may even be that this reaction will come about through writings full of bile and bitterness, even though there is a way of reaching an agreement, safe from any error. This is by making exact inventories, on either side, of patients submitted to regular treatment, and seeing what the proportion of duly cured people is compared with the total number. Such a calculation, of which I give an example in the following section, can save much superfluous discussion by simple comparisons, and show clearly which of the two methods is to be preferred.

NOTES TO FIFTH SECTION

1. *Ubi perperam aliquid dixit aut fecit, fame, vinculis, plagis coercendus est.* Celsus, lib. III, chap. XVIII. *(When he has said or done something wrongly, he should be punished by hunger, chains, or beatings – Ed.)*
2. Has Dr Willis not at times deferred a little too much to the accepted practices in allowing the guardians who led patients for walks in the fields to return blows for blows; thus giving an independent and dangerous latitude to their brutality?

---

[8] I record this invariable collaboration for the good as a rarity in mental hospices, and it may well be that in a few centuries it will have become widely adopted.

3. It is proposed to meet another objective with the disciplinary water jet of which I have spoken elsewhere (paragraph 192), in which case the deranged patient's head is drenched to bring him back to order.

4. Dr Esquirol has carried out some experiments on himself with respect to the effects of the water jet, on which he will no doubt next publish the strange details and results. The liquid reservoir was raised to ten feet above the head; the water was at ten degrees below atmospheric temperature; the column of water was four lines in diameter and fell directly on the head; it seemed to him as if a column of ice was shattering on his head. The pain was very acute when the fall of water occurred on the fronto-parietal suture. It was more bearable when it was aimed onto the occipital. The head remained numb for more than an hour afterwards.

5. Very violent patients brought in have usually been managed at home by strong robust men who keep them firmly fixed on their own bed with handkerchiefs round their hands: the patient then takes advantage of the least moment of respite to make fresh efforts to overcome the resistance he is up against, thus keeping him in a permanent state of exasperation. On the contrary, in the hospice, all movements are restricted at the same time by the camisole with straps which are out of sight because they are attached at the back. Then, however much the patient struggles initially, all her efforts are useless and she does not see why this is; she often ends up becoming resigned and tranquil and her irascibility gradually subsides. Patients are also often seen who are said to be very furious at the time of their admission, and who become calm a few days later.

6. This is no doubt opening the door to a host of minor treatments so often arbitrarily used in medicine, giving them a high price; but sound judgement achieves surer results with more important measures without neglecting those which are merely ancillary.

7. Amongst the melancholic patients some thought their head was filled with heavy material and others imagined theirs was empty or dried out. One of them thought his head had been amputated on the orders of a despot. His physician, Philodotus, to persuade him otherwise, had a lead hat made which he told him to wear. The weight of it served to convince him that his head was still on his shoulders. A man who had been bitten a few days previously by an unknown dog convinced himself that he had rabies, and even assured his brother one day that he was overcome with the desire to bite him. The latter pretended to share his views but answered that the curate would easily be able to cure him with the help of certain prayers or spells. The priest supported him in this trickery and the credulous melancholic patient no longer had any doubts about his cure. These psychological steps were aided with the help of a supposed antihydrophobic drink. Following this well planned experience the illusion evaporated and nothing of the exclusive and dominant idea of rabies remained.

8. I do not need to recall the other physical methods for combating melancholia since they largely relate to those called for in insanity. Hellebore of Antycire was famous for this in antiquity and all the precautions used to make it less dangerous are known. One must not lose sight of the results of long experience; but therapeutics today makes it possible to substitute other purgatives of varying strength more likely to give similar effects with less unpleasant consequences.

9. Here I could add another example of a similar cure of melancholia with irresistible urge to suicide in a clockmaker who had long been tormented with thoughts of destruction, and who was drawn as if involuntarily to a house out in the country to avoid any interference. One day he armed himself with a pistol and went into a wood; but he

misaimed and just shattered his cheek. A violent haemorrhage began and meanwhile he was recognised by a shepherd and taken back to his own house to be looked after. The wound healed slowly, but a change of another kind took place in his mental outlook; be it from the shock of the event, the large volume of blood which was lost or some other unknown cause. There was no longer any trace of the former wish to kill himself. This example is certainly not one to be imitated; but nevertheless it shows that a sudden fright or very acute and profound ailment can sometimes change the disastrous inclination leading a man to suicide.

10. This symptomatic diarrhoea must be distinguished from that which is benign and pain-less, whether provoked or spontaneous. Feriar (*Medical histories* etc) reports the exam-ple of a derangement largely cured by an emetic drink which acted for a few days as a purgative. A robust woman of twenty-five years, maniacally insane for a few yeas, had dropped into a state of fury. She took some tartar emetic *(potassium antimony tartrite)* in small doses just enough to maintain a constant state of nausea. A vesicatory was also applied to her head and this, continued for seven or eight hours, was followed by a marked improvement. But recovery was still some way off, so the emetic was given in whey for fifteen days, and looseness of the bowels was encouraged with a little magne-sia. Following this treatment an opium preparation was added, given in the evening at bedtime, and a drastic purgative was finally given. Recovery gradually took place and after a month's trial she was discharged as cured from the Manchester hospital, four months after her admission.

11. Dr Esquirol's private establishment for deranged patients is situated between the Boule-vards and the Jardin des Plantes; and within its boundaries it contains a kind of orchard full of shrubs and trees. This results in it sharing, either through its outhouses or its vicinity, in a huge amount of vegetation. It is agreeably laid out to keep the patients separated from one another, isolating the sexes, the convalescents and those who are undergoing treatment. Each patient has a domestic servant exclusively at his service, who always sleeps near his bedroom or actually within it if this is thought necessary. All external features likely to be saddening are banned, such as iron bars on the windows, big bolts on the doors and ropes to tie patients up. The windows are protected by shutters which are easily opened when there is no fear of the patient jumping out. The furious patients are accommodated on the first floor and their bedrooms are boarded, with their doors opposite the windows. The shutters are opened and closed from outside, and their laths are moveable so that in tilting them they form a kind of flap. Thus everything is combining towards the same objective and is excellently set out for the treatment of distracted reason.

12. I can report an example of this taken from the writings of Valleriola (*Observ. Med. lib. IV*) and worthy of quotation by dint of the spirit of wisdom prevailing here, always pruning the formulae for medicaments with which he is bristling.

A young man lost his reason following an intense and frustrated love affair. In despair his parents begged the doctor to use everything which prudence and wisdom had to offer in the way of help. Removing the deranged young man from places likely to remind him of the loved one was first considered necessary and he was transferred to a nice house in the country with a pleasant outlook. No delights were missing from this stay: elegant gardens, large park, beautiful meadows, lakes and streams of clear water. The air was scented with the perfume of roses, myrtle, lemon trees and other aromatic plants, which all made walks full of interest. The patient's social circle was numerous and composed of chosen friends. There was a simply constant stream of games, amusements and musical concerts. The erotic delusion seemed to give way a little to so many objects of diversion, but former memories at times dragged the unhappy young man back into his earlier distraction. It was next thought best to remove him again from where he was staying and he was moved to a pleasant town, where the good offices of the doctor were fully supported, but the patient was then undermined with a lingering fever and a kind of hectic consumption. Sedatives and a restoring and tonic diet were resorted to, often with footbaths, lukewarm lotions and showers to the head. On some days, while he was in the bath, there were concerts of music and also readings and pleasant conversation. The bouts of delusion gradually diminished, strength and plumpness came back, and finally reason reigned once more.

13. A farmer who had lost one of his sons because of conscription in Year V fell into a deep chagrin, could not sleep and soon showed every distraction of reason. Another son, which he still had, shut him in a room, took all his belongings, treated him extremely harshly and consequently raised his unhappy father's fury to the last stage of violence. The impossibility of caring for him at home being obvious, a transfer order to Bicêtre was obtained and carried out. His bouts of maniacal insanity remained very violent during the hot weather, but calmness followed as autumn faded and continued through the winter. In spring a few laxative drinks given at the first sign of any nervous agitation prevented a following bout, and from then on I felt that towards autumn he would be ready to go back to his family. A letter I wrote to his son remained unanswered; and I had no more success with the local town council to which I had taken care to send two letters through the post. A lady who was very concerned over the fate of the unfortunate farmer took charge of a third letter in which I confirmed he was cured and the urgency of getting him back in possession of his belongings, and this was carried out in spite of the son's influence on the municipal officers. It was with emotion that the following year I saw this good farmer come, with a basket of fruit gathered from his orchard, to show me his gratitude.

14. *Report from the committee appointed to examine the Physicians who have attended his majesty during his illness, touching the present state of his majesty's health*, London, 1789.

15. The necessity of imposing a discipline of severity and constraint on deranged patients is further borne out in an anecdote taken from Duclos's Memoires. Nothing this historian said better shows the impression the figure of the king (Louis XIV) had upon minds than what happened to Henry-Jules of Bourbon, the son of the great Condé. He was subject to vapours which in anyone other than a prince would have been called madness. Sometimes he thought he had been transformed into a dog and barked as loudly as he could. He had one of these bouts one day in the king's chamber. The Monarch's presence impacted on his madness without dispelling it. The patient retired towards the window, and putting his head outside he muffled his voice as well as he could whilst making the expressions of barking . . . If he had always been before Louis XIV's eyes, would he not have been cured of his mental alienation as a result of being in the habit of controlling and restraining himself?

6

RESULTS OF OBSERVATIONS AND CONSTRUCTION OF TABLES FOR DETERMINING THE DEGREE OF PROBABILITY OF CURING MENTALLY ILL PATIENTS

323. In medicine it is difficult to come to any agreement if a precise meaning is not given to the word *experiment,* since everyone vaunts their own results and only more or less cites the facts in favour of their point of view. However, to be genuine and conclusive, and serve as a solid basis for any method of treatment, an experiment must be carried out on a large number of patients following the same rules and a set order. It must also be based on a consistent series of observations recorded very carefully and repeated over a certain number of years in a regular manner. Finally, it must equally report both events (1) which are favourable and those which are not, quoting their respective numbers, and it must attach as much importance to one set of data as to the other. In a nutshell it must be based on the theory of probabilities, which is already so effectively applied to several questions in civil life, and on which from now on methods of treating illnesses must also rely if one wishes to establish these on sound grounds. This was the goal I set myself in Year X in relation to mental alienation when the treatment of deranged patients was entrusted to my care and transferred to the Salpêtrière.

324. An exact account of alienation, and the identification of its distinctive characteristics, had been the fundamental aim of the Treatise that I published in Year IX on this illness. However, a few isolated observations on a way of directing treatment only seemed to me to give dubious results, and it was necessary to run a well conducted experiment for several years to provide the answer to the following question: in a hospice for deranged patients, what internal provisions should be made, what regular order should be maintained and what medical treatment principles should be adopted to achieve the best ratio between the

Medico-Philosophical Treatise on Mental Alienation.
Philippe Pinel. Translated by G. Hickish, D. Healy and L.C. Charland.
© 2008 John Wiley & Sons, Ltd.

number of cures and the total number of admissions? I thought I could start an experiment of this kind in the month of Germinal[1] Year X at the Salpêtrière hospice. The premises were immense and convenient for making the necessary partitions. I was greatly supported by the hospice's administration council and there was no lack of enthusiasm or skill in the man charged to help me to maintain order and supervision in the department. So the establishment made steady progress right from the start, and ever on guard against personal prejudice or error I took care every six months to summarise the registers to see the respective number of cures compared with what was being achieved elsewhere. Cases where treatment had been successful, and those where it had failed, were submitted to an equally attentive examination. After such work, continued for just three months short of four years, that is, from the month of Germinal Year X until January 1st 1806, the general table was constructed which I submitted for the judgement of the mathematical and physical sciences class at the National Institute of France on February 9th 1807.

325. Prejudice and negligence have led most hospices to accept as a principle the complete incurability of all deranged patients. To achieve this, infallible steps are taken: close confinement, acts of harshness and violence, and the use of chains. In a very small number of properly run hospices it is agreed that this illness can be cured; and, what is better, repeated experience proves this. But the summaries of registers made in France as much as elsewhere show that with all known methods only a certain number are cured, and the only target one can set oneself from now on comes down to obtaining a more or less favourable ratio between the number of cures brought about and the total number of admissions. This total is the sum of cures and non-cures. It follows that one must rely on the calculation of probabilities and the use of one of its elementary principles; that is, that the likelihood of an event is measured by a fraction in which the numerator is the number of successful cases and the denominator is the number of possible cases, favourable or otherwise. So it was necessary to keep exact registers of the different species of mental alienation and their respective numbers, and carefully determine the true character of the observed facts to add them to their correct place in the tables, without concealing those where any doubt or uncertainty still remained. It was necessary to avoid wilfully inflating the number of favourable events whilst masking the uncertain or adverse ones, for as Fontenelle commented on the subject of Daniel Bernouilli's book *(De Arte conjectandi)*, the difficulty is that cases where an event may or may not happen escape us, and the more unknown cases there are, the more uncertain our knowledge becomes of which side to take.

326. Two methods are used in the treatment of mental alienation: one, which is very old, consists in rushing the illness along its course with repeated blood-lettings, strong water jets, cold baths or even surprise baths, and close confinement. The other, which is adopted at Salpêtrière, construes mental alienation as an acute illness which has its successive stages of intensity, decline and convalescence, whose order must not be reversed and whose symptoms should be calmed by gentle means, tepid baths, relaxing drinks and sometimes sedatives or very light showers. In particular cases strict yet brief discipline may be used, but always in a kindly way. The propitious art of gaining the patient's confidence should be applied, as long as reason is not entirely shattered.

---

[1] *Germinal – Seventh month of Republican calendar – Ed.*

Which of the two methods is to be preferred? A mere summary of the registers, tables carefully constructed month after month and year after year, in various hospices, and the theory of probabilities will be enough to settle this question, and by using a simple comparison the course which is continuously the most beneficial can be recognised. I begin by publishing the results of the treatment method I have followed. There is nothing more obscure than the nature of cerebral or intellectual functions, so how can one learn to correct their different derangements other than by the results of comparative observation? Or, in other words, should the success of the treatment not be put in a category of events made up following a fixed law of simple events? And to work out its probability, should the experiment that can lead to the event not be repeated a large number of times, to see how many times it actually occurs?

I. RULES FOLLOWED AT THE SALPÊTRIÈRE HOSPICE FOR MENTALLY ILL PATIENTS TO KEEP THE REGISTERS AND CONSTRUCT THE TABLES

327. The patients are sent to the Salpêtrière either from inner Paris or from neighbouring Departments following an order from the police or the general admissions bureau, and after the alienation has been certified. Upon their admission to the hospice their name, age, place of birth and date of admission are written in a register kept in the office. Marginal notes are added about their previous state and the cause of the illness when the relatives can give reliable information, because the minutes about the onset of the illness are kept elsewhere and are not passed on to us. One hundred and seventy-six patients were admitted for treatment from the month of Germinal Year X until the end of Fructidor[2] of the same year; two hundred and eight in Year XI, two hundred and sixty-two in Year XII, one hundred and four in Year XIII, and two hundred and fifty-two in the last nine months of the year 1805. Added together, these figures give a total of one thousand and two patients admitted in the space of four years less three months, which form the substance of my tables.

328. Alienation is just a general term meaning a disturbance of cerebral or intellectual functions. It is important to indicate the respective numbers of the four different species of deranged patients which continuous observation has distinguished. The number of patients affected by maniacal insanity admitted to the hospice year by year can be seen on the general table (Table 6.1). Their total, for the four years less three months, was six hundred and four. Another species of alienation characterised by a state of stupor, sombre moroseness with an exclusive delusion about certain things, yet full use of reason for all other matters, is also seen although less frequently than the first, and this is called *melancholia*. The number of people admitted with this condition varied from year to year, as inspection of the general table shows. Their total, during the four years less three months, was two hundred and thirty, amongst whom thirty-eight were dominated by a violent urge to commit suicide. The kind of death which these women tried to inflict on themselves was to strangle themselves with a handkerchief or bootlace, particularly at night; hiding in their bed. To supervise them more

---

[2] *Fructidor – Twelfth month of Republican calendar – Ed.*

Table 6.1 List of female mentally ill patients at the Salpêtrière over a period of three years and nine months

Type of disease	Years	Number of patients	Admissions without information	Treated elsewhere	Single women	Married women	Widows	Causes Physical	Moral	Periodical	Cured	Deaths Under Treatment	Incurable	Remaining in the hospice
Maniacal insanity with delusions	X	117	42	58	47	58	12	19	42	18	64	13	16	24
	XI	124	38	55	49	58	17	34	58	33	73	6	23	22
	XII	155	60	57	57	69	29	50	74	45	87	9	31	28
	XIII	56	17	42	20	19	12	21	63	14	24	5	7	20
	1805	152	58	46	48	64	24	41	48	17	62	8	12	70
Melancholy with delusions about a single object	X	24	7	7	15	5	4	2	21	6	14	2	4	4
	XI	42	16	11	17	17	8	11	34	7	36	2	3	1
	XII	54	13	27	21	24	9	16	54	12	34	4	4	12
	XIII	14	5	9	9	2	1	4	10	3	10	2	2	"
	1805	38	4	19	20	11	5	13	29	1	20	"	3	15
Melancholy with suicidal tendency	X	6	3	3	1	4	1	2	4	1	3	"	1	2
	XI	2	1	1	1	"	"	"	2	1	1	"	"	1
	XII	9	4	4	2	3	4	2	7	2	4	"	2	3
	XIII	5	2	2	3	"	2	"	5	4	3	"	"	2
	1805	16	1	5	6	8	9	4	13	2	9	3	1	3
Totals	…	814	271	346	316	342	137	219	464	166	444	54	109	207

Dementia													
X	20	15	5	8	4	7	2	2	2	2	1	11	6
XI	32	19	6	5	6	20	3	5	1	6	"	23	3
XII	32	22	8	13	8	10	—	3	2	4	"	14	14
XIII	22	16	2	11	3	7	3	2	"	6	"	10	6
1805	46	15	11	12	15	20	13	14	1	11	1	15	19
Totals ...	152	87	32	49	36	64	30	26	6	29	2	73	48
Idiocy X	9	8	1	6	2	1	—	"	"	"	"	5	4
XI	8	1	6	7	"	1	3	"	"	"	"	5	3
XII	12	9	3	11	1	"	6	"	"	"	"	1	11
XIII	7	5	"	7	"	"	6	"	"	"	"	1	6
Totals ...	36	23	10	31	3	2	19	"	"	"	"	12	24

Observations

1. Treatment of the female patients was started at the Salpêtrière on the 17th of the month of Germinal in Year X. At that time the hospice, which had always been looked upon as a repository for incurably insane women following unsuccessful treatments at the Hôtel-Dieu, held 517 of these. From this number, 52 who showed some hope of cure and were grouped together with those who had been sent from elsewhere for treatment should be subtracted. These are not included in the present table as they belong to previous years.

2. Out of the total number of 444 who were cured, 15 are omitted who could be considered as such but were handicapped or of limited understanding since an early age and were brought by treatment to the point of being able to undertake supervised work.

3. Women with dementia or idiocy admitted to the hospice who had been affected by an innate disposition, advanced age, or by excessive treatment attempted elsewhere, were grouped with the other patients in the hospice considered as incurable. In cases of fortuitous dementia twenty-nine cures were achieved.

carefully it was customary to make rounds during the night or to position the suspects in a dormitory facing a street light.

329. Dementia characterised by incoherence of ideas and feebleness of cerebral functions without agitation or fury is often the effect of advanced age, and can also be produced by other incidental causes. I counted one hundred and fifty-two of these cases in the indicated length of time, and sixty-four of this number had been reduced to this condition by advanced age. Finally, the last species of alienation remaining for me to speak of, which is named *idiocy*, consists of a more or less complete abolition of the affections of the heart and the absence of ideas. This state is almost always innate and dates from birth; and the total number of alienated patients with this species was thirty-six during the four years less three months. It is the distinction of these different species of alienation which has provided the basis of the construction of the various tables summarised in the general table I am publishing. It has also been very useful for recording my daily notes and making them more precise and exact. Finally, it has greatly simplified treatment and avoided mistakes which could have been made in a large gathering of alienated patients.

330. The benefits of being able to follow and watch alienated patients of each species during their successive periods of acute attack, decline and then convalescence, the disadvantages associated with freedom of patients in these different stages to communicate with one another and, finally, order and ease of running the service, all called for the separation of the patients into three large divisions according to the species to which they belonged. This was apart from the incurable patients who were confined in special premises, and those with incidental illnesses who also have their infirmary. Patients often have to be moved on from one division to another as their condition changes, or returned to their former division in the case of a relapse. To find any of these patients when somebody wants them or is visiting them it is necessary to record these onward or reverse relocations in a separate register. The register has loose cards which can be moved from one sheet to another and which bear the patients' name with notes about their previous state and a reference number to the page of the first register kept in the office. The respective number of patients belonging to these divisions is clearly variable, but these variations are restricted within certain limits. So at an inventory on the 28th Frimaire[3] Year XIII, I found that in the first division, for agitated or more or less furious patients undergoing treatment, there were twenty-four. In the second division, for patients whose illness was declining or who were having just a few periodic recurrences of agitation, there were one hundred and ninety-six. And the dormitory for the fully convalescent held fifty-nine people, whose reason only needed to be completely restored so that they could return to the outside world. Full recovery is achieved above all by means of manual work, and so a sewing room is situated close by this division.

One should not be surprised to find such a small number of patients in the first division, as often very delirious or furious persons are admitted to the hospice whom gentle means bring quickly to a state ready for transfer to the second or third division. The secret of a well-run hospice is to reduce to the *minimum* the number of patients needing strict seclusion in special premises. In the twenty-four lodges reserved for the most agitated patients there are often only six or eight which are occupied, and sometimes just three of four, and the other patients in this division retain some element of liberty in their individual premises, so that those

---

[3] *Frimaire – Third month of Republican calendar – Ed.*

who are strictly confined hardly make up 2 % of the total number of patients undergoing treatment, thanks to the general system of gentleness and freedom adopted in the hospice.

II. DERANGED PATIENTS ADMITTED WITH NO INFORMATION REGARDING THEIR PREVIOUS STATE, AND PATIENTS TREATED ELSEWHERE BEFORE ADMISSION TO THE HOSPICE

331. Deranged patients are often admitted for reasons of public safety or in some other manner, and we are left without the report certifying the cause of the illness or other subsequent events. We are thereby deprived of much useful knowledge for managing the treatment. The fourth vertical column of the general table is devoted to this kind of inventory. Thus out of one hundred and seventeen people struck by maniacal insanity, forty-two were admitted for treatment in Year X with no information about their previous state; thirty-eight out of one hundred and twenty-four in Year XI; and eighty out of one hundred and fifty-five in Year XII etc. Similar comments can be made regarding the other species of alienation, so that during the space of time my tables cover this applies to three hundred and eighty-one, that is, 33 % of the total. Now this lack of proper information often introduces uncertainty regarding the measures to take in organising treatment. It is also damaging to the use one can later make of the calculation of probabilities, since for this one has to compare the number of cases where a cure can be expected with the number of cases where it failed. And how can this be done without precise information about the previous state of the patients when they reach the hospices?

332. Consistent experience has shown that the ease of curing deranged patients, and the probability of success, is always related to the recent state of the illness and the benefits of initial treatment. In fact, in certain foreign hospices, patients who have been treated elsewhere and have subsequently relapsed are not admitted. Completely unrestricted admission of deranged patients to the Salpêtrière gave me a distinct disadvantage. It is enough to have to account for one's own mistakes. I have always noted this circumstance when I knew about it and took care to enter in the fifth vertical column of the general table the number of patients admitted following one or two treatments undergone elsewhere. Thus in the last half of Year X, out of one hundred and seventeen manically insane patients admitted, fifty-eight had been treated elsewhere by other methods; fifty-five out of one hundred and twenty-four in Year XI; and thirty-seven out of one hundred and fifty-seven in Year XII etc. I leave aside reporting the similar results for melancholia, dementia and idiotism, since this can be checked by simple inspection of the table. Broadly speaking, out of one thousand and two patients, three hundred and ninety-eight had been treated elsewhere or brought from another hospice, 33 % of the total.

III. PREDISPOSITION TO MENTAL ALIENATION ACCORDING TO AGE, MARITAL STATUS OR CELIBACY

333. A particular table inserted into my *Treatise on Insanity* published in Year XI attests that this illness mostly manifests itself between the age of puberty and the age of forty-five to fifty years, and that, judging from data about a large group of patients, it occurs most

frequently in men between their twentieth and fortieth years. A simple summary of the registers has given comparable results for women, so that in Year IX sixteen insane patients were between eighteen and twenty years of age, thirty-nine between twenty-five and thirty, twenty-five between thirty-five and forty, and twenty-one between forty-five and fifty. This same law of progressive increase and then decrease likewise occurred for the Years XI and XII. Year XIII was an exception to this rule which could have depended on some incidental cause. But I must not omit a comment arising from simple comparison of the notes I took at Bicêtre and at the Salpêtrière. In men insanity had not appeared earlier than puberty and, on the contrary, in the hospice for deranged patients at the Salpêtrière, this illness was seen nine times before puberty in Year XI, and eleven times in Year XII. Could it be true that the development of reason, like its derangements, is more precocious for women than men?

334. Melancholia is also more common at adult age, between the twentieth and fortieth years of age; but it does not appear, like insanity does, before puberty. It was the same with incidental dementia. But senile dementia, as its name implies, occurs at very different stages in life: thus in Year X this alienation developed twice in the sixtieth year, six times between the sixtieth and seventieth, and once in the ninetieth. In Year XI three cases of dementia similarly came on towards the sixtieth year, ten between the sixtieth and seventieth, and five between the seventieth and eightieth years; with similar results for the subsequent years. Generally speaking there were sixty-four sufferers from senile dementia taken to the hospice during the four years less three months. They were brought in that state, some from decrepitude, others profoundly disturbed, and a few others from abuse of alcohol.

335. Does marriage predispose to mental alienation as much as celibacy or widowhood? To throw some light on this question I have made precise summaries in the registers, and I have devoted three vertical columns in the general table to data relating to this matter. This was all the easier because these various states of the patients were carefully noted in the hospice registers, and on this point there were very few exceptions. But, in another context, certain mortality tables such, for example, as those of M. Deparcieux in France and M. Vargentin in Sweden, have shown that married women generally live longer than spinsters, and that the number of the former is sometimes double that of the others. In the hospices one cannot draw any conclusion from the numerical relationship seen between the two states, indicating a greater or lesser predisposition to contracting maniacal insanity or melancholia. I can only suggest as doubtful the conclusions that can be drawn from the preponderant number of unmarried women who have fallen into dementia, no matter what this number may be according to the summary of the registers. It is always more than double and sometimes four times that of married women. I will finally reveal, as an established fact, without deriving any conclusions, that the number of girls fallen into idiocy was, in Year XI and Year XIII, seven times greater than that of married women in the same condition, and eleven times greater in Year XII. So one can simply presume that for women marriage is a kind of protection against the two most deep-seated and often incurable species of alienation.

IV. VARYING INCIDENCE OF ALIENATION DEPENDING ON ITS CAUSES

336. Such a title refers to matters which could only be developed in this second edition of my *Treatise on Insanity* because they stem from anatomical research and from other details

on the determining causes of alienation. By confining myself within the limits I set myself, I will observe that the lack of precise information about the previous condition of many deranged patients can in some ways be harmful to the progress of science. But it cannot cast any doubt on the usual origin of mental alienation since, in view of the most exact and most often repeated information obtained in other cases, one learns that it recurs every year or even every month, with little variation and showing a kind of constant conformity. In general, at the time of arrival of a patient at the hospice, it can be stated in advance, and with a strong probability, that her state has been determined by some such physical or mental cause.

337. Simple inspection of the general table (ninth and tenth vertical column) is immediately convincing that the same causes determining melancholia or maniacal insanity can also, depending on their intensity and the individual sensitivity, lead to dementia and possibly even to idiocy, although the latter point is less certain. The most common physical causes have been an inherent predisposition, the suppression or arrest of monthly periods, an accident during a confinement, abuse of alcoholic beverages and head injuries. Causes which can be called *mental* have been a dreadful fear, frustrated love, reverses of fortune, domestic crises or ecstatic religious devotion (2).

338. It is strange to see, from a simple summary of the registers, a kind of constant or min-imally varying relationship between the number of mental causes of the women's insanity and the total sum of causes either mental or physical; the first always remaining predomi-nant. This ratio was 61 % in Year X, 63 % in Year XI, 58 % in Year XII, 57 % in Year XIII and 54 % in the last nine months of year 1805. Simple comparison suffices to convince that the number of mental causes is still more preponderant in melancholia than in insanity. It made up 80 % of the total number in Year XI and 83 % in Year XII. The following years gave similar results. It also seems that there is a marked difference as regards the frequency of repetition of certain causes for the various species of alienation, and that whereas do-mestic chagrin most often leads to insanity, ecstatic religious devotion more often ends in melancholia. Sad and frustrated love on the other hand seems to be an equally productive source of these two species of alienation. Finally, it seems that the frequency of incidental causes can vary from year to year. Thus in the last six months of Year X the number of melancholic patients suffering from religious scruples or terrors was 50 % of the total of determining causes, but was reduced to 33 % in Year XI and 18 % in Year XII.

339. The frequent lack of precise information about people with dementia makes it difficult to draw any conclusion about the respective frequency of particular causes. For idiocy a simple inspection of the general table only reveals physical causes, that is to say an inherent defect, for most of the cases about which it has been possible to gather exact information.

V. TREATMENT METHOD FOR DEMENTED PATIENTS SUGGESTED BY THE NATURE OF THE PRECIPITATING CAUSE AND CONFIRMED BY THE CALCULATION OF PROBABILITIES

340. There is nothing more obscure than the nature of cerebral or intellectual functions, and surely the mechanism of their derangement must therefore be equally impenetrable? So the method to adopt in treatment cannot be known *a priori* and can only be deduced

through repeated experiment conducted with the wisest caution. It is no doubt permissible to mistrust treatment which is hallowed by immemorial use, which views alienation as consisting of too strong a rush of blood to the head. We can see many hundreds of patients in the hospices who were formerly treated along these principles and have become incurable. These illnesses were often interrupted for a certain time but then became established, and subject to periodic recurrences which it has no longer been possible to prevent. So I have felt it wiser generally to leave the illness to go through its different stages of acute state, decline and then convalescence, without disturbing or reversing its natural course too much. I would vary secondary curative measures depending on the several species of alienation or particular character of the responsible cause. But above all I count on the powerful resources of discipline by establishing a consistent order in the hospice in which all parties would work together in the most favourable way (3) towards the slow gradual restoration of reason. This method has been developed in the previous two sections and here I confine myself to putting them to the test of the principles of the calculation of probabilities, gathering together the results of a genuine experiment over nearly four years.

341. A treatment method primarily subject to the fundamental rules within the hospice, and varied according to the various species of alienation, or indeed their different periods, can only result from a large assembly of measures which are successfully combined and designed to lead to the same end – the restoration of reason. It constitutes a complicated project whose different elements could only be deduced by attentive examination of the symptoms and the more or less successful results of an enlightened experiment. However, its benefits can only be properly appreciated from simple summaries of regularly kept six-monthly registers, maintained for a long time, correcting or improving matters wherever possible. Subsequent confirmation results from the construction of tables drawn up after a few years to identify precisely the respective numbers of patients cured. Thus progress is slow, but sure, towards an end which is perhaps far away but must always be kept in sight, toward which one is guided by a constant comparison of the reports received between the number of cures and that of admissions, either from reports previously obtained at the same place or those regularly kept from other hospices (4). But to be conclusive this assumes the closest supervision over the maintenance of the various registers, great accuracy in the construction of the tables, regular notes on the most common origins of alienation, a thorough examination of the condition of people discharged as cured from the hospice, a precise determination of the respective numbers of cures and relapses and, finally, identification of cases which must still be considered as doubtful or equivocal, and of the number of adverse cases where treatment has failed. In other words, the elementary notions of calculation of probabilities need to be applied; something which has, of yet, only been done for the hospice at Salpêtrière.

342. Lack of information about several patients (fourth vertical column of the table) who are admitted every year to the hospice has not prevented me from determining the precise number of the different species of alienation, since each of them identified themselves through specific symptoms. So from the start I kept notes on maniacal insanity as precise as on other species of alienation in order to know the effective number of cures; and thus every six months I made a strict list of the results achieved. One hundred and seventeen patients afflicted with maniacal insanity had been admitted to the hospice during the last six months of Year X, and out of this number sixty-four had been cured; which is 54 %. The ratio was 58 % in Year XII, which was even better. It was then sustained with minor variations over

the following years and taking the results of four years less three months I counted three hundred and ten favourable outcomes out of six hundred examples of insanity, which gives a ratio of 51 %, indiscriminately including cases of deep-seated insanity and those of recent onset.

343. Simple inspection of the general table shows that the results were even more encouraging in cases of melancholia, for during the last six months of Year X, out of eighty melancholic patients, forty had been cured; thirty-six out of forty-two were cured in Year XI, and taking the overall results of four years less three months, the ratio was one hundred and fourteen to one hundred and eighty-two, that is to say 62 %. But here, as in a large number of cases of insanity, success often depends not only on medical treatment but again on the enthusiasm of the hospice director who lives amongst the patients all the time, skilfully counters their delusions whilst constantly seeking to win their confidence, and bringing them by the rule of regular manual work to a new chain of thoughts and ideas. I felt I also ought to consider another variety of melancholia separately, those characterised by a strong inclination to commit suicide for no apparent reason. It appears more often in some years than others, for I noted six melancholic patients of this kind in the last six months of Year X, two only in the whole of Year XI, nine during Year XII, five in Year XIII and sixteen during the last nine months of 1805. Apart from the attempts some melancholic patients make to strangle themselves with a handkerchief or lace, others refuse all food to die of starvation. The unremitting care and diverse means which then have to be used to shield them from an inevitable death cannot be imagined. This variety of melancholia seems more resistant to treatment than the other: three out of six were cured during the last six months of Year X, four out of nine in Year XII and nine out of sixteen in the last nine months of 1805. Taking the overall results of four years less six months, a ratio of 20 to 38 is found; that is 52 %. A cure is also easier when the condition is of recent onset.

344. Dementia is a reason for excluding patients in some hospices for the mentally ill in England, and indeed it is often partly the result of advanced age. So one must not be surprised by the hardly favourable ratio which a summary of the Salpêtrière registers gives in this respect. Taking the results obtained during four years less three months, out of one hundred and fifty-two demented patients, only twenty-nine were discharged as cured – 19 %. Idiocy gave an even more discouraging ratio, for out of thirty-six patients in this state, none could be returned to reason. What favourable development can be hoped for in such a condition which is often innate? Out of the total number of idiots, there were nineteen for whom information about their previous state could be obtained: their idiocy was innate which always implies incurability.

345. So in general it is only in rare cases of incidental dementia or non-innate idiocy that treatment can be successfully applied. It is particularly maniacal insanity and melancholia that can undergo this kind of degeneration. This makes the success of the resulting treatment all the more doubtful, especially when these last cases have been treated elsewhere or are of longstanding duration. If one includes, in the same calculation, the four species of alienation of which I have just been speaking, without imposing any restriction, it is clear that the ratio I have obtained between the number of cures and the total number of admissions is 473 to 1002; that is, 47 %. If one wishes, on the contrary, to exclude the cases of dementia and idiocy, which are scarcely susceptible to treatment, and are not admitted to English hospices,

from the figures of this ratio, then this will be 444 to 814, that is, 54 %. This includes with no distinction, maniacal insanity and melancholia considered of recent onset or deep-seated or after one or several previous treatments. These latter cases offer little hope of cure.

VI. LENGTH OF TREATMENT NEEDED TO PREVENT RELAPSES

346. Generally received opinion sees maniacal insanity and melancholia as unlikely to be soundly cured and as being subject to endless relapses. This same opinion seems abundantly confirmed by the example of nearly all hospices in France that are managed without method and where the patients are generally detained all their lives. Elsewhere the usual treatment with repeated blood-lettings is often followed by a temporary remission of symptoms, but is liable to make the alienation periodic and leads one to look upon it as incurable. One of the fundamental goals adopted at the Salpêtrière was to avoid such consequences and produce a sound and lasting cure. This aim determines the curative methods and internal regulations put in place in this hospice, separating the patients into three large divisions, as I have already indicated, which provides the facility to consider the different periods of the alienation separately, adapting the right method of treatment to each, and transferring the patients from one division to another if a relapse appears or upon the first sign of one approaching. In this way it is possible to determine with much more precision the time of complete restoration of reason and the patient's return to the bosom of their family. This has led me to research the duration needed for treatment in order to avoid relapses following discharge from the hospice.

347. A simple summary of the registers shows remarkable variations in this duration, even when the maniacal insanity is of recent origin. Eighteen cures took place in Year XI in the second month of treatment, and nine in Year XII. In a few less serious cases of alienation arising from domestic chagrins, frustrated love or following confinements, the first month has sometimes been enough; but most often the treatment has lasted for three or even four months. Indeed eight persons were cured in the third month in Year X, five at that time in Year XII and eleven in 1805. But when the maniacal insanity is long-standing, or has been disrupted elsewhere in its course by ill-devised or unsuccessful treatment, then treatment has only been rewarded with success after the eighth, tenth or twelfth month and in some cases even after two years, when it is prolonged in order to consolidate the recovery when this has been possible. Most of these patients become incurable. Maniacal insanity resulting from a severe fright, or preceded by relapses, or following the menopause in women, is also more difficult to cure. Thus in the last six months of Year X, eight deranged patients were only cured after one year's treatment and four after one and a half years; and in Year XI nine were not cured till after a year had gone by, and three after a year and a half of treatment which was alternately resumed and suspended; for it often requires great skill to allow nature the time to built up her resources and salutary efforts.

348. The exclusive delusional focus of melancholic patients for certain objects and their sombre character yield with difficulty to treatment. It is rare to obtain marked success in the first or second month unless their confidence has been won and the vicious chain of ideas thereby broken, dissipating their imaginary delusions. In Year XI, eighteen melancholic patients recovered between the fifth and eighth month, four in the tenth month, three after

one year and four after a year and a half. In Year XII, eighteen were cured between the third and sixth months, and twelve between the sixth and ninth. The nature of the determining cause also exercises a large influence on the ease and slowness of the cure. Melancholia resulting from domestic chagrin or an intense urge that has been frustrated may yield without difficulty in the space of a little time using isolation and a few other simple measures; but it is much more resistant if it stems from a fright, the consequence of confinements or an entirely imaginary and unfounded jealousy. The obstacle is even more difficult to overcome if it arises from extreme exaltation of religious principles or endlessly recurring scruples. How can one make the voice of reason heard by people who only obey supernatural inspirations, and who look upon those trying to cure them as blasphemers and persecutors, and who, as one of these patients expressed it, have changed their room into a sort of solitary retreat (5)?

349. It is interesting to compare maniacal insanity and melancholia with one another from the point of view of the usual length of treatment required, and to see the difference between these two species of alienation in this regard. In Year X, out of sixty-four maniacal insanity patients cured, fifty-six were cured during the first or at the very most during the second year; seventy-two out of seventy-three in Year XI, eighty-two out of eighty-seven in Year XII, and so on. More delayed cures have been very rare and can hardly be attributed to anything but some fortuitous incident or indeed a kind of change through advancing age. Similar examples seem to happen less often in cases of melancholia, for in Year X only two like this could be counted, as well as in Year XII, and none in Year XI. It seems that when melancholia does not respond to a certain length of treatment the patient continues to retain the same sequence of ideas and his sombre character, without any hope of recovery.

350. Following the preceding research I naturally had to be led, using the ordinary process of calculation, to determine the average length of treatment. With this in mind I first determined it for each year, and obtained for the total of these years; in the case of maniacal insanity five and a half months, and for melancholia around six months. This included both patients of either kind sent to the hospice at the beginning of the attack of the illness, and those who had undergone one or more treatments in other hospices, who are always very difficult to cure and often incurable. The length of treatment would be roughly halved if solely people who had not been treated elsewhere were sent to the hospice.

351. In fact it is noted, from a simple summary of the registers, that most of the cures achieved each year only took place in the case of the first, second or, at the most, third attack of maniacal insanity or melancholia. These are precisely the cases which are susceptible to cure in the first, second, third or, at the very most, fourth month of treatment.

VII. RELAPSES OCCURRING AFTER CURE AND DISCHARGE FROM THE HOSPICE

352. One of the objectives demanding the greatest attention in following the methods adopted at the Salpêtrière is, as I have just said, avoiding relapses. But are we fortunate to have met this goal, leaving only the relapses occurring after discharge arising from accidents which could not be foreseen whatever prudent measures had been taken? Here there is no authority

to refer to other than the results of experiment – in other words the number of recurrences had to be carefully recorded together with the circumstances which may have preceded or caused them. This number can only be very close to the truth in a hospice where mainly women of lower class are admitted, who become the sole responsibility of their family if they relapse and who are brought back to us. The cases I am going to outline will cast light on the most common cause of relapses.

353. An exact summary of the registers shows that in the course of four years less three months covered by the general table, and out of a total of four hundred and forty-four patients cured, seventy-one relapsed after a varying interval. Now I must point out that out of the last number, twenty had already had one or more attacks treated elsewhere prior to their admission to the hospice, and that on the discharge certificate I had added a restriction and warned of a fresh relapse failing major steps to avoid it. Sixteen other patients relapsed because their first discharge, insistently demanded by the family, had been premature and they had been warned of this danger. I must also comment that out of that last number, ten have been treated again and cured with no recurrence. So out of the total there are thirty-six relapses which cannot be blamed, to speak the truth, on treatment received at the Salpêtrière. Out of the other thirty-five patients, reliable information showed that fourteen of them had been plunged into misery and deep dismay by their aversion to work or the loose-living of their husbands; very common causes of alienation. Six others fell back into their earlier excesses of drink, which is another frequent cause of deranged reason. Finally, a return of melancholia through extreme religious scruples has again led to a breakdown in eight people, and the other six were drawn into a state of alienation as a result of blind jealousy or frustrated love. It remains doubtful whether, as in the other cases, this was a recurrence of the former illness or the onset of a new one. Whatever interpretation one may put on these relapses, they illustrate the well-established boundaries within which their respective number is confined and the most common causes which have produced them. It is indeed difficult to believe that in the eventual progress which science will achieve, it will never be possible to prevent them, since they derive from the powerful influence which long-established habits exert on the human heart. But is this a reason for not considering these favourable events as cures followed by relapses, which can also be subject to a calculation of probabilities?

VIII. REGARDING THE PROPORTION OF SUCCESSES AND FAILURES IN THE TREATMENT OF ALIENATED PATIENTS

354. Once a clear picture has been obtained of the respective numbers of favourable and contrary incidents, the fundamental principle of the calculation of probabilities will always be simply and easily applied. In this way, in every hospice where the true nature of what makes alienation curable or incurable has been discerned, just a simple inventory of the cases of each kind is needed to know their respective number. But at the Salpêtrière the lack of clear information about the previous state of several patients (fourth vertical column of the table) has often prevented any knowledge of these two states and their inventory, so it was necessary to find an alternate way of proceeding. This alternate way consisted of making a count of all the patients remaining in the hospice at the end of the four years less

three months and who had been treated unsuccessfully during that period. Now this total number, which amounted to two hundred and twelve, included one hundred and fourteen people affected with maniacal insanity, ten with melancholia and forty-five patients who had sunk into dementia or idiocy; that is to say one hundred and eighty patients about whom clear knowledge had been gained and who had been given one or more treatments elsewhere. Out of the other thirty-two, seventeen could be counted whose condition was doubtful and continued to be treated with a more or less warranted hope of cure; there were ten about whom no information could be obtained; and the other five, although well known as having been admitted to the hospice soon after the onset of the illness, had nevertheless not been able to be cured. So it follows that the patients treated unsuccessfully elsewhere constituted the great majority of the incurable patients still in the hospice. Their ratio was 85 % whereas that for patients with a recent onset was no more than 7 %, even including ten patients in the calculation about whose previous state no precise information could be received. So there is a probability of 93 % that the treatment adopted at the Salpêtrière will be successful if the alienation is recent and has not been treated anywhere else. And I must point out that relapses occurred among these cases only when their discharge had been premature because of family pressure and it was not considered that their reason was fully restored.

355. It could be objected that as the mortality of women receiving treatment was fifty-six during the space of time covered by my table, some patients accepted as having been cured might have succumbed to other incidental illnesses and so there remains some doubt over the respective number of patients of recent onset returned to society. But I can rank it as one of the most noted facts that the illnesses and deaths in the hospice are almost always found among patients who are worn out by earlier treatments and so weakened at their admission that they are usually sent to a particular infirmary which is nearly always full of patients in this condition or incurable. The many inventories made of patients in these infirmaries show that the illnesses which are most often fatal there are either ataxic or adynamic fevers, simple or complicated with pulmonary catarrhs, or lingering hectic fever which is sometimes associated with pulmonary phthisis or fulminating diarrhoea, which shows that these patients were previously exposed to the most debilitating risks. It transpired from an inventory made in one of these six months periods that out of seventy patients who had died in the infirmaries, either regarded as incurable or submitted to treatment, sixty-two had succumbed from different wasting illnesses (6) which the method followed at the Salpêtrière avoided for people who were solely treated there.

IX. DOUBTFUL SUCCESS OF TREATMENT IN CASES OF ALIENATION WITH INCONCLUSIVE DIAGNOSTIC SIGNS AND SYMPTOMS

356. The path followed in all branches of natural history, and the continual care taken to identify objects by means of distinguishing signs, can greatly clarify the method to be adopted in medicine. And this model can be followed more or less closely in certain illnesses, though it falls short of achieving any real degree of precision and correctness in some others. I have tried in vain to distinguish all cases of alienation and group them

by detectable signs into two large classes: those susceptible to being cured and the others who are incurable. Symptoms which are sometimes very violent may equally feature in an alienation which can, or cannot, be cured. When the disorder is deep-rooted, this is generally an ill omen, but sometimes there may be unexpected exceptions (7). A case of alienation judged from all the similar cases as being curable may encounter unforeseen obstacles in the course of treatment, either from the staff or the internal rules holding up progress, or from some incident which no human prudence could anticipate, or finally through some fault in applying the curative steps which have been poorly adapted to the character of the illness or to the particular variations of age, weather or temperament. For when one judges oneself harshly, how often does one not find oneself a long way from a particular goal one glimpsed yet cannot reach!

357. The inventory made at the end of the period covered by my table gave examples of these doubtful or equivocal cases. There were eight people in a deep-rooted state of insanity, in whom slowly progressive changes seemed to point to a complete return of reason in the future. Five melancholic patients were also in an equivocal state and their delusions were partially dissipated in such a way as to anticipate either a favourable or an adverse outcome. In two other examples all that remained of alienation was an insuperable aversion to work, which nevertheless was necessary to survive. Finally nothing could be made of a weakness in understanding affecting two other persons whose convalescence seemed equivocal. These seventeen cases of alienation could be regarded as equally liable to a successful or unsuccessful outcome: something which is always an obstacle to an accurate application of probabilities and an obstacle which the future progress of science will no doubt find out how to overcome.

358. It is certainly the doubtful cases which cause difficulties over the certificates of cure enabling each person to go back into society after treatment. The established authorities require this kind of guarantee from the doctor. These attestations must be sufficiently nuanced and be expressed without restriction when the alienation is accidental and of recent onset and convalescence has proceeded in orderly stages. One must proceed with some reserve if the hospice admission was preceded by one or two attacks even though recovery appeared straightforward. Fear of future relapses should be greater if the patient has had repeated attacks in the past or has had unsuccessful treatments elsewhere. There are many more reasons for concern if convalescence is incomplete and the relatives strongly press for a premature discharge. It is from repeated experience, and sometimes even having made mistakes, that one learns to step carefully and not compromise public safety.

359. A fundamental report of the successes and failures of treatment of the Salpêtrière patients, and the establishment of the resulting numerical ratios, show rather clearly the extent to which experimental medicine is capable of making sound progress by applying the calculation of probabilities. The benefit of this method will always be rightly questioned if only the favourable results are included. Whatever the divergence of opinion on the treatment of deranged patients may be, a genuine result confirmed by accurate summary of the registers following upon experience gained over nearly four years cannot be denied. And it cannot be contested that, as long as the hospice is directed along the same principles, there will be the same degree of probability in favour of any deranged patient who is admitted there. This degree of probability is estimated at 93 % provided the alienation, whether

maniacal insanity or melancholia, is of recent onset and has not been treated elsewhere. Determining this ratio would have been much simpler and immediate if exact information about the previous condition of the patients could always have been available in the hospice, the number of favourable and contrary cases could have been identified, and if it had not been necessary to resort to roundabout paths. I have nonetheless provided a genuine example of the method which should be followed. Precise records of alienation henceforth maintained in other hospices, and carefully drawn up general tables, will be able to set up so many comparisons for correcting or perfecting treatment methods and provide a solid basis for further research on the calculation of probabilities applied to one of the greatest objects of public welfare.

X. GENERAL RESULT OF TREATMENT OF DERANGED PATIENTS AT THE SALPÊTRIÈRE IN THE YEARS 1806 AND 1807

360. The large establishments for deranged patients are at risk of deteriorating, like all human institutions, and perhaps even more than any others. What energetic and constant supervision has to be exercised over all areas of the department by the staff! Is the doctor himself not liable to relax the vigour of his duties? And how else can the effects of all the abuses be noticed other than by comparing the results of different years and finding a respective reduction in the number of cures? It is again the calculation of probabilities which facilitates this.

Year 1806

361. The biggest difficulties to overcome, as in previous years, arose from the incomplete information received about the earlier condition of many of the patients, whether sent by the police or by the central admissions bureau. Moreover, there can be no agreement about the success or failure of the treatment without starting off from a firm base derived from regular and repeated observation. Indeed it is recognised as much in England as in France, first: that idiocy and dementia are generally incurable, so that at the Saint Luke hospice in London such patients are not admitted. Second: that maniacal insanity unsuccessfully treated elsewhere, not recent and begun more than three months earlier, or complicated by a state of paralysis, is looked upon at the same hospice as being incurable. These observations fully apply at the Salpêtrière, but at this hospice more latitude is allowed for the duration of the maniacal insanity, and for success of the treatment all that is asked for is that the onset does not go back longer than one year and that it is not passed on by hereditary transmission.

362. The number of patients treated during 1806 includes those sent to the hospice during the year and those who were still there at the end of 1805, giving a total of two hundred and thirty-two. This excludes in each case persons reduced to a state of idiocy or of dementia who were being given shelter but were not susceptible to treatment (although I tried this on a few using more vigorous methods). But forty-three must be subtracted from this number: they were treated without success. According to the registers, they should be added to the

number of deep-seated and reputedly incurable alienations. Indeed, in many of these cases, the maniacally insane or melancholic state went back for four, often six, or even ten years. It sometimes went back as far as fifteen or even twenty years. It is also recognised, according to notes recorded in the registers, that some of the patients had been unsuccessfully treated elsewhere using very potent methods and that consequently no success was achieved with treatment which nevertheless it was thought worth trying. From this it follows that the number of patients treated with justified hope of a cure during this year is reduced to one hundred and eighty-nine, out of which one hundred and sixty were discharged home according to the most accurate summary of the registers, giving a ratio of 84 %. The unfavourable prospects resulting from the lack of correct information about the original cause of the alienation should, moreover, not be forgotten. This often led to uncertainty over the choice of direct intervention.

363. Objections derived from the number of relapses are now irrelevant, since these must be attributed only to the imprudence the families sometimes showed in removing convalescent patients before their full recovery, in spite of the repeated advice they were given. The experience acquired in the hospice enables one to recognise the exact time when calm is fully restored and the functions of understanding are back to their natural state, and a relapse after returning into society is no longer to be feared. One only has to look at the certificates I give at the time of discharge, and which are kept in the admissions office, to satisfy oneself that all the doubtful and equivocal cases were pointed out and that there was no relapse which had not been foreseen.

364. The greatest mortality amongst the patients in the hospice generally affected the women with senile dementia, of advanced age, reduced to a languid state, with which the hospices were overcrowded and who had elsewhere gone through stages of exhaustion and indigence. Thirty-three of these died during the year 1806, as well as six persons reduced to a state of idiocy. Amongst the melancholic patients in the hospice, only nine were lost in the year, and the cause of their death was clear since it was due to an insuperable repugnance for taking any food despite all the steps that were tried; and these steps are very varied (paragraph 212). Maniacal insanity is generally associated with a state of vigour and good health, and it is very rare for patients of this kind to become sick in the hospice, especially in view of the care taken to give them all the freedom compatible with their condition, and letting them satisfy their appetite and have healthy air to breathe. But badly planned attempts made earlier to cure them, either elsewhere or within the family, the abstinence to which they are generally condemned, or the misleading appearances of an acute and frenetic fever which can simulate insanity, reduces some of these patients to the most deplorable state. And a number of them succumb some time after their admission. In certain cases an ataxic fever has been confused with a state of maniacal insanity and then the patient has come to die in the hospice. This accounts for sixteen deaths amongst the maniacally insane patients during the year of which I am speaking.

Year 1807

365. The number of patients treated in 1807 includes those who remained at the end of the preceding year and those who were sent to the hospice during the course of the year

concerned, making a total of two hundred and ninety-nine. To arrive at an accurate ratio between the number of cures and the number of admissions one needs to subtract from the total number, 1) three epileptic patients who were returned to their division having recovered their reason, 2) thirty-two patients who arrived at the hospice in a state of senile dementia, 3) eighteen paralysed patients, since constant observation shows that the complication of paralysis with alienation is incurable, 4) fourteen persons who descended into idiocy either original or incidental, 5) twenty with an hereditary maniacal insanity which had become habitual for at least nine years or more, and 6) nine patients in a deep-seated melancholic state. The total number of these patients amounts to ninety-six who must be regarded as not amenable to treatment and dismissed as incurable, following fruitless attempts tried on some of them. This figure subtracted from the total number of admissions leaves two hundred and three.

366. This last number must be further reduced following subsequent information obtained on several patients during the following years as the relatives were able to provide it. It was indeed noted that amongst the remaining two hundred and three thought to be amenable to being cured, fourteen maniacally insane patients had been in that state for seven years or more, nine melancholics were of an early date and, finally, ten cases of dementia and thirteen of idiocy had to be counted. These various numbers added together give a total of forty-six incurable cases and the failure of treatment must in no way be blamed on a defect in the method which was followed. On subtracting this number from the two hundred and three, one is left with one hundred and fifty-seven patients who were amenable to standard treatment. On the other hand the number of cures, which has been recognised as being one hundred and twenty-six, should be increased by ten patients subsequently returned to society in the year 1808; which results in the ratio between the number of cures and that of admissions being one hundred and thirty-six to one hundred and fifty-seven: that is to say 87 %.

367. A medical report should reveal the variations in mortality in a public establishment in order to identify and if possible reduce the causes. The simple inventory of the illnesses occurring in the hospice in 1807, and the accompanying circumstances, will make it easy to judge how the doctor stands in this respect regarding these unfortunate outcomes, even though they are essentially irrelevant to the state of alienation. Twenty-two very old patients were reduced to a state of senile dementia after suffering a major distress. Eighteen fell into a paralysed state with distraction of reason through earlier mismanagement of treatment and ended up succumbing. Eight melancholic patients were victims of wilful starvation despite all expedients taken to get them to eat, and three passed away in a state of complete idiocy. Six very old women sent from the Hôtel-Dieu arrived extremely debilitated as a result of lying in bed too long. Seven maniacally insane patients died of what is known as *malignant* or *ataxic* fever. Six other patients succumbed from scurvy, phthisis or attacks of apoplexy. Combined, these numbers make a total of seventy, giving a result which is scarcely encouraging if one does not bear the previous comments in mind. It is easy to see that the outcomes achieved in 1806 and in 1807 were 84 % and 87 % respectively, whereas it had for the previous years been 93 %; always by comparing the number of possible cures with the total number of admissions. The main reason for this set-back seems to me to stem from the complete lack of precise information about the precipitating cause of the alienation and of the remedies already used before the patients were admitted to the hospice. This, in

many cases, led to great instability in the treatment in these later years: in any case these patients were managed following the same methods. So it seems to me that the admission formalities need to be perfected. But should I not seek out other matters for reform and always be my own strict judge?

NOTES TO SIXTH SECTION

1. Medicine encompasses two distinct parts. One is purely descriptive and has as its objective the precise history of the phenomena of illnesses. This is already very advanced and its teaching makes fresh progress daily by taking the course followed in all the other branches of natural history as a guide. The other part of medicine, still shaky on its foundation under the name of *therapeutics*, only contains vague precepts whose application is perhaps more difficult and uncertain than a total absence of similar knowledge would be. In their special treatises on illnesses authors only mention a few successes and throw a veil over their failures. Hence blind empiricism features on a par with true knowledge and in this respect medicine can only take on the character of pure science by applying the calculation of probabilities.
2. In some instances I have referred to the same patient twice when a mental cause coincided with a physical cause: thus a violent fit of anger or deep chagrin was often combined with the circumstances of a confinement or the suppression of monthly periods. This resolves a kind of contradiction one might find between the lack I complain about of information received about the previous condition of a large number of patients, and the sum total of the numbers shown in the ninth and tenth columns of the general table.
3. The internal regulations of a hospice for deranged patients have to be far from being limited to a simple surveillance like other public establishments for the infirm. There has to be a special study of each of the patients in order to control their lapses, avoid anything which might aggravate them, never lose their confidence, or at least always know how to regain it, and the staff must be severely restrained. This task, which is so difficult, is fulfilled at the Salpêtrière with as much enthusiasm as skill by M. Pussin. who contributes so powerfully to the curing of patients through this kind of mental treatment.
4. Regularly maintained results obtained in a few hospices, national or foreign, have been publicised and this is where, in a public count from the Bethlehem hospital in England *(Observations on Insanity,* by Haslam), the ratio was 34 %. Recently it became known that in the hospital for the mentally ill in Berlin the ratio in 1803 was 117 to 413, or 28 %. At St. Luke's Hospital, where only favourable cases of recent onset are admitted, the ratio over five years was 2811 to 6458, which makes 43 %. But in order to contribute to the progress of science it is necessary to take a much more limited time, assume fixed control in the hospice and a treatment method whose elemental parts can clearly set, and then one is able to see a definite relationship between effect and cause.
5. The deep-rooted delusions of melancholic patients can most often only be dispelled by the timely seizing of a favourable opportunity. One of them claimed to have had a vision which announced that her death was inevitable during the course of the year. Every means successively taken to dissuade her failed and it was only after the whole year had gone by that she was finally lost for words. Soon her delusion completely evaporated and shortly afterwards she was discharged from the hospice.

6. Seventeen were victims of adynamic or ataxic fevers, twenty-five perished with a lingering or hectic fever, and twenty with fulminating diarrhoea.

7. A women suffering from deep melancholia for four years felt a strong urge to commit suicide and had been treated in vain in another hospice. Her distraction, which was heinous, consisted in wanting to kill somebody else in order to submit herself to the severity of the law since she was prevented from killing herself. She had such a distaste for life that in spite of her horror of committing a crime, she would do it, as she put it, to escape the cruellest torments – that of being alive. Every mental and physical method tried for nearly two years at the Salpêtrière had been ineffective and it was only after this period that her reason appeared to recover. Ten months of tranquillity and complete absence of her delusion were scarcely sufficient to reassure me and make me agree to her being discharged, but finally her cure seemed so sound that her request was granted and she returned to society. How many times during the first two years had she not been put in the same category as the other incurable patients!

7

CASES OF ALIENATION WHICH ARE INCURABLE AS A CONSEQUENCE OF MALFORMATIONS OR OTHER CAUSES

368. It is difficult to know the origin of the universally held opinion on the mentally ill found among ancient jurists: *semel furiosus semper præsumitur furiosus*[1] (1). Is this a mere opinion based on popular prejudices, or really the outcome of facts gathered in public asylums where the patients were isolated from society and considered to be incurable? Zacchias, in his medico-legal questions, put strict limitations on this general proposition and amongst the various cases which gave little hope of cure he pointed especially to those with an organic structural defect of the skull or brain. It is important to examine the clarification which further anatomical progress together with the particular direction I have followed in my own research has been able to bring to this subject.

369. Morgagni drew too general an inference about the density and consistency of the brain of mental patients, as more frequently repeated observations have subsequently shown. But the strict path he followed in his anatomical dissections and the historical display of observed facts will always be a model of wisdom and precision no less than of a healthy criticism. One has often had occasion to notice, like him, effusions of lymph in the ventricles of the brain, engorgement of blood vessels, changes occurring in the choroid plexus and corpus callosum, and small calcareous concretions in the pineal body etc. All these observations are confirmed every day by similar research. However, it must be agreed that in other brains of mentally ill patients none of these physical defects are found, nor any change in the physical structure of these parts. What is more decisive, these changes are sometimes seen in other quite different cases and following certain illnesses which have no connection with mental alienation such as epilepsy, apoplexy, convulsions and ataxic fevers. Besides, what enlightenment can come from a long list of all the changes occurring in the brain substance or meninges if they are isolated from a historical and detailed account of the

---

[1] *Once mad, always presumed mad – Ed.*

Medico-Philosophical Treatise on Mental Alienation.
Philippe Pinel. Translated by G. Hickish, D. Healy and L.C. Charland.
© 2008 John Wiley & Sons, Ltd.

earlier circumstances preceding these particular cases, and if the physical or mental cause of the alienation, its exact character, its progress, the treatment given, the incidental illnesses which developed during its course and everything which specially distinguished it are all omitted? Indeed sometimes the organic defects, instead of being seated in the brain or its coverings, are situated in the abdominal viscera and consist mainly in morbid changes seen in the substance of the liver, stomach or intestine, all of which increases the difficulties even more and should always call for caution against hasty judgements. It is with this in mind that the diaries of observations which I kept in the Salpêtrière hospice were completed. I will publish their individual case histories, together with any more I am able to write up, as I have already said (paragraph 320). When their numbers are sufficient it will only be a case of drawing general conclusions from them with the appropriate exceptions and modifications. Here I will restrict myself to the irregularities and defects in conformation which the structure of the skull can show in a few cases of alienation, first making some comments showing how rare these cases actually are.

I. PERIODS OF LIFE WHEN INSANITY FROM MENTAL CAUSES IS MOST LIKELY TO DEVELOP

370. A single result of numerical calculations about the periods of life offering the greatest likelihood of alienation reveals in general how rare malformations of the brain or skull must be. I have made an exact count of the number of insane patients transferred to the Bicêtre during Years II and III of the Republic, carefully noting their respective ages. To set out the results of the calculation better, I took care at the end of each year to draw up a table in which the periods of age were divided into tens of years, from the first to the sixtieth decade, so as to incorporate the ages of the different patients. I noticed that out of the total number of seventy-one who were admitted to the Bicêtre in Year II of the Republic, only three were included between the ages of fifteen and twenty years and not a single one before this lower age at the time of puberty. Twenty-three other patients were intermediary from the twentieth to the thirtieth years, fifteen from the thirtieth to fortieth years and the same between forty and fifty. There were nine between fifty and sixty, just six from then to seventy, and none after that age. I obtained a similar result for Year III of the Republic, in as much as no patient's age was found to be before the age of puberty. Two decades of years comprising from twenty to thirty, and from thirty to forty, embraced most of the patients. There was a smaller number in the years between forty and fifty, and the least number between fifty to sixty. An exact summary of the Bicêtre hospice registers over ten consecutive years serves to confirm the same facts, as I show in Table 7.1:

371. The particular predisposition for alienation of understanding at certain periods of life that are more liable than others to stormy passions fits in well with the result of facts observed in the hospices. In the inventory of patients which I made at Bicêtre in Year III of the Republic, I recognised that the underlying causes of this illness are most commonly very fiery mental disorders such as fanatic ambition and dashed expectations, religious fanaticism, severe chagrins and thwarted love. Out of one hundred and thirteen patients for whom I could obtain exact information, thirty-four had been reduced to this state through domestic upsets, twenty-four because of obstacles put in the way of a much desired marriage,

Table 7.1   Ages

Patients admitted To Bicêtre	Ages						Total
	15 to 20	20 to 30	30 to 40	40 to 50	50 to 60	60 to 70	
1784	5	33	31	24	11	6	110
1785	4	39	49	25	14	3	134
1786	4	31	40	32	15	5	127
1787	12	39	41	26	17	7	142
1788	9	43	53	21	18	7	151
1789	6	38	39	33	14	2	132
1790	6	28	34	19	9	7	103
1791	9	26	32	16	7	3	93
1792	6	26	33	18	12	3	98
9 last months Year I	1	13	13	7	4	2	40
Year II of Republic	3	23	15	15	9	6	71

thirtythrough events in the Revolution and twenty-five through fanatical zeal or terrors of the next life. Certain professions also predispose to maniacal insanity more than others, and this especially applies where a vivid imagination, continually in a state of excitement, is not counterbalanced by a culture of the functions of understanding, or else where understanding has become exhausted through too much dry studying. Thus on consulting the registers of the hospice for deranged patients at the Bicêtre there are many priests and monks listed, as well as people from the countryside who have become deranged as the result of fearful prospects for the future. There are many artists, painters, sculptors and musicians, a few poets enraptured by their versifications, and a big enough number of lawyers and public prosecutors. On the other hand, there are no men seen there who habitually exercise their intellectual faculties, such as naturalists, clever doctors, chemists and, for the strongest of reasons, no geometricians.

372. These preliminary observations indicate in advance how rare lesions or deformities of the skull must be among deranged patients, since at adult age ossification of the bones of the head is complete and mental disorders cannot change it. It just remained to check this truth by frequently repeated autopsies and accurate research. Greding, the German author (2) who has devoted himself particularly to this kind of work, says that out of one hundred mentally ill patients he found three enlarged heads and two very small ones. He also speaks of certain skulls which are remarkable for their thickness or for the particular shape of the frontal bone, which sometimes appeared to him to be small and contracted, or for compression of the temples, or roundness of some heads whereas others are oblong. But it can be seen how vague and indeterminate these observations are, for the author has not used any accurate method for measuring the dimensions of these skulls, so he consequently could not compare them with one another in any exact way. There are, besides, varieties of the skull which are common in all sorts of people, even aside from the case of alienation, so these must be left aside in research on deranged patients to avoid false reasoning and not to take as a determining cause something which is just a fortuitous factor coincidental to the insanity. This is enough to show that I have followed a different method in the anatomical research I have carried out in the hospices.

373. A fairly common opinion attributes mental alienation to defects of the brain and, especially, to variations and disproportions of the skull. It would no doubt be a great doctrinal subject to investigate whether goodly proportions of the head should be looked upon as the external sign of excellence of the faculties of understanding. A first step might be to take the ancient sculptor's masterpiece (3), the Python Apollo, as the model, then put in the second row the heads of men most successfully organised for the fine arts and sciences, and then go down through all the successive degrees of disproportion of the head and intellectual capacity to the man who has fallen into dementia or idiocy. But observation does not confirm these plausible speculations, for one sometimes finds the most perfect shapes of the head associated with the most limited discernment and sees, moreover, remarkable variations of conformation co-existing with all the attributes of talent and genius. However it is no less interesting and useful for scientific progress to establish certain clearly observed facts from new research, to examine the varieties of conformation which seem immaterial to free use of the functions of understanding, to note especially the skull deformities which coincide with obvious disturbances of these same functions, and finally to indicate the species of mental alienation which depend more particularly upon faults in symmetry or capacity of the bony parts of the skull or smallness of its dimensions in comparison with the full stature.

374. Camper, in his research on facial feature differences, had to turn all his attention towards what he called the facial line in order to best grasp the characteristic and consistent features of the face of the different peoples of the world. The basic consideration I am attending to concerns the shape and dimensions of the skull cavity but I have had to direct my research differently. I examined the relationship between the heights of different heads with their depth in the direction of the main axis of the skull, and with their size at the anterior and posterior parts of this same bony structure, in order to be able to recognise the defects in symmetry in the corresponding areas and compare the volume of the head, or rather its perpendicular height against the full stature, in the live subject. To achieve greater accuracy in determining these relationships it was necessary to have a basic example or benchmark for comparison; and what better could I turn to than the admirable proportions of Apollo's head, using the dimensions taken by Gérard Audran (4)?

375. But I must not disguise the obstacles experienced when one wishes to apply the principles of mathematical science to this research. Nothing looks less amenable to exact measurement than the cavity formed by the collection of skull bones. First, at the bottom, there are various recesses and irregular protuberances; and above one just sees the crude appearance of a partial ellipsoid whose anterior convexity is different from the posterior, and whose lateral parts are flattened. The result of this is that a section through the skull parallel to its base only has a remote resemblance to an ellipse and cannot lend itself to any kind of calculation. So I was limited to mechanical methods to measure the dimensions of the skull in a most approximate way. To initially establish a fixed position for all the heads, like Camper[2] I put a prop under the occipital foramen of such a size that the extremity of the nasal apophasis and the upper border of the external auditory canal were in a line parallel to the horizontal plane. I then constructed a parallelepiped such that the two vertical planes which cut at right angles are fixed in a stable manner on the horizontal plane whilst the two other vertical planes can slide whilst remaining parallel to the first two and thus adapt

---

[2] *Physical dissertation on differences of facial features* etc, Utreich, 1791.

themselves to the different head volumes. The superior plane resting on the top of the head is loose and takes up a horizontal position with the help of a spirit level. With this arrangement, the respective distances of the parallel planes give the most exact impression one is able to form of the three dimensions of the head, taking care that the anterior plane does not descend below the coronal apophasis to let the bones of the face move forwards. With a live subject, I use curved compasses to measure the respective dimensions of the head and skull. In this way one has an object for comparison between skulls of different shapes and volumes.

II. VARIETIES OF HEAD DIMENSIONS AND CHOICE OF PARTS TO DRAW

376. A continual source of mistakes, in the pathological anatomy research carried out by Greding, was quoting as the cause of alienation certain varieties of skull shape which might coincide with this illness but might also be found on death in people who had never been alienated. To avoid these mistaken judgements I have examined and measured large number of heads taken either from the collections of the Natural History Museum, from the exhibition rooms of the School of Medicine or from elsewhere. With the aid of curved compasses I have also taken the dimensions of the heads of various people of either sex who have been, or still are, in a state of alienation. I have noticed that in general the two most striking varieties, either of an elongated skull or a short skull approaching a sphere, occur independently with no association with any free exercise of the function of understanding. However, I have noted that there are certain skull malformations associated with a state of alienation, especially with dementia or inherent idiocy. To make these facts clearer, I thought I should have some heads drawn which establish a range through their difference or similarity and seem to bear out some kind of relationship between certain structural faults in the skull and the state of the functions of understanding.[3] First I had the shape of the head of an insane woman drawn who died at the age of forty-nine years (Plate I, Fig. 1). The shape was elongated, for the height of the head was less than its length; and I set it against the skull bones of a person of sound mind who had died at the age of twenty years, which is different from the preceding one (Plate I, Fig.3) by what is called roundness or sphericity of the head. For the end of the same plate I kept the drawing of a very irregular head of a young person who died at the age of eleven years (Plate I, Figs 5 & 6) in a state of complete idiocy. At the beginning of the second plate I show the head with an elongated skull of an insane man aged forty-two who had been completely cured for about seven years (Plate II, Fig. 1). In contrast to this shape I put the very rounded head of a young man who died when twenty-two years old, and who I can vouch was gifted with the healthiest judgement (Plate II, Fig. 2). I end with the drawing of the head of a young man of twenty-one years, reduced to a state of complete idiocy, which is remarkable for the extreme disproportion of the shape and dimensions of the skull (Plate II, Fig.5). The two heads thus completing the plates must be the principle object of my anatomical considerations.

377. Anatomical examination of the heads of two maniacally insane women, one who died aged forty-nine years (Plate I, Figs 1 & 2) and the other at fifty-four (Plate I, Figs 3 & 4), has again confirmed the considerations I had about the most common causes of maniacal

---

[3] See Plates I and II on pages 191 and 192.

insanity, which are deep mental afflictions, and on the age-periods representing the greatest likelihood of developing these. In other words it is not a manifestation of a particular conformation which cannot be found in skulls picked out at random. The head of one is simply like the elongated form, and that of the second reverts to the shape of short heads. The frontal flattening of the one, which seems to form an inclined plane, and the perpendicular elevation of the other are variations which are often seen and from which one cannot make any deductions either favourable or adverse about the faculties of understanding. However, it is different with the skull whose picture I am suppressing here and which I carefully kept on the death of a girl of nineteen years who has been in a state of idiocy from birth. The length of this head is the same as that of the two other maniacally insane patients, but its height is one centimetre more than the second and two centimetres above the first, whilst its width is less. This gives this head a disproportionate degree of height and a lateral flattening common in congenital idiocy. I have noticed each of these two features in two young idiots still living. Such changes are attributed to nearly all the cretins in the Vaud area.

378. I have tried to look at this skull again from a different point of view, contrasting it with another skull which is well-formed. I had corresponding sections made of each of them, passing through the most prominent part of the frontal bosses and the upper quarter of the lambdoid suture. I thus established a means of making a comparison between the two irregular ellipses resulting from these sections and I saw that, in the well-formed head, the two near-ellipses are set in a symmetrical manner around the central axis, so that the combined axes drawn from the right anterior part to the left posterior part, and those from the left anterior part to the right posterior part, are approximately equal. On the other hand, in the malformed skull, the two near-ellipses are not symmetrically positioned on the two sides of the axis, and the one on the right has a more pronounced curvature at the front whilst it is the opposite posteriorly. The near-ellipse on the left is shaped the reverse to this so that posteriorly there is a bigger curvature with a smaller one anteriorly. This difference, which is plain to see, is even more obvious on measuring the combined axes, for those going from right to left measure twenty-two centimetres and those going from left to right only measure seventeen centimetres. I have found the same structural peculiarity in the head of an eighteen-month old baby and the difference in the combined axes was even one and a half centimetres. Was this infant doomed to live in a state of idiocy? This is something that was impossible to say from the little development which had yet taken place in his mental faculties.

379. I must not omit another malformation in the head I am describing, having to do with the thickness of the skull wall. This is everywhere twice the normal, for it mainly measures one centimetre, and even a little more anteriorly, consequently reducing the large and small axes of the internal ellipse. It would be easy to calculate how much the internal capacity of the skull is reduced by this increased thickness if the constituent bones formed a regular ellipsoid, since one would only need to determine the mass formed by the revolution of an elliptical space whose greater and lesser axes would be known. However, the general irregularity of the shape of the skull denied me such a calculation and I restrict myself to remarking that, since such masses are between them like the cubes of their equivalent dimensions, it must be concluded that whatever the irregularity of their shapes may be, the increased thickness diminishes the internal capacity of the skull in a remarkable manner.

380. Do the abnormalities of conformation I have just drawn attention to in the skull of a person who died in idiocy, with its flattening at the sides, lack of symmetry between the right and left parts and, finally, its thickness, which is double the normal, not seem to show that everything has combined to make the internal cavity housing the brain smaller? But I must also be careful to avoid jumping to conclusions and I restrict myself just to recording details without yet deciding whether there is an immediate and necessary connection between the state of idiocy and the malformations I have described. The youngster was in the most complete state of idiocy since infancy. She occasionally made inarticulate sounds but showed no sign whatever of intelligence or affective state. She ate when food was held to her mouth, did not appear to have any sense of her own existence and was reduced to a purely automatic life. She died of scurvy last year, which had caused haemorrhages at the base of the skull and seemed to have affected the brain substance so much that I could reach no decision regarding its softness or specific gravity.

381. On first sight of one idiot patient the most striking thing was the expanse of the face compared with the smallness of the skull, but there was no animation in the features of his physiognomy and nothing to correct the impression of absolute stupidity. There was great disproportion between the height of the head and the full stature, a flattening of the shape of the head at the top and temples, a dazed look and a gaping mouth. The whole scope of his thoughts was limited to three (5) or four confused ideas, poorly expressed by so many half-articulated sounds. He had hardly enough intelligence to convey food towards his mouth, a lack of sensation so bad as to be unaware of passing urine and faeces, a weak heavy tottering gait, extreme inertia and an apathetic aversion to any kind of movement. There was a total absence of the very natural attraction which leads mankind to reproduce: an attraction which is sufficiently potent in the case of the cretin as at least to give him some sense of his existence. This ambiguous creature whom nature seemed to have placed at the extreme fringes of the human race for physical and mental qualities was the son of a farmer and had been taken to the hospice for deranged patients at Bicêtre about two years earlier. He appeared to have been afflicted from infancy with the same character of nonentity and idiocy.

382. The extreme disproportion between the height of the head of the idiot patient (Plate II, Figs & 6) and his full stature was easy to appreciate at first sight; but to define it exactly it was necessary to take the dimensions of the head with curved compasses, relate its height to that of the full stature and then compare this ratio with that of the best proportioned statures. So I have embarked on these tasks using new measures, and found that the height of this idiot patient was eighteen decimetres and the height of his head alone was eighteen centimetres. So the ratio of his whole stature to the height of his head is 180 to 18, or in other words the head is only 1 to 10 of the total stature. On the other hand the patient whose head I had drawn (Plate II, Fig. 1) and who formerly only had periodic attacks of maniacal insanity, has a much better proportion for the head compared with the total height. The latter is in fact seventeen decimetres and the head height twenty-three centimetres; so the one in relation to the other is 170 to 23, or 7.4 to 1. In this case the total stature is approximately seven and a half times the height of the head, which comes much closer to the ratio provided by the Apollo, since in the latter case the full stature is seven times the height of the head plus three and a half units, according to Gérard Audran. So how excessively small in relation to the full stature is the idiot patient's head, since it is only one tenth of the full stature, implying a very significant malformation the likes of which I have

not found in the numerous heads whose dimensions I have taken! On the other hand nothing is commoner than finding heads in society with too flattering proportions. In other words, for them to be in the right proportion to the rest of the body, the height should be greater. But this conformation only gives one more assumption regarding intellectual faculties, and as anyway there are other ways of judging a man, for example on the basis of his words and actions, it is ignored.

383. Ancient artists gifted with the most refined tact and rare sensitivity of observation could not miss having views on the exact proportions which go towards the head's beauty. No doubt it is this which led to Apollo's being divided into four parts by equally spaced horizontal planes (paragraph 116). One of these parts begins at the hair margin on the forehead and extends to the vertex. The shape of the patient's head (Plate II, Fig. 1), like that of a well-shaped man, is not very far from this set ratio. For the total height of his head is twenty-three centimetres and that of the face is seventeen centimetres. On subtracting one from the other there are six centimetres of difference which, compared against the total head height, gives a ratio closely approaching that of 1 to 4 found on Apollo's head. On the contrary, the height of the idiot patient's head is eighteen centimetres and the height of the face is fifteen centimetres: subtraction gives three centimetres difference which is only one sixth of the height, showing how much the vault of the skull is depressed, and consequently its capacity is diminished.

384. This diminution is even more pronounced from another aspect. For it is seen that in well formed heads a horizontal section taken of the skull through the upper third of the temples gives an irregular ellipse, such that the double coordinate passing through the anterior third is always well under that of the posterior third. The patient's head (Plate II, Fig. 1) comes close from this aspect to well-formed heads, for the posterior double coordinate is longer by two centimetres than the anterior. By contrast these two lines are approximately equal in the head of the idiot patient (Plate II, Figs 5 & 6), as I have checked with the curved compasses, so that the skull section I referred to would give a kind of ellipse which is almost regular. This shows the extent to which the posterior lobes of the brain must be reduced in volume by this particular conformation. However, one cannot say that this lack of capacity is the sole and unique cause of the deficient development of mental faculties.

385. One of the heads which is the most remarkable for its shape and the smallness of its dimensions seems to me to be the one which I have had represented (Plate I, Figs 5 & 6), and which I kept on the death of the young idiot patient whose singular character has been described above (paragraph 179). Here I leave out the anatomical considerations to which examination of this head gives rise, and which could lead to finding some sort of correspondence between certain physical lesions of the brain and some marked changes affecting the functions of understanding. I will limit myself to giving an idea of the excessive smallness of this head, comparing its volume with that of a child of seven years gifted with exceptional intelligence.

	Head dimensions of seven-year-old child	Head dimensions of eleven-year-old idiot
Length	1 decim. 8 cm	1 decim. 3 cm
Width	1 decim. 3 cm	0 decim. 9 cm
Height	1 decim. 6 cm	1 decim. 3 cm

386. All other subsequent details of the irregular shape of this head and the variations in volume of other patients, and all the comparative calculations on which this is based, viewing the collection of bones of the skull as a near-ellipsoid, will be set out in a memorandum which I mean to read at the Institute at one of our special meetings.

III. CASE OF ALIENATION THAT BECAME INCURABLE THROUGH ACCIDENTAL CAUSES

387. There are some simple truths in medicine which good souls have recalled since the furthest antiquity, and which are neglected when treatment proceeds without a system. The best way of curing illnesses, Hoffmann[4] said, stems from nature's beneficial efforts; and this general maxim can be successfully applied to mental alienation by removing the obstacles which can set themselves against this beneficial trend! On the contrary, have we not followed a retrograde path in propping up certain hypothetical opinions for managing treatment? Maniacal insanity, it has been said, *is generally incurable, so to treat it successfully it must be transformed into a fever, and this is achieved,* it is added, *by copious blood-lettings which weaken the patient and expose him to the contagious elements in the hospice air.* Others have just viewed maniacal insanity as a strong surge of blood to the head, and have endlessly increased the blood-lettings and applications of ice to the head to counteract nature's opposite efforts. A large number of incurable patients who are the sad consequences of efforts to put these vain theories put into practice can be seen in the hospices.

388. On my visits I have often witnessed the distressing spectacle of many patients who have become incurable through foolhardiness, premature visits or discharges before the state of convalescence had become established, or due to the intervention of an authority inclined to interfere with that of the superintendent responsible for internal regulations. One melancholic patient thought she could see her enemies' conspiracies directed against her everywhere and she was convinced that she could be harmed at great distances by invisible means, such as through electric fluid. Her judgement seemed to be sound in every other respect, but she remained agitated for part of the night and subject to intense restlessness. She muttered against the superintendent when he tried to dissipate her delusions, maintaining that she was not mad and that it was a crying injustice to hold her any longer. She took her complaints to other agents in the hospice who were pleased to talk with her and appeared to share her opinion. From then on all confidence in the superintendent and the doctor was lost, and her illness thus persisted for some years with no hope of a cure. Another patient, a widow of an old captain, subject at intervals to a mild delirium, thought she was a special favourite and became proud and haughty, and at the least argument had often threatened to write to the superior authorities. Her vanity made her think she was destined to marry a prince and from then on she would listen to nothing, and indeed neither could her confidence be gained by kindly manners (6) nor her character be tamed by any methods of restraint, so that her condition had become incurable.

389. A devotionally deranged patient, who was equally inaccessible to all the methods of gentleness or discipline which could be used, found a young convalescent patient whom she began to address in a very enthusiastic fashion. She took her aside, spoke to her in an

---

[4] The title of this doctor's dissertation is: *De Optima naturæmorbi medendi methodo.*

inspired tone and told her forcibly that *she must above everything save her soul, not listen to men, who were all treacherous and deceitful.* To these words she added genuflexions and fussing calculated to severely disturb the young person's imagination and set her right back. Relapses became frequent, sometimes on reading certain devotional books, and at other times simply at the sight of a priest or through secret encounters with other fanatics, all of which led to a kind of chronic and presumably incurable maniacal insanity. Devotional delirium seems to spread as if by contagion; and what supervision does it not demand in well-managed hospices! A former nun, who previously thought she had been possessed by the Devil, was relieved of her delusions and had started on her convalescence. By chance she met an old deeply religious woman whose recurring scruples had gone on to become delusional, but who was also on the way to regaining her reason. They joined to pray together, sympathised with one another over their lots and reciprocally inspired each other with new fears. In this way, both of them fell back into a kind of peaceful dementia which no longer left any hope of a cure.

390. What a lot of young people there are who become incurable through not being amenable to the rule of daily work as a result of laziness that is either inborn or acquired from habit! This is what led to the addition of sewing rooms close to the convalescents' dormitories (paragraphs 209, 212 and 213). But many women brought up in the country or those who are accustomed to dealing in produce in the towns cannot apply themselves to this sedentary work, and it was necessary to look for other kinds of work more suited to their tastes and habitual way of life. So it was thought, to meet these needs, that a large enclosure of three acres should be attached to the hospice for deranged patients where they could walk about and where an area could be set side for growing plants and shrubs. A pump was even erected to draw water and conduct it by means of a subterranean pipe into a large reservoir. It was agreed that convalescent patients prone to laziness should take turns on the pump, carrying water, cultivating plants with pretty flowers, clearing away the stones, generally developing part of the enclosure and thus passing part of the day in continuous activity. But at this time jealousies and rivalries between the employees only too common in big establishments caused these healthy arrangements to fail. Under the pretext of a drive to cleanliness, the patients were even told that it was not their place to work and that this task was reserved for *punishment parties* doing the rough work in the hospice. The superintendent, held up in his projects, lost heart and restricted himself to having a few recesses cultivated in the enclosure, which brightened the outlook with some interesting-looking plants. So the general plan was aborted. It was at that time that a little adventuress who had become demented, and whose reason it was planned to restore through the rule of work, made some alliances through idleness with other convalescent patients who were prone to laziness. Their days were spent wandering about, telling tales and half-crazy exploits, and in an inventory I made in one of the following years (in February 1807), I declared several of them to be incurable (7).

391. The incurability of the maniacally insane or those with melancholic delirium from the upper classes of society must nearly always be attributed to the constant habit of inactivity, and the facility to indulge in visions and dreams. A forty-five-year-old lady who was formerly rich fell into misfortune and insanity as a consequence of the Revolution and ended with a chronic melancholia of an unusual kind. She saw nothing around her except the effects of a magic art designed to torment her and everybody near her seemed to be dedicated to this

devious activity. For some time a new delusion joined the first: she thought she was being continually followed by a spirit which watched her, freely entered all the parts of her body, spoke to her and often shared her bed. Hardly had she lain down than she thought she saw a brilliant light which fell on her and overcame her with absolute power. She said at the same time she felt a burning heat and sometimes a kind of numbness. Sometimes this spirit became forward and made her experience the appearances of sexual union; most often the resulting sensation seemed to be a gentle zephyr's breath. She conversed freely with him and maintained she distinctly heard these words: *you have done the right thing, I hold you in my power*. This melancholic patient, in the midst of all these delusional scenes, sometimes remained immobile and trembling, and sometimes her hair seemed to stand up on end. She gave cries of indignation and her neighbours heard her warding off the powers agitating her in a strong and passionate voice. At other times, disturbed by fainthearted terrors, she got up and, with her head bowed to the ground, she embarked upon the most fervent prayers. Physical and mental treatments were already being combined when one day by accident the pupil charged with following her case history lent his hand on her bed, and from then she added him to the number of magicians relentlessly tormenting her. Her mistrust was carried to the extreme, and all treatment became impossible.

392. Idiocy can stem from a malformation of the head (paragraph 375) and so it would be superfluous to try to cure it. But the abuse of blood-lettings during earlier treatment of the maniacal insanity, a severe fright, a sudden suppression of or delays in the monthly periods can also cause it, and then the cure of a few rare cases of idiotism is possible primarily by the use of internal and external stimulants. These were vainly used on a young idiot girl who had experienced a severe fright at a particular time and who is still in the infirmary, where she always seems like a kind of inanimate statue. Success was very pronounced in another young person who was previously deranged and whom the frequency of blood-lettings had plunged into idiocy.

393. Senile dementia is no less beyond the resources of nature and art, and very rarely too can one cure cases that arise from an accidental cause, especially if it is preceded by certain preludes of apoplexy or paralysis. But defects in understanding can become very marked without actually overstepping particular limits. A lady of rare worthiness but who could become very irascible over the slightest matter, ended after eighteen years of marriage by falling into an unequivocal state of dementia. Isolation for five months and the repeated use of a vesiculatory to the nape of the neck partly brought back her former ways and affectionate character. She was particular about her dress and capable of certain sedentary occupations, but a marked weakness of understanding always remained, with a very limited sphere of ideas. The simplest relationship between objects escaped her and she hardly distinguished at home whether it was for her to give instructions or to obey. She only had a confused image of the places where she had always lived and often hardly knew whether she was in the town or the countryside. Her least movements were slow and laboured, her hands were shaky and she retained none of her earlier dexterity. She was reduced to a state of prolonged childhood, but she inspired a tender interest from the memory of the domestic virtues which had gone before.

394. The complication of maniacal insanity with any other spasmodic illness like hysteria, epilepsy or hypochondria, can give rise to unanticipated obstacles to the success of treatment and make it lengthy or even incurable. This truth has been long recognised, but to make it

more striking I think I should report an example of this kind which will always be with me, and which can, moreover, offer a useful lesson to those who, in the excitement of youth, take up the study of any science with more enthusiasm and ardour than discernment and prudence. A young man aged twenty-four years, gifted with a vivid imagination, came to Paris a few years before the Revolution to study law, and he thought he was destined by nature subsequently to play a most brilliant role at the Bar. There was nothing to touch his eagerness to learn. He showed continuous application, spent his life in retreat, kept to an extreme sobriety to give more flight to his mental faculties and adopted a Pythagorean routine throughout the rigour of the term. A few months later violent migraines developed, with frequent epistaxes, spasmodic chest cramps, vague intestinal pain, embarrassing flatulence and greatly enhanced mental sensitivity. Sometimes he approached me with a radiant look of joy and he could not express the utter delight he said he felt in himself. At other times I found him plunged in the horrors of consternation and despair, and he pleaded with me to end his sufferings. The features of profound hypochondria were easy to recognise. I then went over the dangers with him and often beseeched him to change his way of life, but he stuck to his own plans with inflexible obstinacy. The nervous symptoms in his head, lower abdomen and chest increased, there were frequent swings from extreme despondency to convulsive joy, there were faint-hearted terrors, especially in the shadows of the night, and inexpressible anguish. Sometimes he came to find me, melting in tears and entreating me to snatch him from the arms of death. I then took him away into the countryside and a few walks, with comforting talk, seemed to give him a new life. But on his return to his room there were fresh perplexities and his faint-hearted fears returned. He found extra desolation and despair in the increasing confusion of his ideas, the impossibility of devoting himself in future to study and the oppressive conviction of seeing the prospect of celebrity and glory, with which his imagination had been cradled, disappear for the future. Complete alienation soon followed. One day, to take a break, he went to a show, and the play 'A philosopher without knowing it' was being performed. From then on he was assailed with the darkest suspicions. He was quite persuaded that his silly ways had been enacted and accused me of having myself provided the material for the play. The next morning he came to reproach me in a very serious and bitter way for betraying the courtesies of friendship and exposing him to public ridicule. His delusions had no limits. He believed that along public paths he could see comedians, dressed up as nuns and priests[5], studying all his movements to discover the secret of his thoughts. In the shadows of the night he thought he was being attacked, sometimes by spies, sometimes by robbers or assassins, and once he spread alarm in the quarter, throwing open the windows and shouting at the top of his voice that someone wanted to kill him. One of his relations decided to get him to undergo the treatment for maniacal insanity at the Hôtel-Dieu and arranged for him to leave twenty days later with a travelling companion to go to a small town near the Pyrenees. Equally mentally and physically weakened, and constantly swinging between lapses of the wildest delirium and attacks of dark, deep hypochondria, he then condemned himself to complete isolation in the paternal home. He became bored and developed an overwhelming dislike of life, with a refusal to eat and abruptness to all around him. He finally eluded the surveillance of his guardian, fled in his shirt tails into a nearby wood, became lost, expired from weakness and exhaustion through lack of nourishment, and two days later was found dead holding in his hand Plato's famous dialogue on the immortality of the soul.

---

[5] This was in 1783.

395. How different is this to the usual maniacally insane patient who, angered through blind fieriness or full of pompous ideas of his superiority, rages, threatens, always adopts a dominant tone and can drive himself to acts of the greatest violence if his fury is not checked or he is not faced with an imposing show of strength which he cannot hope to overcome (paragraphs 191, 192)! Will his magical delusions and his enthusiasms not become habitual if nobody tries to put an end to them by methods handled with as much strength as skill? So the secret lies in subduing the patient at the right time and convincing him that any resistance on his part would be in vain. All that then remains is to win his confidence with a benevolent approach and clear evidence of being keenly concerned for his happiness. Once this has been achieved, some time is needed to calm his earlier agitation completely and to strengthen his still frail and faltering reason. This is something which can only be accomplished in well-organised public or private establishments. So should one envy the rich man who has become deranged the sad distinction of having himself treated in his own home, where he is waited upon by his servants and often surrounded by his close relatives? And should there be any surprise if the treatment is then lacking in success, as repeated experience has shown me?

396. The high opinion one has of oneself can be so exaggerated, and the habit of ordering others about so ingrained, that the deranged patient may no longer be capable of being restored to order by any kind of discipline: that is to say his maniacal insanity becomes incurable. Examples of patients who believe they are crowned heads are not rare in the hospices for either sex, and how can a delusion which becomes so powerful and so cherished be dispelled? Does M. Vierus (de Præstigiis demonum) not cite a deranged patient so infatuated with his supreme power that he said he was the sovereign of kings: *Rex regum, dominus dominantium, monarcus mundi*. A young girl full of haughtiness, who was once passionate about reading novels, ended by falling into a very violent maniacal insanity from which she seemed to have been cured after several months of treatment at the Salpêtrière. However, the sad thought that her reason had been distracted so injured her pride that she had an insuperable reluctance to reappear in her native area, and everything caused fresh relapses to be feared.

397. This obstacle to recovery is even more difficult to overcome when the most uncontrollable vanity is associated with the best conceived projects and a kind of fury to sow tumult and disorder everywhere. Here is the example given by one of the patients at the Salpêtrière with all the trickery of a deeply thoughtful mind. Several of her companions were first dragged into the project of a plotted escape, treacherously hatched in silence. Then she dictated letters full of abuse to the superintendent and she had even made the atrocious plan of killing him amidst a small carefully staged riot. Sometimes bitter quarrels were instigated between the most tranquil patients. At other times the will to commit suicide was shrewdly provoked or even vaunted as a laudable and courageous act: something which is very dangerous for particular melancholic patients who are only too inclined to this act of despair. Could one stop oneself from setting the most absolute and inviolable isolation against this kind of turbulent rage?

398. All monstrous excesses of vice, the apathetic torpor of indolence, the habit of drunkenness and unbridled abandon to sexual pleasures are as likely to lead to mental alienation as to foment it. Can the most enlightened doctor dispel the effects of the most pressing

inclinations which seem to have absorbed or overwhelmed all the mental faculties? To set against the touching spectacle presented in the sewing room by a large gathering of laborious and peaceful convalescent patients, I continuously have the contrast of a few other agitated women straying inside the hospice for whom no wise advice or any kind of discipline has succeeded in getting to work and who, through their habitual wanderings, have remained stuck in a state of perpetual illness without being able to move on to an established convalescence. Does the whole of society not continually show the same contrast of vices and virtues? And can one hope to cure an alienation which springs from vice converted into a deep-seated habit?

Does the mental treatment of a deranged patient not also become extremely difficult if he has formerly possessed great riches or occupied eminent positions? Can he forget, even in the midst of the confusion and turmoil of his ideas, the brilliance of the dignities with which he was formerly adorned? I have observed, in these cases, that the man vaguely retraces all the pleasures of vanities, often speaking of the millions at his disposal, the rewards he is keeping for those he protects and all the sumptuous titles which his imagination conjures up. He adopts an imposing attitude, always wants to give the orders, and if he obeys a higher authority it is almost always at the same time while retaining his natural haughtiness and inflexibility of character. He is moreover private, full of shrewd reserve in between his petulant sallies, and he adds to a lack of understanding of others in general, the skill of hiding everything from them. So how can the one who is looking after him gain an ascendancy over his mind and win his confidence, which is essential for the gradual return of full use of his reason? We could just as well exclude any rare man of elevated character, full of deep and well-thought-out morality, who invariably sees in social status the noble opportunity to work towards the happiness of the human species.

399. I am not going to indulge in satires. I solely devote myself to medical considerations about the most common origin and the treatment of illnesses of the mind, but I cannot refrain from making a general remark. This is that practice of a universal morality of all peoples does not constitute the dominant taste of the present century, whereas all the other sciences have made great progress. Should the schools and different philosophical sects who brought fame to Ancient Greece instead be revived? Or else should we devote the last years of the education of young people to a serious and profound study of the lives of great men by Plutarch? Whatever answer one gives to these deep questions, one cannot deny medicine the benefit of working powerfully towards the return of a sound morality, giving an account of the evils which result from its neglect, and especially in publishing a series of corroborating facts under the title of *Annals of Mental Alienation*.

NOTES TO SEVENTH SECTION

1. The best way of responding to the jurists' prejudices is to confront them with what has been said in the preceding section about the calculation of probabilities applied to the treatment of mentally ill patients, adopting the principles which were followed in the hospice of Salpêtrière. It is through fully detailed facts that one should find one's way in medicine as in all the physical sciences.

2. I know his work through the English translation and the extract which Crichton has given under the following title: *Medical aphorisms on melancholy and other diseases connected with it.*

3. 'Of all the productions of art which have cheated the fury of time', said Winkelman, 'the statue of Apollo is unquestionably the most astonishing. The artist conceived this work after an ideal model, and only used material necessary for him to carry out his vision and to make it meaningful to him. . . Its height towers above life size, and its attitude is full of majesty... At the sight of this prodigy I forget the whole world; I myself adopt a nobler attitude so as to contemplate it with dignity; in admiration of it I fall down in ecstasy.'

   I am no less a passionate admirer than Winkelman of the Apollo who has become one of the fruits of our conquests and is now held in the Paris Museum; but I look upon him with all the calm of reason and as combining in his head the most beautiful proportions and most harmonious contours which could be seen in men. Indeed it is under the happy Greek climate and through the fine development which gymnastic exercises bring to the body, that this image was conceived and realised in the sculptural masterpieces.

4. I am going to restrict myself to using the proportions of the Python Apollo statue which are most directly related to the objective I have set myself. The head acts as a base for these proportions.

   The height of the head is divided into four equal parts; that is:

   The first part, from the top of the head down to the hair margin, imagining parallel horizontal planes passing through these places.

   The second part, from the top of the forehead to the root of the nose at the level of the upper eyelid.

   The third part, from the root of the nose to the bottom of the nose.

   The fourth part, from the bottom of the nose to the bottom of the chin.

   Each eye seen from the front at a half unit of size; between the two eyes there is a space of half a unit, and the width of the head at this level, at the temples, is two and a half units.

   The width of the head across the cheekbones is two and one-sixth units; the width of the head at the same height but above the ears, at the widest point, is two and a half units or thereabouts.

   The greatest depth of the head from the most prominent point of the forehead between the eyebrows to the most prominent point of the occiput, in the greatest horizontal diameter, is approximately three and two-thirds units.

   The full stature is seven times the height of the head plus three and a half units including the head; so the head is a little more than one-eighth of the full stature.

5. He had been taken to Paris by a gendarme, and from there to the Bicêtre. It appeared that during his journey he had been led by the neck. The ideas which had struck him most deeply are those whose terms he endlessly recalled: *soldier, Paris, neck*. To these very coarsely articulated words he sometimes added *punch*; he seemed to have retained no memory of his family and gave no sign of any affective state.

6. A rough tone or insulting talk presented to a very sensitive person can have adverse and dangerous effects. One of the hospice agents took a keen interest in an elderly nun and when she was convalescent he kept himself informed as to her progress. He then learnt something about her life which she would like to have kept hidden for the sake of everything that was dearest to her, and for which she was publicly reproached. She was so upset at this indiscrete talk that she contracted a deep melancholia and condemned herself to almost total starvation, and a disastrous state of consumption and languor.

7. One of these young girls who I thought was incurable was fortunately separated from her other companions and she was threatened with being taken to the depot at Saint-Denis if she refused to work any longer. This fear was very successful for her; she embarked on knitting and dressmaking for five months with remarkable energy and from then on she was cured. The kind of contradiction into which I fell over her case will not be maliciously missed: but does this exception not confirm the general rule?

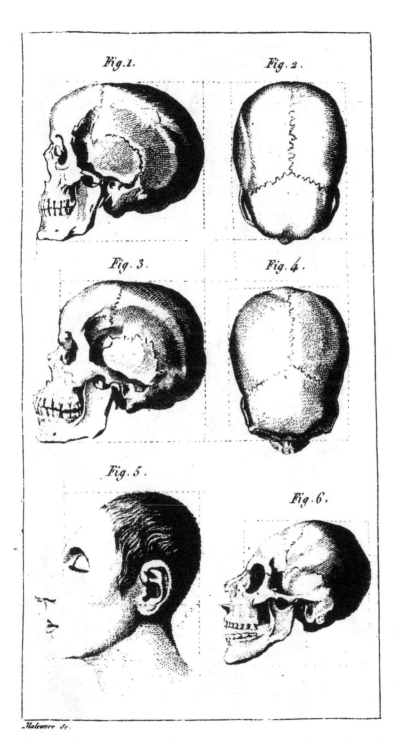

Fig.1.   Fig.2.

Fig.3.   Fig.4.

Fig.5.   Fig.6.

Maleuvre sc.

Plate I

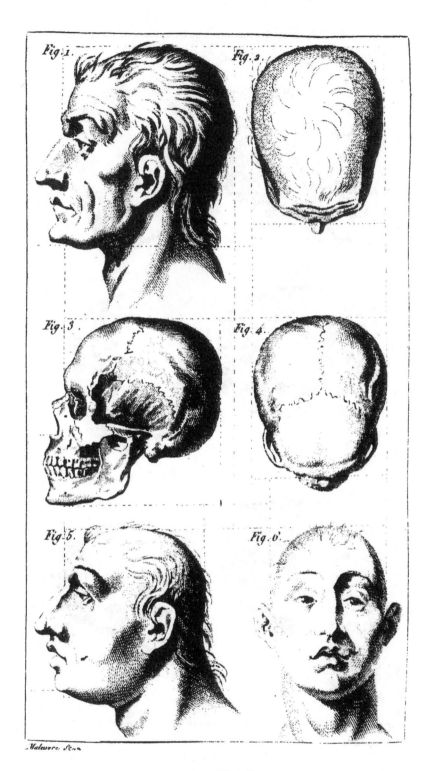

Plate II

INDEX